LITERATURE AND THE CHANGING IRELAND

IRISH LITERARY STUDIES

LITERATURE
AND THE
CHANGING IRELAND

edited by
Peter Connolly

Irish Literary Studies 9

COLIN SMYTHE
Gerrards Cross, Bucks

BARNES & NOBLE BOOKS
Totowa, New Jersey

First published in 1982 by Colin Smythe Limited, P.O. Box 6, Gerrards Cross, Buckinghamshire.

British Library Cataloguing in Publication Data
Literature and the changing Ireland. – (Irish
literary studies, ISSN 0140-895X; 9)
1. Irish authors – History and criticism
I. Connolly, Peter II. Series
820'.9'941 PR8700.C

ISBN 0-86140-043-7

First published in the USA 1982 by
Barnes & Noble Books, 81 Adams Drive,
Totowa, New Jersey 07512

Library of Congress Cataloging in Publication Data
Main entry under title:

Literature and the changing Ireland.

(Irish literature studies ; 9)
Includes index.
1. English literature – Irish authors – History and
criticism – Addresses, essays, lectures. 2. Ireland
in literature – Addresses, essays, lectures.
3. Literature and society – Ireland – Addresses,
essays, lectures. I. Connolly, Peter. II. Series.
PR8705.L58   820'.9'941   81-14930
ISBN 0-389-20234-7 (Barnes & Noble Books)   AACR2

Printed in Great Britain
Set by Inforum Ltd., Portsmouth and
printed and bound by Billing & Sons Ltd.
Guildford, London and Worcester

Contents

FOREWORD

PETER CONNOLLY

These prolegomena must perforce be Janus-faced and serve equally the purposes of afterword and foreword to the occasion which prompts them. The lectures being published here were delivered no less than two years ago at the last major Conference of IASAIL – the International Association for the Study of Anglo-Irish Literature. In July of 1979 it was held for the first time at Maynooth College and with the help of my colleagues in the department of English I had on that occasion the pleasure of hosting what turned out to be a large, lively and fairly happy conference. The cohesion and intimacy of the event was no doubt furthered by its residential nature on-campus but in addition we had the luck that the Irish summer happened on that week of that month for that year. . .

If I must now apologise to all the sundry for the hiatus that has intervened before these lectures come to see the light of print I will plead that one piece of really bad luck extended the normal delays encountered in these matters. At a crucial moment a vital manuscript was mislaid or lost – that of Professor Thomas Flanagan's paper in which he had offered a critical overview of certain aspects of the Irish Literary Revival. From the earliest stages of our programming this had been regarded as an essential topic and hopefully the centrepiece aroung which the other papers might be arranged. Only when our printing schedule had been held up for some eight months – and to no avail – were all hopes of including Professor Flanagan's paper regretfully abandoned. In the present volume its place is filled by the Introductory Essay which was supplied by Dr. Declan Kiberd of the Department of English at University College, Dublin. When offered the commission to do so Dr. Kiberd responded with the highest professional generosity and he has contributed a paper which looks at the 'Revival' from a number of fresh and original angles and in such a way as to propose considerable readjustments to conventional models of that movement. In doing so his article also manages to suggest interesting links with issues raised in some of the other lecture papers included here.

As a rule the triennial conferences of IASAIL have addressed themselves to rather broad areas of Anglo-Irish literature, culture and history and the custom has been to invite IASAIL members to frame a lecture out of their own field of interest but under a capricious umbrella-title which was liberally interpreted by both parties. Obviously this practice does not entitle or enable an editor even of selected papers to elicit *post factum* a tightly organised unity of theme or to impose it on the published volume. The matter of the 1979 Conference originated in a formula as unshaped and open-ended as "Moments of Change in Irish Society 1820–1970" as reflected in literary texts. What emerged in practice were those ever reliable twins of literary historians, Continuity and Change, of which certain instances delineated here link up in an unforced fashion to sketch another outline on the cultural map. In the papers which follow such moments of continuity and change manifest themselves in terms of the mediating language itself (still familiar and foreign source of our unrest of spirit), the practice – in that register – of poetry and short story, the writer's concept of himself and his role, has stances in relation to Irish history. The sheer diversity of the transactions possible between writer, work and the contemporary society is illuminated by a sequence of four or five papers in the middle of this volume – largely, in my opinion, because the critical approaches adopted by the contributors are so catholic, pluralist and free from dogmatic system.

With the minimum of rearrangement from the spoken sequence the papers follow one another roughly according to the chronology of the topics treated. This entails giving the last word to Professor Rafroidi although at the conference itself he had the first word. Perhaps that piece of unforseen symmetry declares its own justice since Professor Rafroidi, then reigning as President of IASAIL, embodied the main driving force behind the 1979 Conference. This is a suitable point at which to acknowledge once more my debt to his organisational powers and to express my warmest thanks to him and to the other members of the executive committee – Terence Brown of Trinity College, Dublin, Hubert McDermott of University College, Galway, and last but not least to Peter Denman of Maynooth.

ACKNOWLEDGEMENTS

The publishers wish to thank the following individuals and organisations for permission to quote from the works they control:–
to Faber & Faber Ltd., for permission to quote from Samuel Beckett's *Waiting for Godot* © 1956, for permission to quote from Seamus Heaney's *Death of a Naturalist* © 1966 and *Wintering Out* © 1972, and for permission to quote from Louis MacNeice's *Collected Poems* © 1966;
to Calder & Boyars Ltd., for permission to quote from Samuel Beckett's *Molloy* © 1954;
to Oxford University Press for permission to quote from Derek Mahon's *Poems 1962–1978* © 1979 his 'Rage for Order';
to the Society of Authors for the Bernard Shaw Estate for permission to quote a passage from a letter by Bernard Shaw, and to the Society of Authors for the James Joyce Estate for permission to quote from the works of James Joyce;
to Victor Gollancz Ltd., for permission to quote from Michael Longley's *An Exploded View* © 1973;
and to Michael B. Yeats and Anne Yeats, and to Macmillan Publishers, Ltd., London and Basingstoke and Macmillan Publishing Co. Inc. New York, for permission to quote from the works of W.B. Yeats.

THE PERILS OF NOSTALGIA: A CRITIQUE OF THE REVIVAL

DECLAN KIBERD

'The sceptre of intelligence has passed from London to Dublin', ran the message that Edward Martyn cabled to George Moore at the start of the new century, exhorting the famous exile to return to his native land. The idea that Dublin was a major literary capital in the years of the Irish revival is just one of the many myths which have come to dominate our thinking about the period. It is nothing more than a gorgeous lie, skilfully fabricated by George Moore to provide him with material for his massive and mischievous trilogy *Hail and Farewell*. That lie was immortalised for the wide world in the syndicated wisecrack that a literary revival occurred because five or six people lived in the same town and hated one another cordially. But the facts show that most of them didn't reside in Dublin for any great length of time. W. H. Auden dryly observed that if one looked at the career of Yeats, the avowed leader of the movement, it was extraordinary how often he contrived to be out of Ireland, spending almost as many years of his career in foreign countries as in Dublin. The paths of Yeats and Shaw were more likely to cross in Woburn Buildings or in Bloomsbury than on the steps of the National Library in Kildare Street. Shaw had abandoned Dublin in 1876 and later complained that it offered its young men a life that was hardly bearable, producing in them 'a certain futile derision and belittlement that confuses the valuable and serious with the base and ludicrous'. He returned in the summer of 1905, and then only 'to please my wife'. He could not bear the prospect of revisiting the port from which he had emigrated almost thirty years earlier and so he managed to land at Cork, journey up through the midlands and enter surreptitiously 'through the backdoor from Meath'.

Shaw's sentiments about his native city never changed. He could fully understand why James Joyce should wish to leave such a dreary place, but not why he should want to recall it in such meticulous detail in his works. In 1922 when Sylvia Beach wrote to Shaw, soliciting a contribution to support the publication of *Ulysses*, Joyce

1

bet her a box of cigars that the wealthy dramatist would send no help. Shaw sent only his good advice:

> I should like to put a cordon round Dublin to round up every male person in it between the ages of fifteen and thirty, force them to read it, and ask them, whether on reflection they can see anything amusing in all that foul-mouthed, foul-minded derision and obscenity. You are probably a young barbarian beglamoured of the excitements and enthusiasms that art stirs up in romantic youth; but to me it is all hideously real: I have walked those streets, and known those shops, and taken part in those conversations. I escaped from them to England at the age of twenty, and forty years later I have learned from the books of Mr. Joyce that slack-jawed blackguardism is as rife in young Dublin as it was in 1870. . . . It is, however, some consolation to find that at least one man has felt deeply enough about it to face the horror of writing it all down . . . I must add, as the prospectus implies an invitation to purchase, that I am an elderly Irish gentleman, and that if you imagine that any Irishman, much less an elderly one, would pay 150 francs for a book, you know little of my countrymen.

Joyce was jubilant at winning his box of cigars and the accolade from Shaw that 'as long as Ireland produces men who have the sense to leave her, she does not exist in vain'.

Joyce may have seen in Shaw's letter yet another statement of his own reasons for exile. In his published work, the young Joyce liked to offer high-falutin' explanations of his flight from the nets of nationality, language and religion, but the real reasons were probably a good deal more practical and economic. He loitered long enough after graduation to realise that Dublin could offer him no post suited to his accomplishments at a reasonable living wage. Moreover, however exciting the literary techniques of *Dubliners* and *Ulysses* may be, it is clear that the world which those books evoke was a place of endless monotony and dreary provincialism, of listless and impecunious youths walking in aimless circles round the town and dragging a wooden stick against the rusty railings of a decaying Georgian street. *Ulysses* is in fact a massive endorsement of Shaw's statement of 1921 that 'to this day, my sentimental regard for Ireland does not include its capital. I am not enamoured of failure, of poverty, of obscurity, and of the ostracism and contempt which these imply; and they were all that Dublin offered to the enormity of my unconscious ambition'. In the same year, Sean O'Casey was earning his living as an unskilled labourer, whose friends stole sheets of paper and lead pencils from their office benches to enable him to press ahead with the work that led to *The Shadow of a Gunman*. When the play was a runaway success in 1923, the dramatist's reward was a mere four pounds. Three years later, he too had gone.

The real question must surely be: whose revival? There was certainly no great change in the conditions of the Dublin poor in the early decades of the century, which began with the announcement that the death-rate in Dublin 'has reached the awful proportion of 46 per 1000, while in English cities it is 18.0 or 19.0' (*The Medical Press*, 17 January 1900). By 1913 the Government Housing Commission revealed that one-third of the population of the city lived in tenements, with over 25,000 families crowding into 5,000 houses, most of which had been declared unfit for human habitation. Over 20,000 of these families lived in a single room and many houses contained more than 50 people. Each year, as the Joyce family knew to its cost, one person in every ten found himself evicted for non-payment of rent. The average wage for men was 14 shillings for a 70-hour week. The First World War did not bring the promised boom in the economy, because the production of consumer goods was drastically reduced and this led to even greater unemployment. Moreover, the government reneged on its promise to clear and rebuild the slums, offering the excuse that everybody must concentrate for the present on the war effort. The sole beneficiaries of war were the Irish farmers who enjoyed a rapid rise in the price of basic foods, but only at the expense of the urban poor, whose condition in 1918 was worse than ever.

Among the middle classes, life was seldom harsh but always dull. As always, Joyce is the best guide to the realities of their lives. He laughed with ordinary Dubliners at the eccentricities of George Russell and even after quitting the city was careful in letters home to ask his brother if A.E. was 'still nibbling away at cabbages in Rathgar'. Genteel Dublin enjoyed a joke as well as ever and extended a fool's pardon to most of the city's writers, but it never paid them the compliment of taking their ideas seriously or of buying their books in any great numbers. At the height of the revival in 1902, J. M. Synge despairingly concluded that he must write with an eye as much on an English as an Irish audience, because 'the Irish reading public is still too limited to keep up an independent school

3

of Irish men of letters'. In a later essay in this collection, Thomas Kilroy makes the point that modern Irish society is unscathed by the subversive implications of its own artists. The main reason for this may lie in the fact that the major artists chose to live most of their lives abroad and, by way of justifying their withdrawal, set themselves up in opposition to the official culture. The growing fame of a Joyce or an O'Casey in Europe seemed but a further reproach to the philistinism of the Irish middle class, which reacted with the wounded pride of a spurned lover and entirely broke off the relationship.

Even the writers who remained had little effect on their society. Yeats's noble speech on divorce surprised his political backers and probably ensured the premature termination of his senatorial career. The very fact that he was appointed to the senate in the first place was due less to his political philosophy than to the shrewd awareness on the part of the Free State government that nobody in Dublin took Yeats's politics seriously. According to Conor Cruise O'Brien, 'the Dublin of the Arts Club liked to treat Yeats's politics as a joke', a tradition which went back to Percy French's comical account of the poet's campaign against the visit of Queen Victoria to Ireland:

> And there must be a slate, sez she,
> Off that Willie Yeats, sez she.
> He'd be better at home, sez she,
> Frinch-polishin' a pome, sez she,
> Than writin' letters, sez she,
> About his betthers, sez she,
> Paradin' me crimes, sez she,
> In the Irish Times, sez she.

During his late flirtation with the Blueshirts, that attitude of affectionate condescension may have protected the poet from reaping the fascist whirlwind, but in most other cases, the same attitude had the effect of protecting society from the revolutionary social implications of the plays of an O'Casey or a Shaw. Amidst the affluence of more recent decades, such good-natured condescension is offered to writers not in the affectionate jibes of Percy French, but in the annual dispensations of the Arts Council, which serves the government and deflects the subversive trajectory of art by converting literature into Culture. As Kilroy shows, nowadays art is accepted by the establishment because it is also Art, something which can be neutralised and transformed into a further testimony to the tolerance of the liberal mind. The denial of art persists, but the name of the game has changed, as the middle-brow comic song becomes institutionalized under a policy of repressive tolerance.

To anyone who examines the cultural and intellectual life of Dublin in the early century, this final defeat of the artist by the middlebrow will not seem surprising. The quality of the city's newspapers was truly abysmal and the provinciality of their concerns was brilliantly captured by Joyce in *Ulysses*. If the newspapers were dull and uninspired, the so-called radical journals were often surprisingly reactionary. Under the editorship of Patrick Pearse, the Gaelic League's *An Claidheamh Soluis* offered intelligent comment on the national scene, but it also carried advertisements for Cork textiles and woollens, with the assurance that there were no Jews among the firm's employees (this just a matter of months after a minor pogrom in Limerick). However, the crusading periodicals reserved their greatest wrath for the art of the Abbey Theatre and the formidable pens of D. P. Moran and Arthur Griffith were wielded in the assault on Synge. For all their national zeal, both men were philistines who might have been employed to advantage by A. A. Zhdanov in the Russia of the nineteen-thirties. They viewed all art as photography, all plays as documentaries, all novels as studies in social realism, and never for a moment suspected that the plays of Synge might have a metaphorical meaning. Contrary to current critical opinion, they never accused Synge of iconoclasm but rather of inaccuracy, resulting from an incomplete knowledge of rural Irish life. 'Men and women in Ireland marry lacking love', said Griffith in his attack on *The Shadow of the Glen*, 'Sometimes the woman lives in bitterness – sometimes she dies of a broken heart – but she does not go away with the tramp'. It was useless for Synge to reply that his art was not to be taken literally, but rather as an account of 'the psychic state of the locality'. Such modernist nuances were beyond the intellectual scope of nation-builders.

The universities, which could have played a major role in educating the emerging nation, remained curiously dormant when they were not being positively perverse. Trinity lapsed even deeper into its self-imposed isolation when in 1899 J. P. Mahaffy tried to block the adoption of Irish by the Commission of Intermediate Education with the assertion that it was impossible to get hold of a text in Irish which was not religious or indecent or silly. The fact that Mahaffy knew no Irish did not blunt the ardour of his exposition, which was supported by Robert Atkinson's declaration that he would not entrust a Gaelic text to his daughters, lest it give them a shock from which they might not recover for the rest of their lives. When Professor Atkinson's Gaelic scholarship was shown to be faulty, a couplet spread like wildfire through the land:

> Atkinson of TCD
> Doesn't know the verb 'to be'.

Douglas Hyde, the president of the Gaelic League, was saddened by the intransigence of his former university and he wrote of Mahaffy: 'How I wish that he and his colleagues would recognise the fact that a new intellectual Ireland has arisen and strive to place their university *en rapport* with it.' Such hopes were vain. Trinity continued on its plunge into isolation, well captured by the young Beckett in some chilling pages of *More Pricks Than Kicks*. Mahaffy was subsequently elected to the Provostship and in 1922 one of his backers offered the immortal comment that the publication of *Ulysses* proved only one thing – 'that it was a mistake to establish a separate university for the aborigines of this island, for the corner-boys who spit into the Liffey'. But the National University men who so swelled the river did not honour the book either. *The Dublin Review* spoke for all patriotic Catholics with its avowal that 'the Irish literary movement is not going to find its stifling climax in a French sink' and went on to lament the fact that 'a great Jesuit-trained talent has gone over malignantly to the powers of evil'. It was the revenge of Cranly – and of all those other upright undergraduates of the National University who had evoked Yeats's scorn with their campaign against immoral literature:

> Where, where but here have Pride and Truth,
> That long to give themselves for wage
> To shake their wicked sides at youth
> Restraining reckless middle age?

The Gaelic League did a great deal more than any other institution to further the education of the Irish in this period. It fulfilled for Ireland the function discharged by the Adult Education Movement in England, at a time when educational opportunities were drastically limited. According to one historian, 'it remained unchallenged also as a provider of entertainment, especially of Irish music and dancing, in those days when cinema, radio and television were as yet unknown'. Something of the spirit of this enlightenment may be discerned in the account of a visiting Frenchman, L. Paul-Dubois:

> But the stranger is most forcibly struck when he attends some Irish class in a poor quarter in Dublin, or even of London, and perceives how serious, deep and infectious is the enthusiasm of the crowds, young and old, clerks and artisans for the most part, with an 'intellectual' here and there – who are gathered together in an ill-lit hall.

The early success of the Gaelic League was nothing short of miraculous, for when Douglas Hyde set about its foundation in 1893, he discovered to his horror that there were only six books in print in Irish throughout the land. Although there was still a substantial Irish-speaking population in the Gaeltacht areas of the west, its members were almost all illiterate in the language. Outside the Gaeltacht the situation was even worse. Hyde observed wryly that only six members of the Gaelic Union, the immediate predecessor of the League, could speak Irish properly. His own ideas came to fruition in a public lecture in 1892 under the title 'The Necessity for de-Anglicising Ireland', where he argued that the mistake of previous leaders of nineteenth-century Ireland had been to confuse politics and nationality, to mistake political campaigns for national campaigns. Leaders such as O'Connell had thrown over Irish civilization while they professed in good faith to fight for Irish nationality. They had exalted the unending fight against England into a self-sustaining tradition and had forgotten the very things which had originally made their country worth fighting for – the native language, dances, games and music. Hyde pointed to the anomaly of 'men who drop their own language to speak English, nevertheless protesting as a matter of sentiment that they hate the country which at every hand's turn they rush to imitate'. He saw Irish as a spiritual language and English as the language of vulgar commerce and believed that 'if something were not done quickly, the Ireland of monuments and cottages will be inundated by a flood of black spuming factories, travelling salesmen

7

and cockney corner-boys'. His exaltation of frugal peasant virtues had an immense influence not just on Yeats and Synge but also on the political vision of the future nation mapped out by Collins and de Valera. Hyde resolved to speak Irish on all possible occasions and writers in Dublin noted with amazement how the native language seemed to froth through his moustachioed lips like porter. Moore wickedly remarked than when Hyde reverted on occasion to his stuttering brand of English, one could well understand why his greatest desire was to make Irish the first official language.

The initial aim of the League had been the preservation of Irish in the Gaeltacht, but after its outstanding early successes, its scope was broadened to include the restoration of the language as the normal medium for the whole people. In the years after the Parnell split, the movement flourished, when young Catholics and Protestants turned with visible relief to a cultural rather than political form of nationalism. Hyde envisaged it as a strictly non-political organization and at first the policy of summoning both Unionist and Nationalist to its banner worked. The redoubtable Dr. O'Kane of Belfast registered as a member, with the declaration that he might be an Orangeman but could not forget that he was also an Ó Catháin. The League was strong enough in Belfast in 1899 to cram a public meeting at which an MA of Trinity College called for the teaching of Irish in schools. The Protestant Bishop of Ossory wrote in approval of 'a platform on which all lovers of our dear native land could meet as nationalists in the truest sense of the word'.

Soon the League was the strongest single secular organization in the country. Its 58 branches in 1898 had swelled to 600 by the start of 1904. According to one contemporary observer in that year, its classes, summer schools, festivals and magazines constituted 'the only National University that Ireland possesses'. During that year Hyde toured America in triumph, collecting money that was badly needed by the Irish Parliamentary Party. The party saw that it must capture the League or be beaten by it, and was bitterly disappointed when Hyde politely declined the offer of a seat in parliament. In the end the League was captured not by the constitutionalists but by Sinn Féin. By 1907 the novelist J. O. Hannay (George Birmingham) was writing to Hyde: 'I take the Sinn Féin position to be the natural and inevitable development of the League's principles. They couldn't lead to anything else . . . I do not myself believe that you will be able to stride the fence for very much longer. You have, in my humble opinion, the chance now of becoming a great Irish leader, with the alternative of relapsing into the position of a John Dillon. It will be intensely interesting to see which you choose. Either way I think the movement you started will go on, whether you lead it or take up the part of Frankenstein who created a monster he could not control.'

Hannay was right and Hyde soon lost control of the monster. In retrospect, it was a measure of the man's political naiveté that he could have hoped to woo thousands of Unionists with that opening lecture, which included such a phrase as 'this awful idea of anglicisation'. The very violence of his own language was bound to stir up his more ardent followers, as when he said that 'every speech we make throughout the country makes bullets to fire at the enemy – isn't it a wonder they don't stop us?' He was merely using a colourful metaphor, borrowed in all innocence from Tomás Bán Ó Concheanainn, with no realization that real bullets would soon fly, fired by young men who had been to school in the Gaelic League. Hyde had no real interest in politics and it was that which allowed him to win such widespread support. It was that, also, which finally broke his power, as the radicals under Pearse sought to translate their cultural nationalism into a more brazenly political commitment. They saw that Hyde's policy was founded on a contradiction, in the sense that no non-political organization could ever hope to save the Gaeltacht without a massive programme of industrial and legislative reform. Hyde had held that it was more important to be Gaelic than to achieve a merely political separation; but Pearse demonstrated that as long as the British ruled from Dublin Castle, the Gaeltacht would continue to decline. So his call was for an Ireland not merely free but Gaelic, not merely Gaelic but free. His own policy was progressive, but it had its flaws, not least of which was the lack of strong support for it within the Gaeltacht itself. In *Allagar na hInise* Thomás Ó Criomhthain tells of how he rebuked his Blasket neighbours for their failure to support the republican movement. 'Abair an focal "republic" i nGaoluinn', he said one day to a friend. 'Ní féidir liom' said the islander. 'Agus is beag a chuir a soláthar imní ort ach oiread' replied the laconic Tomás. Nowadays, one has only to watch the crowds outside Mass on a Sunday morning in the Gaeltacht, as they snatch up copies of the *News of the World* and disdain the more chaste delights of *Inniu*, to appreciate just how little headway the cause of political separatism made in the west. This failure of Pearse has been described by David Greene as a continual weakness in the national movement: 'In retrospect, it is

9

hard to see how the revival of Irish, unsupported as it was by any demand from the Gaeltacht, could be conceived as anything but a political device.' Nevertheless, Pearse's insistence that only a programme of industrial development could save the Gaeltacht proved to be not only correct, but also way in advance of the thinking of the time. 'The language and industries are interdependent,' said Pearse, 'and whoever has a living care for one cannot be unmindful of the other'. Such unashamed modernism would not have recommended itself to Hyde, who saw the Gaeltacht as a refuge from the spuming factories and cockney corner-boys.

Unlike Hyde, Pearse was a radical and in 1912 he called on Leaguers to settle in the west, to make a commitment over and above the wearing of badges and the ritual intonation of the 'cúpla focal'. But they didn't. Sean O'Casey noted how most Leaguers, far from living among the peasantry, were scared to be seen with city labourers and he recalled how members of his own branch had winced at his workingman's muffler. He complained bitterly that Hyde's followers had confused 'the fight for Irish' with a 'fight for collars and ties' and that they continued to live in the choicer suburbs, 'lisping Irish wrongly' in a Gaelic esperanto which bore scant relation to the living language of the west. It was little wonder that by 1913 Pearse could announce that 'the Gaelic League, as the Gaelic League, is a spent force'. He was careful to add, in another speech the following year, that 'what will be accomplished by the men of this generation, will be accomplished because the Gaelic League made it possible'. Hyde was disgusted at such militancy and when at last, at the Dundalk conference of 1915, the League adopted an uncompromising nationalist stance, he resigned his presidency amid tears and a very widespread regret. He said of his departure: 'My own ideas had been quite different . . . so long as we remained non-political, there was no limit to what we could do.' What is surprising in that context, however, is the degree of overlap between Hyde's keynote utterances as leader and the final policy statements of the men of 1916. Consider this speech by Hyde:

> The moment Ireland broke from her Gaelic past, she fell away hopelessly from all intellectual and artistic effort. She lost her musical instruments, she lost her music, she lost her games, she lost her language and popular literature, and with her language, she lost her intellectuality. Only with the restoration of her language could all these things be restored.

10

The influence of that passage on the thinking of Michael Collins is as subtle as it is immense:

> We only succeeded after we had begun to get back our Irish ways, after we had made a serious effort to speak our own language; after we had striven again to govern ourselves. We can only keep out the enemy by completing that task . . . The biggest task will be the restoration of the language.

It has been said of Hyde that if he had any politics, he was probably a Unionist with a small 'u'. He never said anything in favour of Home Rule and he ended his career as he began it, a golf-playing grouse-shooting Anglo-Irishman. His real enemies were not Unionists or Nationalists, but something far more powerful – modern ideas, the city and the socialist ideal. He could never quite come to terms with the fact that the circulation of Larkin's paper, *The Irish Worker*, was always far higher than that of *An Claidheamh Soluis*. It is the socialist analysis of Hyde's work which most sharply exposes his own shortcomings and those of the movement he led. Sean O'Casey reported the disquiet of a comrade in his autobiography; albeit in rather spiteful language:

> – A bit of an oul' cod, the same Hyde, whispered Donal, nudging Sean to take notice. Look at him: oh, wouldn't he like to number on the Coiste Gnótha a few dukes, earls, viscounts, barons and a host of right honourables! For the people, maybe; with the people, maybe; but not of the people. The Fenian Brotherhood waste their time trying to trick him into being a revolutionary even for an hour. Jasus! Listen to his Déunta in Éirinn Irish! Harsh as the crow of a worn-out old cock . . . It doesn't come natural to the man and I'm afraid it never will.

During the Dublin 'Lock-Out' of 1913, Hyde chose to invoke the 'no politics in the League' rule when the issue was that of employers versus organized labour. He disliked Jim Larkin and tried to have Pearse disciplined by the Gaelic League, after Pearse had written an article in Irish, praising Larkin as the only man in the country with the guts for action. All of which proves that Hyde had foolishly equated anglicization with modernization. According to Joseph Lee,

11

'he equated virtually everything existing in his youth with "real" Irish, even though it may well have been an earlier import from England, and denounced virtually every development during his adult years as 'anglicisation'. In his zeal for kneebreeches, for example, he came close to crying "down with trousers" as the battle-cry of his brave new Ireland. Hyde in fact populated his ideal Ireland with a nation of stage-Irishmen, mimicking reality in Irish instead of English. He dreaded the threat of a modernised Gaelic Ireland as intensely as the prospect of a modernised anglicised Ireland.'

Hence his attacks on Pearse and Larkin, his distrust of burgeoning government, his denunciations of popular culture.

That same snobbery in Hyde which so distressed O'Casey had a powerful appeal for other sections of Irish society, especially in small county towns where 'real distinctions of wealth and rank were so small that only a competition in snobbishness could seem to provide them'. So the Gaelic League projected an ideal self-image of the Gael as a descendent of ancient chieftains and kings. Irish Ireland countered the petty 'seóinín' or West Briton, who asserted his superiority by imitating the manners of the English, with its own form of inverted Gaelic snobbery. Anything English was *ipso facto* not for the Irish, as it might seem to weaken the claim to separate nationhood, but any valued cultural possessions of the English were shown to have their Gaelic equivalents. Thus was born what Seán de Fréine has acutely called 'the ingenious device of national parallelism':

English language	–	Irish language
English law	–	Brehon law
Parliament	–	Dail
Prime Minister	–	Taoiseach
Soccer	–	Gaelic Football
Trousers	–	Kilt

It mattered little whether these devices had a sound basis in Irish history, for if they did not previously exist, they could be invented. So, because Englishmen were sensible enough enough to wear trousers in their inclement climate, it followed that the romantic Irishman must have worn a kilt. This pleased the revivalists with its connotations of aristocracy, of Scottish chieftains and kings. Unfor-

12

tunately, the garment never was Irish and subsequent social historians have proved that the Irish wore trousers long before the English (and were reviled for it). This did not deter a whole generation of enthusiasts from unveiling their knees to the luckless Irish public, nor did it reduce Hyde's enthusiasm in expounding the superiority of knee-breeches over trousers. Some devious souls tried to have it both ways, as in George Moore's recommendation that tartan trousers be worn to his Gaelic lawn-party at Ely Place. *An Claidheamh Soluis* contributed to this pan-Celtic lunacy when it announced its own inspired compromise: 'We condemn English-made evening dress, but evening dress of Irish manufacture is just as Irish as a Donegal cycling suit. Some people think we cannot be Irish unless we always wear tweeds and only occasionally wear collars.'

Robert Kee has marvelled at just how heated these debates could become and has suggested that the success of the Gaelic League// Sinn Féin axis may be explained by 'the opportunity it extended to a snobbishly afflicted middle and lower-middle class to assert a new social self-respect'. O'Casey felt the contempt of a socialist for such pretensions to respectability, whereas Synge voiced the contempt of a mandarin class for those underlings among whom he sat at the first performance of *Casadh an tSúgáin* in 1902, 'girls jabbering in very bad Irish to young clerks pale with enthusiasm'. It was left to Joyce, however, to write the most lethal satire on the careerism of some Leaguers in his short story entitled 'A Mother'. The respectable Mrs. Kearney sees in the League a chance to promote not the cause of Irish but her daughter's musical career:

> When the Irish Revival began to be appreciable, Mrs. Kearney determined to take advantage of her daughter's name and brought an Irish teacher to the house. Kathleen and her sister sent Irish picture postcards to their friends and those friends sent back other Irish picture postcards . . . People said that she was very clever at music and a very nice girl, and, moreover, that she was a believer in the language movement. Mrs. Kearney was well content with this . . .

Kathleen secures a position as piano accompanist at a series of concerts in aid of the Éire Abú Society, but when the functions are poorly attended and the society cannot afford to pay the fee, the mother creates a nasty scene and insists on every last penny. Joyce saw just how closely the new social self-respect could verge on hard-nosed bourgeois materialism. The fight for collars and ties was on with a vengeance. In accordance with Hyde's instructions in the lecture on de-anglicization, prizes and medals were awarded to those families who could claim to have spoken Irish in a given year; and similar policies of official grants and governmental bribes were later to be applied with spectacular largesse and no success in the Free State. Such ploys characterized the Ireland of the revival as the land which lost the leprechaun but found the pot of gold.

George Moore was no socialist, but he was outraged by Hyde's cultivation of a distinctly middle-class ethos for the League. He alleged that Hyde curried favour with all sections of the rising Catholic bourgeoisie, 'members of Parliament, priests, shop-keepers' and that 'by standing well with these people, especially the priests', he had become 'the archetype of the Catholic-Protestant, cunning, subtle, cajoling, superficial and affable'. It was that affabil-ity which made him acceptable to de Valera as the first President of Ireland in 1938, under a constitution which effectively signed the civil rights of Irish Protestants away. It was, moreover, a con-stitution which illustrated the depths to which the language had sunk after the noble ideals of 1893, for although it declared Irish to be the first official language, it was originally written in English and only then translated into Irish. This meant that the version in Irish was to have ultimate authority and would prevail over the English version, even in the event of a mistranslation. The constitutional hypocrisy about the other National Aim was no less obnoxious. It claimed the whole island of Ireland, including the six counties, as the national territory, though specifically excluding the Orange State from the jurisdiction of the Dublin government, 'pending the re-integration of the national territory'. It was a superb example of government by duplicity, for while seeming to claim the six coun-ties, it actually gave formal recognition to partition. Hyde was a godsend to a government committed to such policies for, by making him President, the politicians seemed to honour both the native language and the Protestant tradition while in fact their legislation displayed a callow contempt for both. By making such an affable man the leader of the state, the government could deflect the far-reaching implications of the movement which he had once led, while the erstwhile crusader was (to borrow Kilroy's phrase) 'flat-tered by the ease with which society could contain him'. His eleva-tion illustrated not only the magnitude of the nation's debt to Hyde, but also how unimportant his ideas had become. To make a revolutionary safe, one need only give him a seat in parliament.

While Hyde presided in Dublin, the Gaeltacht continued to decline. Although the farmers of Ireland were cossetted by successive governments, the Gaeltacht was not and Pearse's demand for an industrial programme in the area remained unanswered. The real powerlessness of the League may be measured by the fact that in the three decades of its greatest influence up to the census of 1926, the total number of Irish speakers had declined by over 120,000, from a figure of 700,000 in 1891. Both Connacht and Munster had lost about 100,000 Irish speakers. The limited success of the League is attested by the rise in Leinster from 14,000 to 101,000 but most of these enthusiasts were learners rather than fluent speakers of the language. For all the initial success of the League in having Irish recognised as a legitimate school subject, the fact remained that in 1921 only one primary school student in four was being taught the subject. The accession to power of a native government did alter the situation, to the extent that more and more people outside the Gaeltacht claimed to know some Irish, from 240,000 in 1911 to over 700,000 in 1961; but, as M. W. Heslinga has argued, this means little more than that, with wider educational opportunities, more people in Great Britain have become French speakers. The failure of successive governments to tackle the real problem in the Gaeltacht is registered by the drop in the number of its native speakers to 70,000 in 1961, just one-tenth of the number recorded seventy years earlier. The remaining nine-tenths had gone to earn their livings in places like Birmingham and Boston.

The gains made in the east in no way compensated for such a drastic decline and much of the ballyhoo surrounding the League had little basis in reality. At the height of its power in 1906, it could boast of a total membership between 75,000 and 100,000, but most (like Kathleen Kearney and, indeed, the young James Joyce) attended meetings more for the sociability and the music than for the painstaking study of a new language. Even those classes that did meet were run on crude and unsophisticated lines. According to Daniel Corkery, 'the teacher, hardly ever paid, in most cases was himself a student of the language, and often not much ahead in knowledge of those he taught'. Desmond Ryan recalled that 'stock phrases were bandied around without too much regard for sense or context, and many folk contented themselves with sending cows to wells and leaving salmon on tables, and alas, eventually the books of

O'Growney along with them'. Stephen MacKenna's letters to Synge, with their ritual use of stock Gaelic idioms but without a single Gaelic sentence, are all too typical of the phenomenon. It is now conceded by a government report that although thousands were registered as members of the League's classes every year, it is unlikely that more than a few hundred achieved fluency. The brand of Irish spoken by the remainder has been dismissed as 'twaddle' by J. M. Synge and explained by R. A. Breatnach:

> Compelling large numbers of teachers and others, in a matter of months, to teach, use, adopt and develop it in accordance with the particular needs of a more advanced social milieu, has led to the development of a 'hybrid speech', a travesty of Irish, pronounced as if it were English.

Such a dialect is now spoken by many speakers outside the Gaeltacht, among whom one must number the television announcer who signs off each evening with a cheery 'sin a bhfuil anocht'. He, too, has resigned his part in the comedy and been changed in turn. Needless to add, the store of the words and the quality of Irish in the Gaeltacht has been adversely affected by these developments.

All this is to judge the Gaelic League harshly with the dubious benefits of hindsight and to neglect the vast achievements of Hyde in his day, achievements in the face of popular despondency and the sneers of his own class. Hyde was the most important scholar-in-waiting to the Irish Revival, supplying Yeats with folk-tales and themes, providing Synge and Lady Gregory with the basis of their dramatic dialect, and offering all and sundry his own pleasant little plays in Irish. Yet, though he was a fine scholar, he never created any lasting play or poem in the language. His achievement, in so far as it existed, *was* political, whether he liked it or not. By his campaigns, he had forced the British government to accept postal parcels addressed in Irish, he compelled the Committee of Intermediate Education to establish Irish as a school subject, and he won recognition for Irish as a language of instruction of Gaeltacht schools and as a compulsory qualification for those who wished to matriculate at the National University. By 1908, when he became first Professor of Irish at that institution, the battle seemed to be won and Hyde was soon immersed in scholarship and crowned with laurels. In fact, the battle was only beginning and despite the sacrifices of Pearse and Collins it was never really joined. The Ascendancy gentleman went on to preside over a country where Irish was a dreary compulsion, a threat rather than a gift, in schools where now thousands instead of hundreds lisped Irish wrongly. He was convinced in his gentle and self-effacing way that his career had been something suspiciously like a success, but all the time there were more native speakers in Birmingham than in Galway. It was a victory of sorts for Hyde, but not quite the Gaelic Ireland of his youthful dream.

It is something of a paradox that a lower-case unionist should end his career as first president of the Irish Free State, but that can be no great surprise to the student of previous Irish revivals. The implication of Cathal Ó Háinle's essay in this collection is that the eighteenth-century revival was less a spontaneous outpouring of nationalist feeling than a desperate strategy adopted by the more liberal unionists who knew that their backs were to the wall. Charlotte Brooke hoped above all that her work should be read in England, where the common view was that the Irish were a barbarous and uncultivated people. This was held to be true not only of the peasants, but also of the landlord class, of whom Goldsmith had written that they 'spent more money on breeding horses in one season than they had in two centuries on learning'. Such evidence gives the lie to Yeats's absurd idealization of these hard-riding fellows. All the contemporary accounts suggest that while the peasants were scraping a few pence together for the aphorisms of the hedge-school, the Ascendancy were busy shedding what little culture they retained. 'All their productions in learning amount to perhaps a translation of a few tracts in Latin', reported Goldsmith, 'and all their productions in art to nothing at all'. Charlotte Brooke hoped to clear the reputation of her class and to arouse a greater respect in England for the ancient poetry of Ireland, which displayed 'a degree of refinement totally astonishing at a period when the rest of Europe was nearly sunk in barbarism'. Her call to the English reader – 'were we better acquainted, we should be better friends' – is a warning that they must blend the Gaelic tradition with the English, if they wish to administer a united and peaceful land. It remarkably anticipates the 'union of hearts' policy of Matthew Arnold in the 1860s and it is not coincidence that both calls were issued by enlightened unionists when Ireland was on the verge of rebellion. The confident and noble sentences of Charlotte Brooke's preface to her collection of poetry cannot conceal her fear that, as so often in the past, the English will not understand: 'The British muse is not yet informed that she has an elder sister in this isle; let us introduce them to each other; together let them walk in cordial union between two countries that seem formed by nature to be joined by every bond of interest and amity.' Behind her cultural nationalism lies a deep-seated desire to cement the union and to yoke Ireland to England, not by violence but by culture. Her espousal of Gaelic Ireland was to provide a model for a more enlightened landlordism, which would take an intelligent interest in the culture of the peasantry. The fact that her call seems to have fallen on deaf ears would not have surprised Henry Grattan, who described the recalcitrant landlords as rascals 'standing in the sphere of their own infamy'.

Those who do not learn from history are doomed to repeat it. One hundred years later, the same message was spelled out by Standish J. O'Grady, the father of the next revival and the man to whom (according to Yeats) every modern Irish writer owed a portion of his soul. Unfortunately, Yeats did not study the writings of his hero with sufficient care, for a closer inspection would surely have cured him of his Ascendancy fetish. O'Grady could find no planted lawns or dappled hills among the Protestant aristocracy, which he described in 1901 as 'rotting from the land in the most dismal farce-tragedy of all time, without one brave deed'. Like Charlotte Brooke, he was convinced that the success of rural insurgents was due to the penny-pinching of bad landlords and that the turmoil would cease once the landlords were established as benevolent despots with an active interest in their tenants and land. He wrote his *History of Ireland: Heroic Period* (1878–80) in hopes of interesting his fellow-landlords in the culture of the folk, but failed to read the ominous signs when he was forced to pay for the cost of publication himself. He was a propagandist without a significant audience and even his few disciples scarcely understood the implications of what he said. The Yeats who aspired to 'dream of the noble and the beggarman' and of the perfect courtesy which could characterize that relationship had hardly come to terms with the teachings of his chosen prophet. For O'Grady complained that the great sin of the landlords had been their agreement to negotiate terms with 'the scum', i.e. the peasants. In so far as Yeats learned anything from O'Grady, it was a pathological hatred of modern ideas. The poet who spoke of democracy as a world 'half dead at the top', of 'formless modern fury', of Paudeens fumbling in greasy tills, was harking back to the crusty old despot who berated his own class for

18

capitulating to 'this waste dark mass of colliding interests, mad about the main chance – the pence-counting shop-keeper; the publican; the isolated crafty farmer; the labourer tied to his toil . . .'

O'Grady's contempt for the labourer in the field was exceeded only by his scorn for the failings of his own class. 'Christ save us!', he exclaimed, 'You read nothing, know nothing'. So much for the patronage of the arts, a myth beloved of Yeats. Louis MacNeice was nearer the mark when he wrote that most of the Big Houses contained no culture worth speaking of – 'nothing but an insidious bonhomie, an obsolete bravado and a way with horses'. O'Grady himself was forced to concede that the way with horses did not extend to humans. He berated the landlords as boys with 'a boyish devotion to boyish amusement', who prized their horses but deserted their own wounded comrades. George Bernard Shaw noted the same strange combination of athleticism and cowardice in his account of their life; 'This way of producing hardy bodies and timid souls is so common in country houses that you may spend hours in them listening to stories of broken collar-bones, broken backs, and broken necks, without coming upon a single spiritual adventure or daring thought'. This hardly squares with Yeats's noble vision of lovers and horsemen beaten into the clay, but proves that nostalgic falsifications of an ideal aristocratic past were not the sole preserve of the clerks and shop-assistants of the Gaelic League. There was something quite infectious about the aristocratic fetishism which pervaded all elements of the revival. Indeed, to find a parallel text to O'Grady's *Toryism and Tory Democracy* one need only cite the anti-democratic *snobbisme* of *Parlaimint Chlainne Tomáis*, written about 1650 and published in 1912, with its merciless assault by a dispossessed poet on the newly freed serfs. It is no coincidence that the most quoted poets of the revival were Ó Rathaille and Ó Bruadair, both of whom outdid O'Grady in their eloquent contempt for churls and upstarts. If Yeats's identification with figures of eighteenth-century Ireland has any basis in reality, it must lie in his fellow-feeling with Ó Rathaille, whose deathbed lines he loots for his own assault on the risen people of the twentieth century:

> You ask what I have found, and far and wide I go:
> Nothing but Cromwell's house and Cromwell's murderous crew,
> The lovers and the dancers are beaten into the clay,
> And the tall men and the swordsmen and the horsemen, where are they?

19

And there is an old beggar wandering in his pride –
His fathers served their fathers before Christ was crucified.

The beggar too proud to seek help is the abandoned Gaelic poet and the lines which close the stanza are a deliberate echo of the last line ever written by Ó Rathaille:

Rachad a haithle searc na laoch don chill
Na flatha faoi raibh mo shean roimh éag do Chríost.

A more balanced and intelligently sympathetic account of 'the tragedy of the landlord class' may be found in Synge's essay on 'A Landlord's Garden in County Wicklow'. 'These owners of the land are not much pitied at the present day, or much deserving of pity', he wrote, 'and yet one cannot quite forget that they are the descendents of what was at one time, in the eighteenth century, a high-spirited and highly-cultivated aristocracy'. Yet Synge seemed in two minds about this cautious nostalgia, for he went on to write a sentence which was excised from his published work: 'Still, this class, with its many genuine qualities, had little patriotism in the right sense, few ideas, and no seed for future life, and it has gone to the wall'. A reader of many essays in nostalgia might infer that the Big Houses were laid low by callous rebels and philistine town councillors, but Synge's account proves that the decline came from within and owed more to a combination of fast women and slow horses. His description of Big House culture at the turn of the century is remarkable only for the vulgarity of the life portrayed:

Where men used to collect fine editions of *Don Quixote* and Moliére, in Spanish and French, and luxuriantly bound copies of Juvenal and Persius and Cicero, nothing is read now but Longfellow and Hall Caine and Miss Corelli. Where good and roomy houses were built a hundred years ago, poor and tawdry houses are built now; and bad bookbinding, bad pictures and bad decorations are thought well of, where rare buildings, beautiful miniatures and finely-carved chimney-pieces were once prized by the Irish landlords.

The overall impression left by the period is of poverty in the cities and seedy decay in a countryside wracked by official neglect and massive emigration. The debate between landlordism and peasant

20

proprietorship proved meaningless, for in the event both sides invested more importance in the ownership of land than its creative use. When Horace Plunkett tried to increase the efficiency of Irish farming at the turn of the century, he was accused of trying to consolidate British rule in Ireland by devious means. Co-operation was called 'hellish work' and Plunkett 'a monster in human shape'. When he suggested that economic development was hampered by a lack of self-reliance in the national character, the prelates of the Catholic Church lashed out against the implication that they had weakened the independence of the Irish mind. 'Everything is howled down here except a facile orthodoxy', wrote George Russell in despair, 'independent thought is forbidden'. For this brave declaration he was chastised by D. P. Moran in *The Leader* as 'burnishing Sir Horace's muddy boots'. But he was proved right in the end, when the followers of Moran became the leaders of the new state and proceeded to censor books, ban divorce and outlaw contraception. In the words of Frank O'Connor, they created 'a new Establishment of the Church and State in which imagination would play no part, and young men and women would emigrate to the ends of the earth, not because the country was poor, but because it was mediocre'. Yeats fought bravely against the censorship, citing Thomas Aquinas in evidence against the government's definition of 'indecent' as meaning 'calculated to excite sexual passion'. He praised those Renaissance painters who had used their mistresses as models of the Virgin. But the damage was done. By 1926 the Christian Brothers had publicly burned an English magazine which was alleged to have offered a 'horrible insult to God' by printing the 'Cherry Tree Carol'. By the nineteen-forties, some clergymen were issuing edicts against young girls foolish enough to ride bicycles or play camogie in public, while jazz was banned on Radio Eireann.

It would be unfair, however, to blame the clergy for the great tide of puritanism that swept through the country in the decades of the revival and after. The repression seems to have penetrated even those western islands where the clerical boot seldom left a print on the windswept sands. Tomás Ó Criomhthain ended his haunting account of life on the Blasket with the complaint that the ancient 'scléip', and 'mór-chroí' had been lost in rural life, a clear reference to the prudish schoolmasters on the mainland who had censored some innocently sensual passages from his book. In so far as the clergy were apostles of the new puritanism, this was due more to practical considerations than spiritual imperatives. Most priests were the children of rural farmers, with a shrewd awareness that the great wrong in life was the unnecessary subdivision of the family farm. The inevitable result was that the inheriting son had to delay marriage until the retirement or death of his father, while the other sons were doomed either to the emigrant ship or to the distortions of ingrown virginity. The clergy saw their task as the preaching of a moral code which reinforced these harsh economic realities. The result was that most forms of company-keeping were condemned, many new dances were denounced as immoral and dance-halls began to resemble churches where the men sat on one side of the congregation and the women on the other. It was no wonder that the easy sociability and innocent relaxations offered by the Gaelic League, with the approval of the clergy, proved so attractive to young people starved of other excitement. The real condition of rural Ireland in the period was well captured by Sara Tansey in *The Playboy of the Western World*, when she complained of endless journeys to the priest, 'going up summer and winter with nothing worthwhile to confess at all'.

Seen against this depressed background, Synge's play may be taken, in the author's own words, as the definitive account of 'the psychic state of the locality'. In such a land, the myth of a hero is more a confession of impotence than a spur to battle. The Ireland depicted in his play has lost all its strong men and innovators to the emigrant ship or the prison cell, leaving only the timorous Shawn Keogh to inherit the rocky soil. The energies of the womenfolk find an outlet not in a vibrant sexuality, but rather in the tedious violence of cattle-maiming and the hanging of a dog. The Christy who staggers into the shebeen is seized upon as a hero, but to the critical eye of the audience, he is seen only as an abject copy of Shawn Keogh. The stage directions emphasise that he is 'slight, tired and frightened' and the actor who first played the part was only five feet three inches in height. That such a man should become an instant celebrity is a satirical comment on the emotional poverty of the villagers' lives. This is the major point of the play, which may be taken as an attack on what the dramatist disparagingly called the 'Cuchulanoid' hero. For Yeats, Lady Gregory and Pearse, Cuchulain was the inspiring exponent of the heroic gesture; and the central theme in all treatments of the warrior was his capacity to make violence seem heroic. So potent a symbol was Cuchulain for Patrick Pearse that one of his pupils wrote that at St. Enda's School, 'Cuchulain was an important if invisible member of the staff'. The school's motto was an aphorism attributed to the ancient warrior: 'I care not if I live only a day and a night, so long as my deeds live after me'. What this meant in practice could be strange. One young lad who won a poetry competition in the school was astonished on prize-day to be rewarded not with a Bible, or even a book, but a gleaming new rifle.

Synge could not have viewed this increasing glorification of violence with anything but grave concern. He himself was a staunch pacifist, who had resigned from Maud Gonne's *Irlande Libre* movement in Paris in 1896, on discovering her willingness to start a bombing campaign in Britain. In portraying in his major play an Irish hero who is acclaimed by village girls for a deed of violence, Synge offered what Maxim Gorki was later to describe as 'a subtle irony on the cult of the hero'. His play shows that the so-called fighting Irish can only endure the thought of violence when the deed is committed elsewhere or in the past. But when a killing occurs in their own backyard, they become suddenly aware of that notorious gap between gallous stories and dirty deeds. Far from being another attempt to pander to the British notion of Ireland, Synge's play was an honest attempt to reveal to his own countrymen the ambiguity of their attitude to violence. He seems to have foreseen how Pearse and the men of 1916 would evoke only the jeers of an apathetic Dublin populace. His play is a poignant and painful prophecy of how generations of Irishmen would sing ballads of glamourised rebellion and offer funds for self-proclaimed freedom-fighters, so long as the fighting took place at a safe distance in past history or on the other side of a patrolled political border. He believed that a writer's first duty was to insult rather than to humour his audience, to shock his compatriots into an even deeper awareness of their own dilemmas. His play exploded forever the myth of the fighting Irish and, like Joyce, revealed to his countrymen an even more distressing truth – the fact that their besetting vice was not pugnacity but paralysis. This was also the diagnosis offered by Pearse in his essays of 1914, where he argued that Ireland had lost the right to nationhood because her men had grown decadent and supine. As a socialist and a pacifist, however, Synge could never have endorsed Pearse's final remedy.

There is a great climactic scene in *The Life of Galilio* by Brecht which sums up the difference between the patriot and the playwright. A young idealist named Andrea seems to endorse the thesis of Pearse when he loudly complains: 'Unhappy the land that has no heroes'. But some moments later Galileo offers a more devastating diagnosis: 'No. Unhappy the land that is in need of heroes'.

SOURCES AND REFERENCES

K.H. Connell, *Irish Peasant Society*; Oxford 1968.
Daniel Corkery, *The Fortunes of the Irish Language*; Cork 1954.
Seán de Fréine, *The Great Silence*; Dublin 1965.
Douglas Hyde, 'The Necessity for de-Anglicising Ireland', *The Revival of Irish Literature*; London 1894.
Robert Kee, *The Green Flag*; London 1972.
David Krause, *Sean O'Casey: The Man and His Work*; London 1960.
Joseph Lee, *The Modernisation of Irish Society 1848–1918*; Dublin 1973.
Conor Cruise O'Brien, ed., *The Shaping of Modern Ireland*: London 1960.
'Passion and Cunning: An Essay on the Politics of W.B. Yeats', *In Excited Reverie*, eds. Jeffares and Cross; London 1965.
Sean O'Casey, *Drums Under the Windows*; London 1945.
Tomás Ó Criomhthain, *An tOileánach*; Dublin 1929.
Allagar na hInise; Dublin 1928.
Standish O'Grady, *Toryism and Tory Democracy*: London 1886.
Selected Essays and Passages: Dublin 1918.
Seán Ó Tuama ed., *The Gaelic League Idea*; Cork 1972. See especially Breandan S. MacAodha, 'Was This a Social Revolution?' for many of the statistics quoted in this article.
Desmond Ryan, *The Sword of Light*: London 1939.

AUTHOR AND AUDIENCE IN THE EARLY NINETEENTH CENTURY

KLAUS LUBBERS

The following comments form part of an attempt to develop a rationale for the study of Anglo-Irish fiction. The problem – that of how to understand literature historically – is both old and general. The literary critic is in a much better position than the historian. He can be selective in what he wants to take up, and he can analyze and evaluate according to his own ideas of what literature ought to be. A modern critic is not likely to waste much time with Michael Banim's *Crohoore of the Bill Hook* (1825) or *The Croppy* (1828). He may possibly praise isolated details such as a character, a scene, the dialogue, the description of the Slaney valley, but he will make short shrift of the author on aesthetic grounds. The literary historian cannot do that. These two novels – the one about Whiteboyism, the other about the Wexford Rising – may interest him from points of view that have little to do with the game of intrinsic analysis: (1) the historical material and the way it is treated; the phenomenon of awkward, off-centre, melodramatic plotting that connects the private story only superficially with the public events and that shows the author's cultural distance from the anarchic world at the core of the book; (2) the author's social background, his political ideas, his artistic intentions, the readers he hopes to reach; (3) the author's actual contemporaneous readers and what they thought of his works; (4) the political situation in which a book was written and read.

*

A historical approach shows us a good deal about the peculiarities of literature seen as a process of give and take, of intending and (mis)-understanding. It is only when one studies the reception of an author in conjunction with his (explicit and implicit) intention that one grasps the meaning of his works. This meaning is not, in the first place, what we, living as we do at a later time and often in a different culture, read into them or extract from them, but what contem-

25

poraneous readers – those to whom the author addressed himself – saw in them. Their opinions will differ from ours, but that does not justify our disregarding the limited perception of the primary, i.e., the original audience. Historically, our opinions about *The Croppy* are at best of secondary importance; it is those of the readers of 1828 that count. Michael Banim's intentions and the reactions of his readers are two sides of a coin called the literary process. Such an approach seems to be particularly promising in the case of the Irish novelists, whose writings were so clearly dominated by non-aesthetic considerations. If literary historians have traditionally contextualized works of art in this way, they have usually done so in a rather haphazard fashion.

I have selected the first three decades of the nineteenth century because this period has special attractions for the literary historian: (1) it begins and ends with two political events – the Act of Union and the Catholic Emancipation Act – that were of considerable concern to novelists of all persuasions and that created a climate of expectation on the part of the British reading public; (2) the early Irish novelists took over where the Arthur Youngs, i.e., English writers of Irish travel books, had left off; their focus is wide, i.e., national, their attitude explanatory; (3) it was a time when the novel was still fairly new; its reputation was unstable; it still had functional possibilities denied it later; on the other hand, it allowed as yet of little formal variation – which presented a crux for all of the early writers except Maria Edgeworth; (4) it was a time when British knowledge of things Irish was even more superficial than it was to be later in the century; (5) it was a time when, for want of serious competition, the Irish novelists loomed large on the British horizon – until Sir Walter came along.

I am confining myself to the British side of the reception mainly because, before Griffin, Irish novelists had their books published in London and because they addressed British readers.[1] To complete the picture, one would have to include the Irish and the American reception. The former was controversial from the outset. Irish attempts to build a 'great (nationalist) tradition' began well before the middle of the nineteenth century and culminated in Daniel Corkery's separation of the Irish sheep from the Colonial goats. American critics responded to Irish fiction almost from the beginning. Yet, before the Great Famine, they tended to take their bearings from the British reviews. A new interest in Irish politics, culture, and literature sprang up in the wake of Irish mass emigration to North America and gained momentum with the appearance of the generation of George Moore and Somerville and Ross, i.e., from the late eighties, which is about the time when second-generation Irish-Americans began yearning for fictional news from the Emerald Isle and writers like Seumas MacManus and Jane Barlow started catering to their wants. After 1900, American critics and readers seem to have undergone a long process, painful at times, of re-education, of getting used to a more realistic picture of Ireland than that of the Isle of the Saints or the Celt's Paradise drawn in chimney corners through the turf smoke. This process seems to have been brought about largely by the generations of Joyce, Brinsley MacNamara and Patrick McGill and of O'Flaherty, and, less shockingly, of O'Faolain, and O'Connor. In more recent times, there has been a growing rapport between the Irish writer and his American reading public, a harmony no doubt increased by the fact that writers are again tending to select their materials with a view to transatlantic magazines and publishing houses.

*

Maria Edgeworth's patriotism was the rational, hence selective one of the 'middle nation'. 'As we were neither *born nor bred* in Ireland', say Edgeworth *père et fille* in their *Essay on Irish Bulls* (1802), 'we cannot be supposed to possess this *amor patriae* in its full force: we profess to be attached to the country only for its merits.' [2] In *The Absentee* (1812), Maria introduces 'our hero', Lord Colambre, as a young man in whom 'the sobriety of English good sense mixed most advantageously with Irish vivacity . . .' [3] Her ideal was a bicultural synthesis not of Gael and Colonist, but of the latter and the Englishman. Her Irish *oeuvre*, expressly or implicitly part of her 'tales of fashionable life', i.e., of her novels about the upper classes written for the benefit of the upper classes, follows the general tone of her other moral fictions. Irish materials are used to illustrate didactic ideas of a general character. Her notes headed 'Ormond Objects of this story' list as 'prime object' her intention 'to shew how a person may re-educate themselves . . .' Although she mentions quite a few Irish intentions as well, they are subsumed under 'Secondary Objects'.[4] I.e., even her Irish novels were conceived under the wide roof of her father's educational theories. This subsidiary function of her Irish materials is in keeping with his assumption 'that the Irish tales were too local in interest to last . . .' [5]

27

All the same, Maria's Irish fiction was an eloquent plea for the preservation of the *status quo* in Ireland. If only the absentee landlords would attend to their estates, she kept saying.

The Great Maria became a celebrity on the occasion of her London debut in 1802. Until 1814, she marched, as one critic put it, 'in the first rank of modern novelists'.[6] After that, she was second only to Scott although his praise of her work[7] no doubt helped to make Edgeworthtown for a time another Abbotsford on a smaller scale. The very fact that she was among the few novelists reviewed in the leading British reviews, the *Edinburgh*, the *Quarterly*, and the *Monthly*, was indicative of her renown.

The critical debate was carried on as part of the larger discussion of the novel as such. John Wilson Croker's view of the matter is fairly typical. Reviewing novels for the *Quarterly Review* would have been beneath his dignity had it not been for the fact that 'the customers of the circulating library are so numerous, and so easily imposed upon, that it is of the utmost importance to the public, that its weights and measures should be subject to the inspection of a strict literary police, and the standard of its morality and sentiment kept as pure as the nature of things will admit'.[8] The greatest fault of novels was seen in their 'hold[ing] up false views of life' and in their 'inculcat[ing] pernicious principles of action'.[9] To Croker, the chief sinners were Fielding and Smollett. He was 'convinced that the gay immoralities, the criminal levities, and the rewarded dissipation of Tom Jones and Peregrine Pickle have contributed to inflame, and we will venture to add, to debauch many a youthful imagination'. Hence his maxim: 'A novel, which is not in some degree a lesson either of morals or conduct, is, we think, a production which the world might be quite as well without . . .'[10] This the more so as persons of fashion, to the regret of the *Edinburgh Review*, no longer read edifying essays or apologues or sermons.[11] In other words, the novel was almost expected to assume the function that didactic prose had had while it was still being read. On the strength of their didacticism, Miss Edgeworth's tales almost seemed to transcend their *genre*. Lord Jeffrey paid her a great compliment when he set her apart from the ordinary 'manufacturers of novels' and called her productions 'works of more serious importance than much of the true history and solemn philosophy that comes daily under our inspection'. In correcting erroneous theories of human happiness, Maria was seen as a teacher of the *summum bonum*.[12] *The North American Review* went even further:

In this art of healing the novel-sick mind, Miss Edgeworth is a
most skilful physician. She frames her stories with such pressing
interest as to engage and delight the most fastidious devotee of
fiction; and at the same time interweaves just and philosophical
views of life and sound maxims of prudence. One does not read
even her inconsiderable works, without feeling his moral principles to be invigorated, and learning something of the means, by
which existence is made desirable and useful. On these accounts
Miss Edgeworth ought to be ranked among the great reformers,
who have given a new direction to the faculties and opinions of
mankind, or accelerated them in some laudable course, which
they had already taken.[13]

In statements like these, authorial intention and critical reception
coincide.

Only a minority of readers disapproved of the central position
utility, that pet child of the Enlightenment, held in Maria's word.
Mme de Staël regretted the Irishwoman's 'triste utilité' and so did
Byron and Leigh Hunt. Most of the critics, however, found her
didacticism so much in keeping with their own tenets of social
eudaemonism that, almost from the outset, the daughter must have
felt confirmed in her aims and the father in the pedantry of his
prefaces. Maria's novels were salutary reading, Maria was an
enlightened corrector of her own class, a doctor prescribing a tonic
for patients suffering from *ennui*. As the vices and illusions of
fashionable life had a way of being 'speedily propagated and dif-
fused into the world below', mused *The Edinburgh Review*, they
ought to be exposed in their original sphere; the stream must be
purified at its source.[14]

The national aspect of Maria's novel did not receive much attention. Her Irish works were read as moral tales rather than as
national ones. One did not question the author's pictures of Ireland
until the mid-1820s when the Banims presented Ireland in a quite
different light. From the beginning, one was grateful for whatever
information one got. The well known reactions of George III and
Ruskin point in this direction. One felt a new disposition in favour
of the Irish and compassion for their distresses.[15] One drew tenta-
tive conclusions concerning the probable consequences of the union
between the two sister kingdoms.

Sydney Owenson (who married Sir Thomas Charles Morgan in
1812) stepped into the Gaelic world and inevitably found herself

confronted with the Irish past. Maria Edgeworth had not had much use for history. Her only Gaelic grandee, Count O'Halloran, was a minor, if significant figure; by imputing Unionist ideas to him, she had pocketed him for the Edgeworth side. Irish tradition, to her, had been social backwardness. She had gone so far as to imagine a Catholic landlord of the old type, but she did not recommend him. This was exactly what Miss Owenson did. In *The Wild Irish Girl* (1806), her antiquarian interest in the past gave way to a political one; henceforth, her subject became the pressure of the penal laws on the Catholic gentry.

Maria Edgeworth had had her own class to identify herself with. There had been a type of fiction that she could use – the novel of manners. Sydney Owenson identified herself with the circles in which she moved as a governess and, later, as a lady companion. Hence her mania for projecting herself into Gaelic heroines of superior stock. Sydney herself became the Olivia of *St. Clair*, the Glorvina of *The Wild Irish Girl,* the Duchess of Belmont of *O'Donnel*, the Lady Clanclare of *Florence Macarthy*. She played the fictional role of the wild Irish girl in London society and later put the London episode back into her fiction. ' "This wild Irish princess" ', says Lady Clanclare to the hero, Walter Fitzadelm, ' "has been one of the *lions,* I suppose, of a London season, has been exhibited for her brogue or her howl." ' [16] Since she had no ready-made form to use, she invented one. Her novels, epistolary at the beginning, start out in the way of the 'Stranger in Ireland' type of travel book and then turn into romances with a quest plot.

Her nationalism was emotional and necessarily mythopoeic. It amounted to an imaginative reconstruction of a pre-Protestant Ireland led by Gaelic nobles. No matter how progressive the land-lordism of the rich English commoner Mr. Glentworth – he is outshone by the reinstated O'Donnel of Tirconnel with his bride, the still virginal widowed duchess, with his servant M'Rory, his heavy sword and Bran, his fierce Alsatian hound.[17]

British critics found Sydney Morgan second-rate. She was, as Leigh Hunt said much later, 'So Irish, so modish, so mixtish, so wild. So committing herself, as she talks, like a child'.[18] They criticized the symptoms of haste and negligence, her innumerable classical allusions, her florid style, her incorrect grammar, her pert and flippant attitude, the improbabilities of her plots, her undignified characters, her satires on real or imaginary offenders. She was a woman of more ambition than talent. If one excused her artistic flaws, one did so in view of her liberal aims – 'to reform some of the vulgar prejudices against her countrymen that have been entertained by so many inhabitants of this island', as the *Monthly Review* stated.[19] One saw the political slant of *Florence Macarthy* but there was doubt whether the book would 'reach the hearts of legislators, reform the measures of local magistrates, excite the generosity of the higher classes'.[20] One compared her to Maria Edgeworth and found her wanting and, what was worse, tiresome. Her reputation peaked for a short time with *The O'Briens and the O'Flahertys*, then declined. Like Maria Edgeworth, she outlived her work.

As in the case of Miss Edgeworth, critics were concerned with the function of the novel, i.e., whether it might serve as a vehicle of information. Richard Phillips, Miss Owenson's London publisher, had wanted her to keep fact and fiction apart. He had asked her in 1805 to write a travel book 'on the state of Ireland, the manners and customs of its inhabitants, etc., etc.' in letter form[21] and, when the travelogue had metamorphosed into a novel of sorts called *The Wild Irish Girl*, had shown disappointment. However, he must have known well enough that there was no trusting his Irish authoress because he had at the same time engaged a professional travel-book writer to provide the book that he was afraid Sydney Owenson wouldn't deliver.[22] The critic of *The Monthly Review* remarked, slightly amused at *The Wild Irish Girl,* that

Romances and novels were formerly written to make old women sleep, and to keep young women awake. They interfered not with the serious affairs of the world, but dwelt in a region of their own, and revelled there free and unconfined. It was sufficient if, by a tale tolerably connected together, they amused the mind, and banished *ennui*. – Now, however, they are frequently made the vehicles of the most marked and serious instruction; they are industriously employed to spread the doctrines of methodism, or to warm the mind for the fervours of quietism; sometimes to *illuminate,* and sometimes to beat down the illuminé; – they discuss and settle the most doubtful points in politics; – and instead of being toys to amuse, they have occasionally become extremely useful as mines to blow up, or as battering rams to throw down, whatever is deemed hurtful to society.

He smiled at the author's national stance, at her Milesian pride, and in the end disapproved of her mixed media technique:

It cannot but be obvious that one great end, which the writer of this work proposed to herself, was the bringing the Irish forwards to our view, and to urge with effect their various claims. The purpose is benevolent: but perhaps this is not the way to accomplish it. In a work of this nature, truth and fiction are blended together, and no readers can discriminate what is precisely true on the subject. . . . It must be the statistical man who will essentially benefit Ireland, and not the professed writer of fiction. The latter may reach to the private drawing room, but the former will obtain attention in senates and in councils.[23]

It was not until twenty years later that *The Monthly Review* approved of the political content of Lady Morgan's last novel, *The O'Briens and the O'Flahertys*. The reviewer praised her for steering clear of the 'weeping sentimentalist[s] of the modern school of literary ladies' and for 'having taken a practical part in the real business of life'. The question no longer was whether the novel was a legitimate form for political discussion but only whether the sphere of politics should be 'forbidden to the delicacy of the tender sex'.[24] Times had indeed changed.

In fact, this critic wrote at a moment when the Banims, under the pseudonym 'the O'Hara family' had just launched the first two series of their *Tales* and *The Boyne Water,* the historical novel whose ending aimed at Westminster and the pending case of Catholic Emancipation. While Maria Edgeworth had faced the problem of absenteeism and Lady Morgan had fictionalized the pressure exerted upon the Catholic gentry, the Banims, in taking up the cause of Irish Catholicism, had added a third theme to the Irish novel. Unfortunately, of the letters exchanged between John in London and Michael back home in Kilkenny, we only have the extracts reprinted in Murray's pious, pompous, and pathetic *Life* of 1857. What little was published goes to show that John's explicit intentions (and it was he who suggested to Michael what to write about and how to go about it) were quite modest, rather confined to the regional and the local, and far from being 'national'. John, who had wanted to become a painter and, later, a dramatist, had the painter's eye and the playwright's idea of character. He valued scene and action higher than plotting. As early as 1824, he had asked Michael to describe 'local superstitions' (the result being *The Fetches*). When Michael ran out of material in 1828 and John, because of his sickness, could not write at the pace dictated by publisher and audience, he suggested that Michael fall back on their mother's reminiscences (the result being *The Ghost-Hunter and His Family*). Within the *oeuvre* of the 'O'Haras', we see the national tale being superseded by the local: half of their work is still national, the other half is regional or local. Although in 1832, John spoke of the 'uniform political tendency' of his own and his brother's novels, 'viz. the formation of a good and affectionate feeling between England and Ireland',[25] this was said *post factum* and applied only to five novels covering the period of Catholic discrimination from 1685 to 1825: *The Boyne Water, The Denounced, Crohoore of the Bill-Hook, The Croppy,* and *The Anglo-Irish of the Nineteenth Century.*

The British reception of the 'O'Haras' took place under the star 'of our own inimitable Romancer of the North', as *The Edinburgh Review* put it.[26] Comparison with Scott seemed inevitable since the O'Haras were 'borrowing largely from the storehouse of Sir Walter's machinery'.[27] More interesting is the fact that the Ireland presented by the Banims, certainly a country more remote from the British experience than the Ireland depicted by Maria Edgeworth and Lady Morgan, created problems of understanding. Ireland was still a *terra incognita*. To enter, with due sympathy, into such a story as *Crohoore,* said a critic, 'it would be necessary to come prepared with a much fuller knowledge of the condition, habits, and modes of expression of the lower orders of Irish than could be expected from a mere English reader'.[28] This explains why readers tended to find 'the greatest merit and the most easy charm of these tales' not in their historical and political aspects but rather 'in the sketches, sometimes grave, sometimes humourous, and ever most lively and faithful, which they offer of genuine Irish life.'[29] This is what the *Gentleman's Magazine* had to say about *John Doe*, a Shanavest story: 'It abounds with national traits very faithfully depicted, and exhibits the Irish character in its most varied and antithetical form, in its most contentious bearings, and in its fine and generous enthusiasm: fierce in its revenge, gentle in its affections.'[30] Not a word about Doe's grievances and the rascality of Purcell, the tithe-proctor, land-jobber, gentleman at large, and county magistrate. Part of this failure on the part of the readers was due to melodramatic plotting that often drowned the authors' finer intentions. *The Edinburgh Review* noticed this in *The Croppy*:

> Than the period chosen for this tale, perhaps none in the history of Ireland is more interesting; and it is therefore to be wished,

that the story had been rendered more strictly historical, – that the author had introduced just enough of fictitious private details, to cause us to take an interest in his imaginary actors in the real public drama, and then allowed us to follow with them, easily and naturally, the march of events. But this is not done; on the contrary, we are allowed to see very little of the outbreaking and progress of the Irish rebellion. Attention is diverted from it by a very improbable and unnecessarily complicated plot, so little reconcilable with our notions of truth and nature, that it communicates an air of improbability even to those parts of the narrative which are so.[31]

Still, the message sometimes got across. 'It is pleasant after ages of bad romances in politics', quipped *The Edinburgh Review* about the first series of *Tales*, 'to find thus, at last, good politics in romances.' [32] Especially *The Boyne Water* and *The Anglo-Irish of the Nineteenth Century* seem to have had the effect desired by their author.

In 1831, *The Edinburgh Review* took provisional stock of Anglo-Irish novel writing since 1800. By then, the appearance of new authors had thrown the older ones into perspective. If, before 1800, the Irish character had been misrepresented by Farquhar, Sheridan, and his like, this was because it had always been sketched out of context.

We never saw the Irish grouped – we never trod with them on Irish ground . . . We had seen them alone in English crowds – solitary foreigners, brought over to amuse us with their peculiarities; but we had never been carried to Ireland, and made familiar with them by their own hearths, till, for the first time, they were shown to us by Miss Edgeworth.

But even Miss Edgeworth's achievement had remained incomplete:

Hers is the least dim and distorting mirror in which we ever viewed a reflection of the Irish people. It might, nevertheless, have been wished that she had deepened her views, and extended her sphere of observation . . . There is a careful avoidance of political topics, the bearing of which upon Irish society is too marked and important to be altogether neglected. We even question if it would be possible to discover in her writings that the

Catholics laboured under any disabilities, and that any strong feeling had been excited by the unequal position of the two principal sects.

Lady Morgan pursued the opposite course by indulging too freely in political considerations. It was not before the advent of the Banims (thought to be but a single author) that a Hogarth of Irish life appeared:

His delineations, like those of the English artist, are forcible, true, and characteristic, but too often coarse and unpleasing, – dwelling on the dark side of human nature, and overcharging its loathsome defects; – teaching us rather to hate than to love our species, and occasionally ministering to a pruriency of taste which it is by no means the prevailing sin of modern writers to encourage; yet, at the same time, full of a strength and earnestness which convinces us of the perfect fidelity of the unwelcome representations we are made to contemplate.[33]

Clearly, the British reading public had been prepared for Carleton's even more minute and graphic accounts of the Irish peasantry, which made their debut in 1830.

NOTES

1 A gradual change set in with Griffin who still had London publishers. Carleton prided himself on having been the first Irish fiction writer who ever thought of publishing in his own country and producing his books for 'home consumption' although the latter claim needs some modification. See the 'General Introduction' to the 1869 edition (published in London!) of *Traits and Stories of the Irish Peasantry*.
2 Longford Edition, IV, 186.
3 op. cit., VI, 6
4 Marilyn Butler, *Maria Edgeworth* (Oxford, 1972), 236 f.
5 Butler, 301
6 *Quarterly Review*, VII (June, 1812), 329.
7 In his 'Postscript' to *Waverley*, 'which should have been a preface'.
8 *QR*, II (August, 1809), 146.
9 *North American Review*, VI (January, 1818), 155.
10 *QR*, VII, 332, 331.
11 *Edinburgh Review*, XX (July, 1812), 102.
12 *ER*, XX, 100 f.
13 *NAR*, VI, 156.
14 *ER*, XX, 101.

15 *ER*, II (July, 1803), 401 f.
16 *Florence Macarthy* (London, 1818), III, 93.
17 There is, to be true, a note of historical relativism in her work that modifies her restorative ideas. It begins in *The Wild Irish Girl* and culminates in *The O'Briens and the O'Flahertys* (1828).
18 'Blue-Stocking Revels', *The Poetical Works of Leigh Hunt,* ed. Thornton Hunt (London, 1860), 211.
19 *Monthly Review,* LVII (December, 1808), 382.
20 *American Monthly Magazine,* IV (March, 1819), 340.
21 *Memoirs* (London, 1862), I, 205.
22 John Carr's *The Stranger in Ireland* appeared in 1806.
23 *MR*, LVII (December, 1808), 379, 381.
24 *MR*, n.s., VI (December, 1827), 508.
25 Patrick Joseph Murray, *The Life of John Banim* (London, 1857), 220, cf. 254.
26 *ER*, XLIII (February, 1826), 356 f.
27 *MR*, n.s., IV (January, 1827), 131.
28 *ER*, XLIII, 365.
29 *MR*, n.d., IV, 131.
30 *Gentleman's Magazine,* XCV (July, 1825), 56.
31 *ER*, LII (January, 1831), 417.
32 *ER*, XLIII, 172.
33 *ER*, LII, 411–413.

TOWARDS THE REVIVAL
Some translations of Irish Poetry: 1789–1897

CATHAL G. Ó HÁINLE

The nineteenth century was a disastrous period for the Irish language. It is estimated that in 1788 half of the total population of four million were Irish-speaking; by 1851, after the Great Famine, when the total population was six million, only about 25% were Irish-speaking. And from 1851 onwards, the decline in the use of Irish continued steadily. I do not propose here to go into the reasons for this decline: I simply wish to refer to it by way of illustration of the strange lack of interest in the fortunes of the living Irish language on the part of many of those who became interested in the Irish language and literature of a former era. For, apart from a very few exceptions, no-one made any attempt to stop the flight from the Irish language, and those few exceptions such as Philip Barron in Waterford (1835) and Richard D'Alton in Tipperary (1862), received little support for their practical suggestions and efforts and, as a result, met with almost no success. A few others who could have been influential saw the danger to the living language, but did nothing practical to avert that threat. Thomas Davis, for example, frequently referred to the importance of the Irish language; but in the end he simply went with the tide, and the new nationalism which gave birth to the Young Irelanders found expression in English which was the language of the *Nation*, the newspaper founded by the Young Irelanders in 1842.

In fact it was not until the foundation of the *Society for the Preservation of the Irish Language* (SPIL) in 1876 that a group of people got together to do something positive to save Irish as a spoken language: it was from the SPIL that the Gaelic Union and later the Gaelic League grew.

Thus, the interest taken in Irish language and literature towards the end of the 18th, and in the first three-quarters of the 19th, century was for the most part an antiquarian interest, and was inspired by the romanticism which was fashionable throughout Europe at the time. It was this antiquarianism which gave birth to such learned societies as The Gaelic Society (founded in 1807), The

37

Hiberno-Celtic Society (1818), The Archaeological Society (1840), and The Celtic Society (1845). Writing in 1931, Douglas Hyde enumerated the membership of the Archaeological Society in 1842: its committee had as members a duke, an earl, a viscount and a baron, and among its 260 ordinary members was a liberal sprinkling of civil and ecclesiastical nobility. Hyde mentioned this to show that the society's membership was in large part drawn from the ascendancy, and to give the lie to those who believed that such people had no interest in things Irish.[1] He further declared that it was the songs of Thomas Moore which aroused their interest in the ancient literature of Ireland:

> Those songs directed the attention of the nobility to the ancient glory and deeds of Ireland, without arousing any enmity or bitterness or fear.[2]

His explanation is only partially true: for the success of Moore's *Melodies* was itself due to the popular romanticism. But Hyde's reference to enmity, bitterness and fear is not without foundation. These societies confined themselves to resurrecting ancient texts from the manuscripts and publishing them: this was safe. To show interest in preserving the living language, however, would be dangerous, as it could revive old enmities and fears. Thus it was that when in 1853, the Ossianic Society was founded to publish early modern texts which would not be too difficult for a popular readership, as Hyde says, 'the ascendancy showed no interest in the new society. They did not want modern texts.'[3]

It is against this background of ascendancy romantic antiquarian interest in Irish literature that we must see the work of many of the translators of Irish poetry such as Charlotte Brooke and Samuel Ferguson. And we must further notice that the work of some of them at least was not without 'political' overtones. As we shall see, this was admitted in her own hyper-romantic way by Charlotte Brooke at the end of the 18th century, but it received its most forthright statement in a lecture given by Stopford A. Brooke at the inauguration of the Irish Literary Society in London towards the end of the 19th century.

His lecture entitled *The Need and Use of Getting Irish Literature into the English Tongue* contains many valuable comments and suggestions on the translation of Irish prose and poetry, but the whole 'need and use' of the exercise is summed up by him as follows:

Get [the old tales] out into English, and then we may bring
England and Ireland into a union which never can suffer separation.[4]

However, there was another group of translators whose objective
was anything but unionist! This group was headed by John O'Daly,
a schoolteacher from Waterford, who came to Dublin where he
turned bookseller and publisher. O'Daly and his bookshop in Ang-
lesea Street, are now best remembered for their associations with
James Clarence Mangan. But O'Daly is important in his own right
as the publisher of *Reliques of Irish Jacobite Poetry* (1844), *Irish
Popular Songs* (1847), *The Poets and Poetry of Munster* (first series,
1849; second series, 1860) etc. O'Daly's purpose was not that of the
ascendancy translators i.e. to make the people of England aware of
the literary genius of the Irish, but rather to repair some of the
damage being done to the Irish spirit by the loss of the Irish language:

At a moment like the present, every exertion should be made to
restore, if possible, the sweet and pathetic Songs of Ireland – the
Songs written by the bards at the period of her bitterest woes, too
long neglected – too long forgotten, and give them to the people
and the land they belong to.[5]

O'Daly referred to James Hardiman's work *Irish Minstrelsy* which
was published in two large expensive volumes in 1831:

Ireland indeed stands indebted to Mr. Hardiman for rescuing
very many of her songs from oblivion; but, Mr. Hardiman's
collection was published in such a manner, as to put it entirely out
of the reach of the parties for whom such a work should be
intended, I mean, the *Irish peasantry*.[6]

O'Daly, therefore, planned to publish his collections in slim volumes which could be sold at a penny each which would put them
within the range of the limited financial resources of the common
people.

It seems to me that a broad division can be drawn between the
translations of Irish poetry produced by these two groups, the
ascendancy, unionist, or – more charitably – cosmopolitan, group,
and the insular, or – more accurately – native, group. The first group

tended to translate rather loosely, ignoring the metre of the originals, and, very often, transforming their idiom and colour too. Their aim seems to have been to provide their cosmopolitan audience with a representation of the Irish originals which that audience would find pleasing and acceptable rather than to give an accurate rendering of the originals. The second group, on the other hand, sought to reproduce in English, something of the metres of the originals and to retain their colour and idiom. This distinction, of course, does not provide a basis for assessing the relative merits of the two kinds of translations; but it does draw attention to the fact that they must be judged on different bases: the first, not really as translations at all, but as original poems in their own right; the second as genuine efforts at verse translation. Interestingly enough, the translators who collaborated with James Hardiman belong, in the main to the first group, while J. C. Mangan used both methods.

The first important collection of translations from the Irish was Charlotte Brooke's *Reliques of Irish Poetry* (1789). Other translations had appeared earlier, such as Jonathan Swift's rollicking version of Hugh McGauran's *Pléaráca na Ruarcach*. There were also the translations of Charles Wilson in his *Poems* (1782) and *Select Irish Poems* (1790). But Brooke's work is much more polished than Wilson's, and she also had the advantage of circumstance.

In 1786, Joseph C. Walker's *Historical Memoirs of the Irish Bards* had appeared. This great romantic account of the old Irish poets and their poetry had aroused much interest. Charlotte, who was a friend of Walker's, had provided some translations of Irish poems for this work. She also knew Bishop Percy, and received advice from him. It seems obvious too that his *Fragments of Ancient Poetry* (1760) and *Reliques of Ancient Poetry* (1765) would have been a source of inspiration to her in her work.

A further circumstance was the publication of James McPherson's *Ossian* in the early 1760s. Though presented as a translation of original Gaelic texts, *Ossian* was in fact an original work in its own right and had only a very tenuous relationship with its supposed originals. It greatly angered Irish scholars in Dublin and Belfast who saw the work as a fraud, and who furthermore felt that the Scotsman had stolen their Fenian heroes from them. Charlotte Brooke's reaction is described by Walker:

> When Mr. Macpherson's Ossianic Poems were put into her hands, she was surprised to find in them her favourite Irish tales, decked

with meretricious ornaments; and her blustering heroes . . . so polished in their manners.[7]

Unfortunately when we look at Charlotte's own work we find that her translations from the Irish are themselves so 'decked with meretricious ornaments' as scarcely to merit the name translations. Charlotte Brooke (1740–1791) was born in County Cavan. Her father, a writer of English of some small note, was interested in Irish and instilled the same interest in his daughter. One of Henry Brooke's workmen had two Irish manuscripts and Charlotte frequently heard him read from these to his fellow-workers in the fields. Having learned Irish, she began collecting the songs of the people, intending to translate them into English. The McPherson controversy directed her attention to the Fenian and Red Branch lays. The result is that her book contains four sections: the first two, *heroic poems* and *odes*, consisting mostly of lays (ballads); the third, *dirges*, consisting of one love poem in syllabic metre and four more modern pieces; and the fourth, *songs*, consisting of two poems by Turlough O'Carolan (1670–1788), one by Pádraig MacAlindon (d. 1733), and one folk song.

Irish poetry before that of the present century can be divided into two periods: the first down to 1650, which was the period of syllabic verse; and the second from 1650 to the revival in the early 20th century, which was the period of accentual metres. Syllabic verse has a long history, but from about 1200 it was developed into a rigid system by the schools of poetry in which the professional poets were trained. The basis of the system is syllable counting: each line contains a fixed number of syllables. Stress is ignored, both stressed and unstressed syllables being counted. Each verse consists of four lines and the use of alliteration and rhyme is strictly governed by the rules of the various forms of syllabic metre. The type of rhyme used is quite complex since it involves not only vowels, but also consonants. The ignoring of stress and the fixed number of syllables per line give these metres a poker-faced quality, so that they were known as *dán díreach*, or straight verse. In spite of this quality, these metres could be, and were, used to fine effect in poems of many very different kinds.

Dán díreach, however, properly refers only to the strict forms of these metres in which the rules of syllable counting, alliteration and rhyme were strictly applied. These strict forms were *de rigeur* for the professional poets when composing formal verse for their patrons.

Less strict forms, called *óglláchas*, could be, and were, used in other compositions – e.g. in the Fenian lays.

After the collapse of the old Gaelic order at the beginning of the 17th century, the professional poets and their schools faded away for lack of patronage. With them went *dán díreach* and the stressed or accentual metres became the accepted mode. No doubt these had long been in use, but found no recognition in the formal literary tradition so long as the classical poets held sway. As the term implies, accentual verse is based on a line in which only the accentuated syllables count for metrical purposes, and in general the vowels of the accentuated syllables rhyme according to the pattern of the particular metre being used.

Charlotte Brooke drew her originals from verse of both periods. In general, she managed to retain much of the sense of her originals, but she lost completely their colour, for she used verse forms which bore no relationship to the Irish verse forms, and she introduced additional words and phrases into her translations which not only make them extremely prolix when the originals were quite spare, but also transformed the whole feeling of the verse.

Her statement of intent explains why this should be so:

With a view to throw some light on the antiquities of this country, to vindicate, in part, its history, and prove its claim to scientific as well as to military fame, I have been induced to undertake the following work . . .

I trust I am doing an acceptable service to my country, while I endeavour to rescue from oblivion a few of the invaluable reliques of her ancient genius . . .

The productions of our Irish Bards exhibit a glow of cultivated genius, – a spirit of elevated heroism, – sentiments of pure honor, – instances of disinterested patriotism, – and manners of a degree of refinement, totally astonishing, at a period when the rest of Europe was nearly sunk in barbarism: And is not all this very honourable to our countrymen? Will they not be benefitted, – will they not be gratified, at the lustre reflected on them by ancestors so very different from what modern prejudice has been studious to represent them. But this is not all. –

As yet, we are too little known to our noble neighbour of Britain; were we better acquainted, we should be better friends. The

42

British muse is not yet informed that she has an elder sister in this isle; let us then introduce them to each other! together let them walk abroad from their bowers, sweet ambassadresses of cordial union between two countries that seem formed by nature to be joined by every bond of interest, and of amity. Let them entreat of Britain to cultivate a nearer acquaintance with her neighbouring isle. Let them conciliate for us her esteem, and her affection will follow of course. Let them tell her, that the portion of her blood which flows in our veins is rather ennobled than disgraced by the mingling tides that descend from our heroic ancestors. Let them come – but will they answer to a voice like mine?[8]

She was in fact providing for a romantic public romantic interpretations of verse which had little or nothing of romanticism in it, and she was doing so in the name of cultural unionism.

My first example of her work is from the lay 'The Coming of Connlaoch'. A strange warrior arrives on the shores of Ireland seeking combat. He defeats Conall, one of the great Ulster heroes, and word is sent to the greatest hero, Cúchulainn. When he arrives, he is urged to combat by his compatriots:

> Fáilte ó gach aon roimh an gcoin:
> 'Is mall thangais dár gcabhair;
> atá Conall mar stéad i mbroid
> is céad dár slóigh na choimhideacht.'

> 'Is deacair dhúinn gan bheith i mbroid
> d'éis na bhfear do rachadh i gcosgar;
> is deacair dhúinn dul chum catha
> leis an laoch lér ceangladh Conall.'

> 'Ná smuain gan dul na dháil,
> a laoich na n-arm n-aithghéar,
> a láimh is treise gan teibeadh re neach,
> fuasgail h'oide agus é i gcuibhreach.'

> An tan chualaidh Cúchulainn na lann
> éigin agus cuibhreach Chonaill,
> an curaidh do budh tréine lámh
> téid ag buain sgéala don mhacámh.

> 'Troid má ba héigin dhuit
> nó sgéala thabhairt uait mar charaid:
> beir do rogha, a chiabhuidhe bhog,
> sul ma heagal dhuit do chomhrac.'[9]

Brooke's version of this is as follows:

'Welcome, Cucullin! mighty chief!
Though late, O welcome to thy friend's relief!
Behold the havoc of yon deadly blade!
Behold our hundred warriors bite the ground!
Behold thy friend, thy Conall bound!
Behold – nor be thy vengeful arm delay'd!'

'No wonder (he replied) each foreign knight
Should now insult our coast!
Lost are the souls of martial might,
The pride of Erin's host!
Oh! since your deaths, ye fav'rite sons of fame!
Dismay, defeat, distress, and well-earn'd shame,
Alike our loss, and our reproach proclaim!

For me, my friends, what now remains
When I behold yon mighty Chief in chains
With such a hero's conqueror should I cope,
What could my humbler boast of prowess hope?
How should you think my arms could e'er prevail,
Where Conall-Cearnach's skill and courage fail?'

'And wilt thou then decline the fight,
O arm of Erin's fame!
Her glorious, her unconquered knight,
Her first and fav'rite name!
No, brave Cucullin! mighty chief
Of bright victorious steel!
Fly to thy Conall, to thy friend's relief,
And teach the foe superior force to feel!'

Then with firm step, and dauntless air,
Cucullin went, and thus his foe addrest:
'Let me, O valiant knight (he cried)
Thy courtesy request!
To me thy purpose, and thy name confide,
And what thy lineage and thy land declare?
Do not my friendly hand refuse,
And proffer'd peace decline; –
Yet, if thou wilt the doubtful combat chuse,
The combat then, O fair-hair'd youth! be thine!'[9a]

The whole swing of the metre and the register of the vocabulary is very far removed from the original. Further the ancient warriors have been transmogrified into mediaeval knights who address one another in knightly fashion.

As the story unfolds Cúchulainn kills the invader only to discover that he has killed his own son, Connlaoch. He recites a long lament which Brooke also translated. What scope it gave her to unleash passion and pathos:

> Alas, I sink! – my failing sight
> Is gone! – 'tis lost in night
> Clouds and darkness round me dwell!
> Horrors more than tongue can tell!
> See where my son, my murdered Conloch lies!
> What further sufferings now can fate devise!
> O my heart's wounds! well may your anguish flow,
> And drop life's tears on this surpassing woe!
>
> Lo, the sad remnant of my slaughter'd race,
> Like some lone trunk, I wither in my place! –
> No more the sons of Usnoth to my sight
> Give manly charms, and to my soul delight!
> No more my Conloch shall I hope to see;
> Nor son, nor kinsman now survives for me!
> O my lost son! – my precious child adieu!
> No more these eyes that lovely form shall view!
> No more his dark-red spear shall Ainle wield!
> No more shall Naoise thunder o'er the field!
> No more shall Ardan sweep the hostile plains!
> Lost are they all, and nought but woe remains! –
> Now, chearless earth, adieu thy every care:
> Adieu to all, but Horror and Despair![10]

My next example of Charlotte Brooke's work is her translation of a love poem in strict syllabic metre. At the point in the poem from which this extract is taken, the speaker is praising the lady's beauty. The device he uses is to warn the lady to avoid looking at herself, for her body is so beautiful that, like Narcissus, whose story he has related, she cannot fail to fall in love with herself. He enumerates the parts of her body and praises each in turn: her breasts, her eyes, her hair, and continues:

Foiligh fós an béal mar shuibh,
's an dá ghruaidh mar ghréin tsamhraidh,
barr na gcraobh bhfíthe bhfeachta,
's an taobh síthe soineanta.

Choidhche arís ná féach orra,
glaca míne méarchorra,
troigh ghealmhálla, tráth, is buinn,
sál is seangmhálla séaghainn.[11]

If we abstract from the gymnastics which seem to be required of the lady, or rather forbidden her, we notice that the original is quite sober in metre and expression. Where the adjectives and comparisons are rather flat, Charlotte introduces phrases and adjectives which are much more charged with sensual feeling and emotion, so that her translation can hardly be said to be an accurate reflection of the original:

Hide the twin berries of thy lip's perfume
Their breathing fragrance, and their deepening bloom;
And those fair cheeks, that glow like radiant morn,
When sol's bright rays his blushing east adorn!
No more to thy incautious sight display'd,
Be that dear form, in tender grace array'd!

The rosy finger's tap'ring charms;
The slender hand, the snowy arms;
The little foot, so soft and fair;
The timid step, the modest air;
No more their graces let thine eyes pursue,
But hide, O hide the peril from thy view![12]

Charlotte can be forgiven for not attempting a close imitation of the metre of her syllabic verse originals: there was nothing available to her in the range of English prosody which would even remotely resemble the Irish syllabic metre. Her translations of accentual verse are not so easily excused on this head. Indeed the very nature of her originals demanded some real effort to imitate the music of the originals.

Much of 17th century, and particularly 18th century, Irish verse does not rate very highly as poetry: either because, as in the political verse, the thoughts expressed are purely traditional, or because, as in much of the love poetry, the emotions are not expressed in any sustained way. There do occur, of course, lines and verses of great beauty and feeling, but since in general the poems are weak in structure, they fail as poems. The only structuring element of much of this verse is its music. It was written to be sung, and had the further level of music in the rich patterns of its vowel assonance. The metre of the anonymous love song, 'An Droighneán Donn', is not nearly so richly patterned as much of the verse of the period: it simply requires that two corresponding vowel sounds occur within each line and that each line of a verse ends in the same vowel sound. Even this simple pattern escaped Charlotte Brooke, as did the whole swing of the metre, so that, though she captured the sense of the original reasonably well, its music is completely lost in her translation.

Shílfeadh aonfhear gur dil dó féin mé nuair a luíonn dom mionn,
Is go dtéann dhá dtrian síos díom nuair a smaoiním ar do chomhrá
  liom;
Sneachta síobtha is é á shíorchur faoi Shliabh Uí Fhloinn
Is go bhfuil mo ghrá-sa mar bhláth na n-airní atá ar an droighneán
  donn.[13]

The metrical pattern is:

E: E: X   U
I: I: X   U
I: I: X   U
A: A: X   U

Brooke translates:

When oaths confirm a lover's vow,
He thinks I believe him true: –
Nor oaths, nor lovers heed I now,
For memory dwells on you!

The tender talk, the face like snow
On the dark mountain's height;
Or the sweet blossom of the sloe,
Fair blooming to the sight![14]

47

The *Monthly Review* of January 1793 declared Charlotte Brooke an outstanding poet. We would hardly agree. But the defects of her work should not blind us to its merits. For one thing, she had brought an important selection of Irish poetry into print for the first time; then she had provided reasonably good texts of her Irish originals; and finally she had provided translations, though not very successful ones. She deserved some acclaim, at least the acclaim of a second edition. She did not live to receive this acclaim, though receive it she did when a really handsome second edition appeared in 1816. She also deserved a successor in the field: in fact, in admitting defects in her work, though not the most crucial ones, she hoped for a successor who would improve on her efforts. In this she was not so fortunate. Her successor did not appear until 1831, when James Hardiman published his *Irish Minstrelsy*,[15] and the translations in this work are only slightly better than Brooke's.

Hardiman was a Galwayman who seems to have been a native speaker of Irish and to have acquired his interest in Irish literature from some of the survivors of the old schools of native learning. He was a collector of manuscripts and intended at first to publish a collection of original Irish verse. When he altered his plan and decided to include translations he enlisted his friends as translators.: Thomas Furlong, John D'Alton, Edward Lawson, Henry Grattan Curran, William H. Drummond. Furlong, says Hardiman, aimed 'in his translations . . . to express himself as he conceived and bard would have done, had he composed in English',[16] and it seems that the other members of the team were at one with him in this. Thus their versions are in the same vein as those of Brooke: not always so fulsome nor so wordy, it is true, but nonetheless very much romanticised versions of the originals. A case in point is John D'Alton's version of the *dán díreach* poem lamenting Brian Ború which Douglas Hyde labelled 'a fearful translation', which even showed McPhersonish influence.[17]

In dealing with the verse of the 17th and 18th centuries, the translators, like Brooke, succeeded in capturing the sense of the originals, but missed, like her, all of their music and rhythm, and in dealing with the love songs they oversentimentalised. Take, for example, Furlong's translation of the first verse of the love-song 'Caiseal Mumhan'. The original is:

Phósfainn thú gan bha gan phunt gan áireamh spré,
agus phógfainn thú maidin drúchta le bánú an lae.

'S é mo ghalar dúch gan mé is tú, a dhiangrá mo chléibh,
i gCaiseal Mumhan is gan de leaba fúinn ach clár *bog* déil.[18]

The metrical pattern of this version of the first verse is:

U: U: A: E:
U: U: A: E:
U: U: A: E:
U: U: A: E:

Furlong translates:

I would wed thee my dear girl without herds or land
Let me claim as a portion but thy own white hand;
On each soft dewy morn shall I bless thy charms,
And clasp thee all fondly in my anxious arms.

It grieves me, my fairest, still here to stay,
To the south, to the south, love! let us haste away;
There plainly, but fondly, shall thy couch be spread.
And this breast be as a pillow to support thy head.[19]

This single example will have to suffice as an illustration of the all-pervading tone of the translations in Hardiman's two volumes, the tone of the English drawing-room. Again it must be said, however, that *Irish Minstrelsy* was an important work in that it provided for the first time in print a sampling, even if a rather eclectic one, of Irish poetry from the earliest times down to the 18th century. Thus its scope was much wider than that of Brooke's work. Furthermore it was not without influence, for it was from it that Samuel Ferguson, a member of the Protestant ascendancy, received his first impulse towards that interest in Irish literature which subsequently captured his imagination and dominated his literary achievement. Ferguson's translations, published in *Lays of the Western Gael* in 1865, also lacked the music of the originals, but he did avoid oversentimentalizing so that his translations ring much truer than those of the Hardiman group. His translation of the first verse of 'Caiseal Mumhan' runs as follows:

I'd wed you without herds, without money, or rich array,
And I'd wed you on a dewy morning at day-dawn grey;

My bitter woe it is, love, that we are not far away
In Cashel town, though the bare deal board were our marriage-
bed this day![20]

That, it seems to me, compares more than favourably with Furlong's
translation. It is clear, however, from *Lays of the Western Gael*, and
from his other works, *Congal, Lays of the Red Branch*, that Ferguson preferred composing lengthy poems based on the ancient sagas
to translating. He in his turn, however, had an influence on James
Clarence Mangan. And Mangan, as I have mentioned, was a
member of the O'Daly group. It is to this group that I shall now turn
my attention.

O'Daly's aim, as we have seen, was not to reach into the English
drawing-room, but into the cabins of the Irish peasantry. His first
collaborator was Edward Walsh, who made the translations for
Reliques of Irish Jacobite Poetry (1844) and for *Irish Popular Songs*
(1847). Walsh had a clear understanding of the nature of the Irish
accentual metres, but he was not very successful in *Reliques* in
carrying their sound-patterns over into English. Very often he failed
to achieve a free flow and many of his lines are very lame indeed. In
Popular Songs he was more fortunate. Here he introduced his work
with the following statement of intent:

> One striking characteristic in the flow of Irish verse must princi-
> pally claim our notice – namely, the beautiful adaptation of the
> subject of the words to the song measure – the particular embod-
> iment of thought requiring, it would seem, a kindred current of
> music to float upon. Or, to vary the figure, the particular tune so
> exquisitely chosen by the Irish lyrist, seems the natural gait of the
> subject, whatever that may be, from which it cannot be forced, in
> translation, without at once destroying the graceful correspon-
> dence which gives its most attractive grace to the original.

> Miss Brooke has erred through her versions of the 'Reliques' in
> this respect, and so also, almost generally, have the translators of
> Mr. Hardiman's 'Minstrelsy'.

> I have . . . been careful to avoid that error which I have already
> censured in others – namely, the fault of not suiting the measure
> of the translation to the exact song-tune of the original. The Irish
> scholar will perceive that I have embodied the meaning and spirit
> of each Irish stanza within the compass of the same number of

lines, each for each; and that I have also preserved, in many of the songs, the caesural and demi-caesural rhymes, the use of which produces such harmonious effect in Irish verse.[21]

Even in *Irish Popular Songs* he did not always follow these guidelines; but when he did, his efforts have much merit as accurate translations which carry with them a good imitation of the vowel-music of the originals. His translation of the first verse of 'Caiseal Mumhan' can be compared with Furlong's and Ferguson's and will suffice as an illustration of the merit of his work.

The version of the original is not quite the same as Hardiman's. It is as follows:

Phósfainn thú gan bha gan phunt gan áireamh spré,
a chuid den tsaol le toil do mhuintir' dá mb'áill leat mé.
'S é mo ghalar dúch gan mé is tú, a dhianghrá mo chléibh,
i gCaiseal Mumhan is gan de leaba fúinn ach clár *bog* déil.[22]

Here the metrical pattern is:

U: U: A: E:
I: I: A: E:
U: U: A: E:
U: U: A: E:

Walsh translates:

I would wed you, dear, without gold or gear, or counted kine;
My wealth you'll be, would your friends agree, and you be mine –
My grief, my gloom! that you do not come, my heart's dear hoard,
To Cashel fair, though our couch were there but a soft deal board.[23]

O'Daly's second collaborator was James Clarence Mangan, who provided the translations for the first series of *The Poets and Poetry of Munster* (1849). Mangan knew little or no Irish, at least during the period when he worked with O'Daly, and depended on prose translations made by O'Daly, Eugene O'Curry and John O'Donovan. Only occasionally did he try to reproduce the metrical pattern of his originals, as in 'Caitlín Ní Uallacháin'.

In vain, in vain we turn to Spain – she heeds us not.
Yet may we still, by strength of will, amend our lot.
O, yes! our foe shall yet lie low – our swords are drawn!
For her, our Queen, our Caitlin Ni Uallachain![24]

More typical of his work here is his translation of 'Síle Ní
Ghadhra' in the popular ballad style:

Alone as I wandered in sad meditation
And pondered my sorrows and soul's desolation
A beautiful vision, a maiden, drew near me
An angel she seemed sent from Heaven to cheer me.[26]

Mangan's best success in *Poets and Poetry* was achieved in handl-
ing more humorous pieces, such as the argument between the
poet-publican Seán Ó Tuama and his fellow-poet, Aindrias Mac
Craith. The banter of the original, which is cast as a series of
Limericks, is successfully reproduced:

Ó Tuama: I sell the best brandy and sherry,
         To make my good customers merry;
         But, at time their finances
         Run short, as it chances,
         And then I feel very sad, very!

Mac Craith: O Tuomy! you boast yourself handy
         at selling good ale and bright brandy,
         But the fact is your liquor
         Makes everyone sicker,
         I tell you that, I, your friend, Andy.

         When quitting your house rather heady,
         They'll get nought without more of 'the ready'.
         You leave them to stumble
         And stagger, and tumble
         Into dykes, as folk will when unsteady.[26]

In general, however, Mangan was most successful when he gave
freer rein to his own muse. His translation of 'Roisín Dubh' for
Poets and Poetry has the internal rhymes after the manner of the
original. But it was the freer version, inspired by a prose rendering
by Ferguson, which captured the popular imagination:

O my dark Rosaleen
Do not sigh, do not weep!
The priests are on the ocean green,
They march along the deep.
There's wine from the Royal Pope
Upon the ocean green:
And Spanish ale shall give you hope,
My dark Rosaleen!
My own Rosaleen!
Shall glad your heart, shall give you hope,
Shall give you health, and help and hope,
My dark Rosaleen!

Mangan is perhaps best remembered as a translator for his 'O'Hussey's Ode to Maguire' which is a version of Eochaidh Ó Heodhasa's *dán díreach* poem composed for his patron, the Fermanagh chief, Aodh Maguidhir, when the latter was in Munster during the winter campaign of 1600. Here again Mangan's version was inspired by a prose rendering by Ferguson, and Osborn Bergin has this to say of it:

Apart from the vivid picture of appalling floods and frost and thunderstorms the details are all wrong . . . The great captain who is ravaging Desmond is turned into a poor wanderer, lonely, persecuted and betrayed, cheered only by memories, and warmed only by 'the lightning of the soul'. Mangan's poem must be judged on its own merits.[27]

He might have added that the verse form employed by Mangan is very far indeed from the original. But as a poem in its own right, 'O'Hussey's Ode to Maguire' is not without merit. The first stanza of the original runs:

Fuar liom an adhaighsi d'Aodh,
cúis tuirse truime a ciothbhraon;
mo thruaighe sein dár seise,
neimh fhuaire na hoidhcheise.[28]

The following is Mangan's version of that first stanza:

Where is my chief, my master, this bleak night, mavrone?
O cold, cold, miserably cold is this bleak night for Hugh!

Its showery, arrowy, speary sleet pierceth one thro' and thro',
Pierceth one to the very bone.

If we admit, as I think we should, that Mangan's free versions
have some considerable merit, then we must also admit that his best
work as a translator was not done for John O'Daly, for these pieces
which I have mentioned and others like them did not appear in
Poets and Poetry of Munster. O'Daly was more fortunate in his third
collaborator, George Sigerson, who, under the pseudonym 'Éirion-
nach', provided the translations for the second series of *Poets and
Poetry of Munster* (1860). Sigerson seems to have dedicated his life
to this work of translating Irish poetry, for, as a boy at school in
France he won a prize for a Latin translation of an Irish poem. His
interest bore abundant fruit in the publication of *Poets and Poetry of
Munster*, and more abundant still in the publication more than thirty
years later, of his fine volume, *Bards of the Gael and Gall* (1897),
which contains versions of Irish poetry from the beginning down to
the 18th century. All of his work shows a striking faithfulness to the
original and a certain appealing simplicity. I shall confine myself to a
few examples from the later period.

In 'Gráinne Mhaol' he imitates the internal and final rhymes and
the caesurae of the original:

Above the bay, at dawn of day, I dreamt there came
The beautiful – the wonderful – the dear bright dame!
Her clustered hair, with lustre fair, lit all the vale –
She came a Star, with fame afar, Our Gráinne Mael![29]

That, it seems to me catches admirably the spirit of the original. So
too does the following extract from his translation of 'Seán Ó
Duibhir':

Oft, at pleasant morning,
Sunshine all adorning,
I've heard the horn give warning
With bird's mellow call –
Badgers flee before us,
Woodcocks startle o'er us,
Guns make ringing chorus,

'Mid the echoes all;
The fox run higher and higher
Horsemen shouting nigher,
The maiden mourning by her
Fowl he left in gore.
Now, they fell the wild-wood:
Farewell, home of childhood,
Ah, Shaun O'Dwyer a' Glanna, –
Thy day is o'er![30]

So also does this verse of his translation of an anonymous love-song:

Black head dearest, dearest, dearest!
Lay thy hand, dearest! my hand above!
Small mouth of honey, thyme-scented, sunny –
No heart that lives could refuse thee love![31]

Between the publication of Sigerson's two volumes in 1860 and 1897, no volume of translations had appeared except Douglas Hyde's *Love Songs of Connacht* (1894). To consider Hyde's work would bring us far into the present century so that it is perhaps time at last to stop and ask what is the importance, if any, of the work of these late 18th, and 19th, century translations of Irish poetry?

On the negative side, it must be admitted that John O'Daly's aim of giving back their poetry to the native Irish was not to succeed. The Irish poems and songs which he had translated survived, and still survive, in the original among the speakers of Irish. They were supplanted in the hearts of the nationalistic speakers of English by the ballads and songs of the *Nation*. It must also be admitted that, while the Anglo-Irish might be attracted to read some of these translations, they could be, and often were, I am sure, blissfully unaware of the fact that they were translations: that Ferguson's 'Downfall of the Gael' was a version of a poem by Fear Flatha Ó Gnímh; Mangan's 'O'Hussey's Ode to Maguire' a version of a poem by Eochaidh Ó Heodhasa and his 'Kincora' a version of a poem by Mac Liag; Rolleston's 'The Dead at Clonmacnois' a version of a poem by Enóg Ó Giolláin.

On the positive side, these translations stand as a considerable body of verse, and whenever Irish poetry is now anthologised in English the translations of many of those whom I have mentioned find a niche. There is, too, a certain chain of tradition: Ferguson was drawn by Hardiman's work from his ascendancy antipathy to things Irish to a deep interest in, and affection for, Irish literature. Ferguson in his turn, together with John O'Daly, helped to fire Mangan's imagination and Mangan became the songster of the nationalism which was seeking roots and identity.

In the broader perspective these translations constitute an important segment of 19th century Anglo-Irish literature and are part of a movement under the influence of which Anglo-Irish literature came to maturity at the turn of the century. In this context the importance of these translations is difficult to define. Suffice it to say that they cannot have been totally negligible as a formative influence.

NOTES

1 Dubhghlas de hÍde, *Mise agus an Connradh*, Dublin, 1937, p. 14.
2 *ibid.*; my translation.
3 *ibid.* p. 15; my translation.
4 2nd edn., London, 1893, p. 57.
5 *Reliques of Irish Jacobite Poetry*, Dublin, 1844, preface.
6 *ibid*
7 *Historical Memoirs of the Irish Bards*, 1818 edn., vol. I, pp. 57–8, n.
8 *Reliques of Irish Poetry*, pp. v–viii.
9 *ibid.* pp. 266–7. The metre is a form of less strict *dán díreach* i.e. *óglâchas*. I have edited the text very slightly and offer the following prose translation to assist comparison:
   All welcomed the Hound (i.e. Cúchulainn, the Hound of Cuala): 'Late have you come to help us. Conall is like a steed in bondage, and a hundred of our force together with him.'

   'It is difficult for us not to submit now that none remains of the men who would give combat; it is difficult for us to go to fight the hero by whom Conall has been bound.'

   'Think not of refusing to go to meet him, o hero of the sharp weapons; o strongest hand who would shun no man, free your teacher who is in fetters.'

   When Cúchulainn of the swords heard of the straits and the bondage of Conall, he, the hero of the strongest hand, went to demand that the (invading) youth give an account of himself.

   'O soft-haired one, (he said) choose whether to fight if you must or to give an account of yourself as a friend, lest you have reason to fear combat.'
9a *ibid.* pp. 12–16.
10 *ibid.* pp. 30–1.
11 *ibid.* p. 305. I have used, however, the version of these verses as edited by Tomás Ó Rathile in *Dánta Grádha*, Dublin & Cork, 1926, p. 23. I offer the

following prose translation to assist comparison:

Hide also the mouth which is like a berry, and the two cheeks which are like summer sun; the twining, curling hair, and the quiet, pleasant side.

Never again look on the fine tapering-fingered hands, the sedate instep, indeed, and the soles and the heel which is slender and excellent.

12 *Reliques* . . . p. 196.
13 *ibid*. p. 306. I have used the version of this first verse of the song as edited by Tomás Ó Concheanainn in de Brún Ó Buachalla and Ó Concheanainn *Nua-Dhuanaire: Cuid I*, Dublin, 1971, p. 77.
14 *Reliques* . . . p. 200.
15 London, 1831. Reprinted by the Irish University Press, Shannon, 1971.
16 p. lxxviii.
17 *A Literary History of Ireland*, London, 1899, p. 432, n. 2.
18 *Irish Minstrelsy*, vol. I p. 238; text slightly edited.
19 *ibid*. p. 239.
20 *Lays* . . ., 1888 edn., p. 156.
21 *Irish Popular Songs*, pp. 14, 31–2.
22 *ibid*. p. 168.
23 *ibid*. p. 169.
24 *Poets and Poetry*, p. 133.
25 *ibid*. p. 101.
26 *ibid*. pp. 67, 69.
27 *Irish Bardic Poetry* (ed. Greene and Kelly), Dublin 1970, p. 124.
28 Text from Bergin, *op. cit*., p. 124. Bergin's prose translation runs:
Too cold I deem this night for Hugh; the heaviness of its shower-drops is a cause of sadness; woe is me that this is our comrade's lot, the venom of this night's cold. (*ibid*., p. 268).
29 *Bards of the Gael and Gall*, London, 1925 edn., p. 282.
30 *ibid*. p. 247.
31 *ibid*. p. 295.

VICTORIAN EVANGELICALISM AND THE ANGLO-IRISH LITERARY REVIVAL

VIVIAN MERCIER

> On one of its sides, Victorian history is the story of the English mind employing the energy imparted by Evangelical convictions to rid itself of the restraint which Evangelicalism had laid on the senses and the intellect; on amusement, enjoyment, art; on curiosity, on criticism, on science.
>
> G.M. Young, *Victorian England*[1]

I

It would be outrageous to suggest that the true purpose of the Irish Literary Revival was to provide alternative employment for the sons of clergymen after Disestablishment had reduced the number of livings provided by the Church of Ireland. Nevertheless, the Revival, whose beginnings can be dated about ten years after the Irish Church Act of 1869, did have this unexpected side-effect. Among the leading figures of its first generation, Standish James O'Grady and Douglas Hyde were clergymen's sons, while W. B. Yeats and J. M. Synge were grandsons of clergy. Yeats's paternal grandfather and great-grandfather were both rectors of rural parishes; Synge's maternal grandfather, the Rev. Robert Traill, rector of Schull, Co. Cork, died in 1847 during the Great Famine, of fever caught while ministering to the poor of his parish. Surprisingly, although the Synges were one of the great clerical families of Ireland, we have to go back to the dramatist's great-great-grandfather to find a clergyman in the direct male line.[2]

No doubt the quality of one's ancestors' churchmanship counts more in the long run than the number among them who have sought a livelihood in the Church. Precisely for this reason, I sense something more than coincidence in the clerical antecedents of the writers just mentioned and others who joined their movement. We naturally expect writers and other artists to come from educated

59

families, and virtually every clergyman of the Church of Ireland had received a university education, but the immediate clerical ancestors of Yeats, Synge, Hyde and O'Grady were not conspicuously literary. The Rev. William Butler Yeats, grandfather of the poet, was supposedly involved in the editing of the *Dublin University Magazine*[3] with his friend Isaac Butt – also, by the way, the son of a clergyman – while the Rev. Robert Traill was a classical scholar, translating from the Greek Flavius Josephus's *Bellum Judaicum*. The Rev. Arthur Hyde and the Rev. Thomas O'Grady were competant scholars by the standards of their day, the former being able to teach his sons Latin and Greek, while the latter seems to have been most interested in Hebrew: it is hardly surprising that their sons can be more accurately described as propagandists and scholars than as artists.[4]

If such ancestors influenced their descendants towards a renewal of intellectual and artistic life in Ireland, it is at least conceivable that the impulse came from their religious faith rather than from any literary gift they may have possessed. The Church of Ireland as a whole, both clergy and laity, was powerfully affected throughout the nineteenth century by the Evangelical Revival, which began in the Church of England during the last quarter of the eighteenth. In Ireland, the earlier movement of renewal known as Methodism had had relatively little impact, but Evangelicalism permeated the Church of Ireland to such a degree that by 'mid-nineteenth century . . . the church could safely be described as predominantly evangelical,' though 'it was not until disestablishment was well past, that the majority of the bishops would wear an evangelical label.'[5] There is, then, at least an even chance that any given Irish clergyman ordained during the first half of the nineteenth century would have felt evangelical sympathies; those ordained in the second half were virtually certain to have done so. Furthermore, we do not have to rely upon guesswork alone in regard to the 'views' of the fathers and grandfathers of our four authors.

The authenticity of Thomas O'Grady's vocation may be measured by the fact that it came as a shock to his family, who regarded him 'not only as eccentric, but a "little wild" ' for entering the Church.[6] Elsewhere in his memoir of his father, Hugh Art O'Grady writes:

When Standish was a child the evangelical movement was at its zenith, Cork was its stronghold, and between his father and the famous Bishop Gregg there was a deep friendship. Accordingly he was brought up in a religious atmosphere, whose only parallel today can be found in the Society of Friends. 'To my father and mother', he once wrote, 'the world was filled with spirits good and bad, ministers of God or of His enemy.'[7]

Standish himself studied divinity for two years, but, in his son's words, 'His outlook was too broad, too unconventional, for a Church of Ireland clergyman.'[8] Nevertheless

O'Grady grew to manhood with two possessions, a deep religious feeling, and a minute knowledge of the Bible. The religious feeling, which he never expressed in conversation, came out in his writings on social questions. To him the devil was very much alive in our great civilization, and evils, which others viewed with equanimity, or as mere themes for politics or academic discussions, he treated as 'sheer downright wickedness.'[9]

It should be added that Standish O'Grady not only married a Co. Cork clergyman's daughter but lived to see his eldest son vicar of an English parish.

The Synge family, unlike the O'Grady clan, were staunch Evangelicals even when laymen, as we learn from the *Recollections* of the Rev. Richard Sinclair Brooke, unofficial and rather gossipy historian of the evangelical movement in Ireland. John Synge, the dramatist's grandfather, made Glanmore Castle available for clerical meetings at a time when these were a rallying point for the evangelically inclined; he was 'a skilled Hebraist, and had written, for the use of his sons, an excellent grammar of that language,' which he printed on a hand-press in his own house. John's second son, the Rev. Alexander Hamilton Synge, was Brooke's 'able, pious and devoted assistant' at the Mariners' Church, Kingstown (Dún Laoire), an important centre of Irish Evangelicalism, founded in 1836, of which Brooke was the first minister.[10] Alexander Synge has also been described as 'the first Protestant Missionary'[11] to the Aran Islands, where he arrived in 1851, shortly followed by a schoolmaster. 'We have a little church,' he wrote to one of his brothers, 'two to twenty-five make our congregation, mostly of the families of the coastguards.' Only one further sentence from his letters need be quoted here:

> I get on with the people so far very well, but how will it be when we begin to attack their bad ways, religion, etc., I don't know.

His conception of his mission to the Roman Catholic majority is set forth with painful clarity in those few words. One of the 'bad ways' he soon attacked was the Sunday handball match: surprisingly, the parish priest began demolishing the handball court next day, 'though the rascal had seen them playing there a hundred times before.' One notices over and over again that Anglican Evangelicalism produced two almost opposite effects in Irish Catholicism: offensively, the latter became more Catholic – and more Roman – but defensively it became in certain ways Puritan, as the Aran incident shows. Despite his exemplary death, the Rev. Robert Traill also illustrates the most bigoted aspect of Evangelicalism. He complained that his bishop, 'who is well known as the enemy of all evangelical piety, objects to me on account of my religious sentiments.'[12] Nor was his bishop his only affliction:

> I have waged war against popery in its thousand forms of wickedness, until my life had nearly paid the forfeit. None but those who have had the trying experience can possibly know the state of inquietude and feverish anxiety in which the Roman Catholics, especially in the country parts of the kingdom, keep the man who boldly denounces their abominations. It occurred to me on one occasion to be under the necessity of having two bodies of police armed for my protection.[13]

Many will think it natural that J. M. Synge should have abandoned a faith that could produce such bigoted adherents, but his objections to the milder Evangelicalism taught him by his mother were intellectual rather than emotional.[14] He remained to the end of his short life essentially puritanical in both morals and manners. His nearest brother in age if not temperament, the Rev. Samuel Synge, M.D., has left us a touching, ill-organised memoir, *Letters to My Daughter: Memories of John Millington Synge*. Its burden is that the playwright's life deviated little from what the Rev. Samuel regards as the evangelical Christian norm.[15] As for his beliefs, they may have been partly due to physical causes:

Always, too, remember your Uncle John's health. How often a man's doubts or difficulties that he thinks are in his own soul are really caused by bad health or some trying complaint.[16]

Samuel even blames himself for unintentionally putting his brother astray. When John was in his late 'teens, the brothers 'used to have great discussions on theology.' Samuel admits that, as a typical Evangelical of his time,

> I was very conservative in my way of taking or explaining many of the passages, for instance, in the Old Testament. I now see that I should have been far more help to him if I had said to him to take them either way he liked, . . . as actual historical accounts, or else as parables . . .[17]

Samuel, as one might have expected, ends by convincing himself that John 'died looking to God, I feel sure.'[18] No wonder John wrote of Samuel to his fiancée, Molly Allgood,

> He is one of the best fellows in the world, I think, though he is so religious that we have not much in common.[19]

Samuel seems to have accepted with equanimity the fact that Molly was a Roman Catholic, a response that neither of his grandfathers nor his Uncle Alexander would have been capable of. Evangelical in the fullest sense, he spent the greater part of the years 1896–1914 in China as a medical missionary: he could describe non-Christian Chinese as heathen but not as uncivilised, and was proud that he had helped many Chinese to break off the opium habit 'that was injuring their nation and condemned by all their people as a great vice.' [20]

This brief look at the O'Grady and Synge families shows that Evangelicalism had both attractive and sinister aspects, and, above all, that its influence did not die out in just one generation. The Yeats and Hyde families, on the other hand, retained something of the lax attitude of the eighteenth-century Irish Church: the Rev. John Butler Yeats was born in 1774, while the four generations of clerical Hydes preceding Douglas reached back farther still. Yet the next John Butler Yeats, father of the poet and himself an agnostic, spoke of his whole family for generations as being 'dyed . . . in a sort of well-mannered Evangelicism,' which he attributed to a French Huguenot ancestor.[21] The Rev. William Butler Yeats, during his curacy at Moira, Co. Down, is said to have antagonised his rector by his Evangelicalism,[22] but then few who studied divinity at Trinity in the early 1830's can have escaped evangelical influences. The group who founded the *Dublin University Magazine* in 1833 were Conservatives in politics but mainly Evangelicals in religion: the first editor, the Rev. Charles Stuart Stanford, remained bigotedly evangelical throughout his life; Isaac Butt, his successor from 1834 to 1838, shared Stanford's views at the time, though eventually he was to become the leader of the Home Rule party.[23] It seems unlikely that the Rev. William Yeats was ever a bigot: certainly when he was rector of Tullylish, Co. Down, he 'lived on good terms with the neighboring Catholic priest while remaining unacquainted with the Presbyterian minister.' [24] He was most nearly evangelical in his devotion to the second person of the Trinity, his aim being 'to follow closely in the footsteps of Jesus, to be like him sympathetic and like him affectionate, and like him courteous.' [25] Two of his laymen brothers, however, Henry and Matthew, were unequivocally evangelical. Of Matthew, John Butler Yeats, junior, was to write that 'Bible Christianity' did him 'a great deal of injury – It spoiled him, made him unhappy . . .' [26] Henry's religious ideas resembled Matthew's, 'but he had benefitted by being among clever and altruistic men . . .' [27] John told Matthew's eldest son, Frank,

> . . . You ought to be proud of being descended from the Yeats – Of all the people I have known they were the most attractive and the most spiritually minded – You did not see them at their best.[28]

Despite his agnosticism, John would not have hesitated to apply the phrase 'spiritually minded' to himself, and it can be applied without irony to all his children, though especially to the poet among them, W. B. Yeats.

Douglas Hyde's feelings about the Church of Ireland in his youth were complicated by his feelings towards his father, the Rev. Arthur Hyde, the fourth of his name in succession to have been a clergyman. Douglas's eldest brother was expected to become the fifth clerical Arthur Hyde, but he declined. The next brother, Oldfield, named after his maternal grandfather, the Rev. John Orson Oldfield, Archdeacon of Elphin, may never have shown signs of possessing a vocation. But Douglas seriously considered entering the Church from January 1877, when he turned seventeen, until he began to study law in October 1886. He had taken his B.A. in 1884, passed his final divinity examination in 1885, and was studying theology in 1886, presumably with the intention of obtaining a B.D. As early as November 1878, it was suggested that he enter Trinity College, Dublin, preparatory to becoming a foreign missionary. He recorded his father's reaction in his diary:

> 'T.C.D. be damned! Look at how it made an undisciplined scoundrel of Oldfield, and an agnostic of Arthur. I won't let you through any college! You can be a preacher to your own Irish-speaking countrymen.' [29]

Hyde writes later in the same entry, 'All I got out of the whole affair was two half-crowns when my father cursed T.C.D.' Apparently the father fined himself for cursing, or was it the sons who instituted this system of curbing their parent? An earlier diary entry in 1878 reads

> There was a great argument tonight between Arthur and the Master about the Master's excessive drinking. Arthur said that all the Master's good works and preaching were of no avail as long as he continued like this . . .[30]

It sounds as though the sons' standards of conduct were more nearly evangelical than those of the father. Doctrinally, however, the Rev. Arthur Hyde seems to have been on some points more high-church than evangelical; in this respect, Douglas Hyde deferred to him, or so a diary entry of May 1879 would suggest:

> I had great fun talking to a young Irishwoman . . . who has spent ten or fifteen years in England, about religion etc. She is very low-church. She said the Prayer Book was full of Popery and Romanism, and that the Archbishop of Dublin [Richard Chenevix Trench] had done a great deal of harm imposing Ritualism on us, and so on. I trotted out for her the arguments I heard so often from the Master, but I made no impression on her; she said she was not able to argue. Her thesis was that a person once converted could never be damned. I showed her the chapter in Ezechiel,* and the strong verses in Hebrews, but to no avail.[31]

*Perhaps Ezek. ch. 33, especially v. 13: 'When I shall say to the righteous, that he shall surely live; if he trust to his own righteousness and commit iniquity, all his righteousnesses shall not be remembered; but for his iniquity that he hath committed, he shall die for it.'

Hyde's mood was clearly flirtatious, and he may not have 'trotted out' his father's arguments with complete sincerity, but he certainly shows a thorough familiarity with them. A very suitable conversation for a Victorian Sunday afternoon in London, obviously with a Bible handy!

By 1883 father and son were disagreeing fiercely, not merely about whether Douglas should enter the Church but about fundamental beliefs. One night they 'had a terrible row . . . about belief in the Bible and about angels.' Arthur Hyde seems to have insisted upon interpreting the Bible literally. Douglas 'spent a couple of hours trying to make him understand my arguments against Christianity, which he answered very feebly.' [32] Later the same year, Douglas almost made up his mind to go in for medicine, except that he feared his health would not stand 'the strain of the Medical School.' He adds, 'On the other hand, I always feel a secret aversion against the clerical life, inspired in my childhood by my father's inexcusable conduct.' [33] What that conduct was, other than the overbearing, bad-tempered behaviour already noted, is not known. When the old man was grieving over the death of his wife in 1886, Douglas confided to his diary, 'I still have a certain fear of him, and some of the old hatred, and I have little enough sympathy for his pains and his grief.' [34] As we have seen, Douglas's wavering between the Church and medicine was resolved just after his mother's death by his beginning to study law. One piquant result of his vacillation was the scene at the College Theological Society on 1 March 1885, when he read his essay on 'The Attitude of the Reformed Church in Ireland,' a deliberately misleading title:

> The latter part of the Paper gave the essayist's own opinions as to the position the Irish Church clergy ought to take up with regard to the present Nationalist movement. This position, according to Mr. Hyde, should be one of approval, implicit if not avowed. Such opinions are not very common in the Theological Society [an ironic understatement], and their expression evoked against the essayist many hostile criticisms . . .[35]

Although he never left the Church of Ireland, Douglas Hyde was destined to become a missionary of the Gaelic Revival rather than of the Gospel. If he had taken orders, he might well have become a bishop or even Primate of All Ireland; instead, he became the first President of Éire, Uachtarán na hÉireann.

II

'Evangelical' and 'Evangelicalism' are words whose definitions may be found in any dictionary and most encyclopaedias, but in the course of time their use and meaning have varied greatly. Let us look at two descriptions of mid-nineteenth-century Irish Evangelicalism by two Church of Ireland clergymen of differing views. The first, not wholly sympathetic, is that of the Rev. Professor John Pentland Mahaffy, a man who might have been more at home in Renaissance Italy than in Victorian Dublin but was a dominant figure there, nevertheless:

> The popular preachers of Dublin in 1850 . . . differed from the early Puritans in that these thought an accurate knowledge of the original Bible essential, while their descendants were quite content with the Authorised Version. But so convinced were they of the vital importance of Scripture, that I have actually heard a clergyman . . . assert the verbal inspiration of the English Bible, on the ground that the same influence which guided the pens of the original writers could not have failed to guide . . . the translators . . . Regarding therefore the Bible, as they understood it, [as] the absolute rule of faith, they nevertheless acquiesced in the formularies and ritual of the Church of England . . . They never quarrelled with the Book of Common Prayer; they read through the service devoutly every Sunday . . .[36]

But 'the real work of the day,' according to Mahaffy, was the sermon:

> In this discourse, which often occupied three-quarters of an hour, it was [the minister's] absolute duty to set forth the whole Gospel (as he understood it), so that any stray person, or any member of the congregation in a contrite condition, might then and there attain conversion (which was always sudden) and find peace.[37]

In discussing the dogma preached by these popular Evangelicals, Mahaffy says, 'They were distinctly Calvinists'; this may possibly have been true of the 'half-a-dozen eminent preachers' that he has in mind, but a belief in predestination was not characteristic of Irish Evangelicals as a whole: those who had felt the influence of John Wesley were of course Arminians, while others adhered to various shades of opinion on the spectrum between extreme Arminianism and extreme Calvinism.[38] All, however, were 'distinctly anti-ritualists,' in Mahaffy's words, and as he says:

> They did not hesitate to preach that all those who had not embraced the dogma of justification by faith were doomed to eternal perdition. They believed as strongly as Massillon in 'the small number of the elect.' They were not afraid to insist upon the eternity of the very maximum of torture . . . But on the other hand, they had the firmest belief in the future bliss of those that were saved, and upon their deathbeds looked forward with confidence to an immediate reunion with the saints who had gone before. They even had strong hopes of seeing visions of glory on their deathbeds. These strong convictions gave them a zeal and fervour in their preaching which we look for in vain in the cautious and critical discourses of the present day.[39]

Mahaffy's final judgement on these preachers is rather severe, though I find it difficult to decide whether his viewpoint is that of the Broad Church or that of the High Church – perhaps a little of both?

> Their logic was often at fault; they felt no difficulties about the origin of evil, or the reconciling of moral responsibility with necessitarianism. They boldly preached that while man was free to do evil, and therefore responsible for it, he was unable, owing to Adam's transgression, to do any good thing of himself. And yet they never doubted the benevolence of the Deity, though they called every conversion a miracle. They lived saintly and charitable lives, though they inveighed against the value of good works. They controlled their congregations as spiritual autocrats, though they denied all efficacy in apostolical succession. They were excellent and able men, proclaiming a creed which has over and over again produced great and noble types of men, though most philosophers would denounce it as a cruel and even immoral parody of the teaching of the Founder.[40]

Lest anyone should mistakenly think that the Evangelicals were as chary of mentioning the name and person of the Founder of Christianity as Mahaffy is, here is a quotation from R. S. Brooke to redress the balance:

. . . wherever the Gospel of Christ is told forth with fervour, feeling, and simplicity, the people in this country, both high and low, throng to listen, and are never weary in so doing. Ritualism may dazzle the senses, Rationalism delight the intellect, but it is only a *full Christ*, all-sufficient in life for an holy example, all-sufficient in death for an atoning sacrifice, all-sufficient in glory to sanctify and help us by the impartation of His grace – it is only this Christ, like a full ocean breaking upon a thousand shores of feeling, and reaching and touching every realm of thought and life – it is this, and this only, that can, through the Spirit, go down and speak to the heart, and wake up its every pulse to the reception and enjoyment of a life which, begun then, will outlive death and last for ever.[41]

Not a logical definition, certainly, but an attempt to convey the essence of evangelical teaching in its ideal form. If this passage, written by Brooke in his seventies, makes salvation seem a little too easy of attainment, it should be read in the light of the fourth 'lecture' or sermon in his *Christ in Shadow* (1858). There he defends the doctrines of election and predestination – without claiming to understand God's motives in decreeing them – but at the same time rejects, as having no scriptural authority, 'the dogma of particular atonement.' He believes rather in 'the doctrine of universal atonement, or that Christ died for the sins of the whole world.' In sum,

. . . we shall be damned or saved according as we *believe or do not believe in Christ*.[42]

But the individual member of Brooke's congregation is left wondering whether his own belief is strong enough and pure enough. Justification by works is a more comforting doctrine than justification by faith, because one's good works are quantifiable, or seem to be, but it is anathema to Evangelicals. The Rev. James Thomas O'Brien, one of the first Irish Evangelicals to be made a bishop, describes it as 'what is common to all false religions – the being enabled to look for forgiveness to some outward acts . . .' Elsewhere in the same episcopal charge, he writes:

It is impossible to say what amount of superstitious observances – what extent of tyranny over the reason and conscience – an enlightened age will submit to, in return for having religion transferred to externals, and being allowed to look more to man than to God – to what is done without us than what is done within.[43]

Perhaps Bishop O'Brien was right in claiming that 'a sense of the presence of God is intolerable to fallen man,' who would prefer his religion to 'interpose something between this dreaded being and his soul.'[44] Surprisingly, however, an almost perfect answer to such fears had been given by a pioneer Evangelical, the Rev. Benjamin Williams Mathias, chaplain of the Bethesda Chapel, Dorset Street, Dublin, 1805–1835. In a letter (perhaps to his fiancée) he wrote:

> One thing I would enforce on you and on myself, is, to recollect that the motives of God's love to us are drawn from himself, not from us. He loves us because he is *love*. He has mercy because *he will have mercy*. Instead then of judging as we are apt to do, whether God loves us, by looking whether there be anything in *ourselves* to induce that love, let us rather look to God and consider whether there be anything in *him* to lead him to love.[45]

The above quotations stress four of the five essential tenets of Evangelicalism – and at least mention the fifth – listed in the following succinct definition:

> . . . the utter depravity of unregenerate human nature, necessity for conversion, justification of sinners by faith, free offer of the Gospel to all mankind, and the divine inspiration, authority and sufficiency of Holy Scripture . . .[46]

Irish Evangelicals found it difficult to agree on the correct interpretation of the dogma summarised as 'free offer of the Gospel to all mankind.' Besides insisting that Jesus Christ's redemptive sacrifice of himself on the Cross was offered for the whole human race, not the members of a narrow sect, it clearly implied the duty of undertaking or supporting foreign missions. Did it also, then, justify missions to one's fellow-Christians who were not convinced of the sufficiency of Holy Scripture or of justification by faith alone without works? Those who gave a positive answer to this question ultimately brought Evangelicalism into disrepute.

One of the early manifestations of the evangelical revival within the Church of England was the founding of the Church Missionary Society in 1799: its purpose was to bring Christianity, as understood by Anglicans, to the non-Christian world, and particularly to Africa and Asia. The Church of Ireland followed suit fifteen years later, when the Rev. B. W. Mathias, the Rev. Robert Daly (later Bishop of Cashel), and several laymen founded the Hibernian Church Missionary Society.[47] The priorities of Irish Evangelicals, living in a predominantly Roman Catholic country, differed from those of their English brethren: hence it was only two years after the founding of the British and Foreign Bible Society in 1804 that Mathias, after consulting some fellow-Anglicans and 'the ministers of different denominations in Dublin who professed to value the word of God,' joined in founding the Hibernian Bible Society.[48] The eighteenth-century torpor of the Church of Ireland had resulted in, among other symptoms of neglect, a scarcity of bibles in English; bibles in Irish, for a variety of reasons, were almost unobtainable.[49]

Contrary to the probable intentions of Mathias, within a few years the Hibernian Bible Society – almost inevitably, perhaps – came to resemble a proselytising agency. Given the traditional attitude of the Roman Catholic Church towards unguided reading of the Bible, an organisation that proposed to supply what were in effect Protestant bibles (though 'printed without note or comment') in Irish or English to any who wanted them was bound to cause friction between the two religious communities. In fact, as pressure built up for Catholic Emancipation (legislated in 1829), many branches of the Bible Society became centres of aggressive Protestant propaganda.[50] Another evangelical body, the Irish Society (founded 1818), took matters a step farther: its aim was to teach Irish-speaking peasants to read the Scriptures in Irish to their neighbours.[51] Thanks to what the Rev. William Sewell was later to call the 'extraordinary and magical influence over the people' of the Irish language,[52] these scripture-readers were expected to – and did – make a number of converts. While insisting that it was not an out-and-out proselytising agency, the Irish Society had to stress the number of conversions that its activities fostered if it wished to go on collecting funds.

It was in the 1830s that the more extreme Evangelicals began an overt campaign of proselytism against the Roman Catholic Church in Ireland. Events during the first half of the decade alarmed the entire Church of Ireland: the 'tithe war' began in 1830; in 1831 the supposedly 'godless' national system of education was introduced;

in 1833 the Church Temporalities Act, which was seen as an instalment of disestablishment, received the royal assent.[53] Some Evangelicals were in a sufficiently unChristian mood to want to hit back at what they saw as an unholy alliance of the Whigs and the papists. The most generally acceptable reaction proved to be the founding of the Church Education Society in 1839: it provided Anglican-controlled primary education in competition with the national schools until disestablishment and beyond; every Evangelical supported it, and many others besides.[54] Not content with this defensive action, some chose to attack. The chief centres of proselytism were one or two of the poorer parishes in the city of Dublin and some impoverished areas on the west coast.[55] Relatively successful missions were established by the Rev. Edward Nangle on Achill Island[56] and by the Rev. Charles Gayer, an Englishman, in the Dingle Peninsula. Gayer was helped by one of three local Irish-speaking converts, the Moriarty brothers, from a well-known Kerry family.[57]

In 1849 the most notorious and for a time the most successful of proselytising agencies, the Society for Irish Church Missions to the Roman Catholics, was founded by the Rev. Alexander Dallas, with headquarters in London at Exeter Hall, that hotbed of evangelical societies. Dallas was an Englishman, rector of Wonston in Hampshire, and his chief function in the I.C.M. was to raise funds throughout the British Isles, but he had many Irish allies, especially in Counties Galway and Mayo.[58] The late Anglican Archbishop of Tuam, the Rev. Power Le Poer Trench, who died in 1839, had encouraged missionary work in his archdiocese: apart from Nangle's Achill Mission, it had been carried on chiefly by the Irish Society. Trench's successor, the Rev. Thomas Plunket (later Lord Plunket) – who as a result of the Church Temporalities Act ranked only as Bishop of Tuam – encouraged Dallas, as did the Rev. Hyacinth D'Arcy, landlord and then rector of Clifden, and the Rev. William Conyngham Plunket, later Lord Plunket and Archbishop of Dublin. Given such support, a substantial minority of the Connacht clergy engaged in missionary work; recruits, including the Rev. Alexander Synge, were brought from elsewhere in Ireland and from England. There was also a mission church at the Irish headquarters of the I.C.M. in Townsend Street, Dublin. The great irony of the Connacht mission was that its converts, shunned by the neighbouring Roman Catholics and educated for white-collar occupations at the mission schools, found themselves forced to emigrate to America or the British colonies.[59] Despite the tremendous decline in the Roman Catholic population, due to famine and emigration, between 1834 and 1861, in the latter year the proportion of Anglicans in the total population of Ireland was only 11.9 per cent. This represented a small increase over the 1834 figure of 10.7 per cent., but the total membership of the Church of Ireland had declined by almost 160,000.[60]

Professor Desmond Bowen believes that the initial success of the Irish Church Missions in Connacht was one of the factors leading to the selection of the Rev. Paul Cullen (later Cardinal Cullen) as Archbishop of Armagh in 1849 and to his being authorised to summon the Synod of Thurles in the following year.[61] Among many other Catholic countermeasures taken at that time, it is interesting to note the visits by missioners from England to Dublin, Connacht and Ulster – reclaiming converts from Protestantism and heartening the faithful. Their activities seem a peculiarly appropriate response to Dallas.[62] The long-term consequences of his campaign included, in all probability, the prevailing Counter-Reformation spirit of Irish Catholicism during the next hundred years and the advancing of the date for the inevitable disestablishment of the Church of Ireland.[63]

On the mythical level – the most vital one for poets – what Bowen calls 'The Protestant Crusade' had important consequences also. That Dallas should have begun his missionary campaign while the Irish people, especially in Connacht, were still reeling from the blows of the Great Famine of 1845–47 made a particularly sinister impression on the Irish mind, both conscious and unconscious. The evangelical missionaries were accused of bribing starving people with food, of making them sell their Catholic birthright literally for a mess of pottage. The term 'souper' for a convert to Protestantism was already in use before the Great Famine, at least in Dingle:

> . . . a benevolent Protestant lady of the town set up a soup kitchen to sell food to the poor. Those who bought from her were immediately labelled 'soupers,' and accused of apostasy.[64]

Ever since the Reformation, any Catholic Irishman who changed his religion was assumed to have done so purely for worldly advantage. The Gaelic poetry of eighteenth-century Ireland includes many satires against those who were believed to have betrayed their religion and their nationality because of the higher material and social status of Protestants in a period when Roman Catholicism

73

was virtually proscribed.[65] Not until the nineteenth century, however, were converts accused of selling their faith for bare existence.

At the height of the famine in 1847, tens of thousands more might
have died were it not for the soup kitchens, usually manned by the
local Church of Ireland clergyman and his household and financed
by Quaker relief organisations. Bowen writes:

> In most cases religious issues were put aside during the actual
> famine crisis. The Catholic clergy were so much in the saddle, as
> they brought the last rites of their church to the sick and dying,
> that they were content to accept a division of labour whereby the
> administration of temporal relief was left to the parson and his
> family. But inevitably – as the Quakers noted – the person who
> actually managed the boiler and the distribution of food, was
> accused of partiality, and the ugly issue of souperism began to
> divide the people. Once the charge was made the distributor of
> relief was guilty until proved innocent – and how was innocence
> to be proved?[66]

If Synge's grandfather the Rev. Robert Traill had survived the
Famine, he would have been peculiarly vulnerable to such charges
because of his avowed Evangelicalism and anti-Catholicism, yet his
conduct in 1847 seems to have been accepted on all sides as heroic.
Had it not been for the timing – and for some of the dubious tactics –
of Dallas's campaign, the untrue charges of 'souperism' might have
faded into oblivion. Bowen reluctantly concludes, however, that
'there is much to suggest that one of the agencies whose missionaries engaged in souperism was the Society for Irish Church
Missions to the Roman Catholics.'[67]

Only those who are aware of the history and mythology of souperism can grasp the full significance of the fact that W. B. Yeats's *The
Countess Cathleen* was the very first play presented by the Irish
Literary Theatre (8 May 1899). Only they, too, can appreciate the
full irony of the fact that this play about devils buying Irish souls for
gold should have been denounced as anti-Catholic.[68]

III

Besides the theological and political effects just described, the
Evangelical Revival in Ireland had moral, social, and even intellec-

tual consequences. In discussing the corresponding English movement, Noel Annan gives priority to its moral results:

> Evangelical morality was the single most widespread influence in Victorian England. It powerfully influenced the Church of England, was the faith of the Methodists, and revived the older Nonconformist sects; it spread through every class and taught a clear set of values. The peremptory demand for sincerity, the delight in plain-speaking, the unvarying accent on conduct, and the conviction that he who has attained a Higher Truth must himself evangelise, leap from the pages of [Leslie] Stephen's books and proclaim him a child of the Evangelical tradition.[69]

All of these values can of course be traced in the Church of Ireland Evangelicals and their descendants, but I think the most striking difference between the average nineteenth-century Irish Anglican, lay or clerical alike, and his eighteenth-century counterpart must have been the former's seriousness of manner – an outward and visible sign of intellectual and moral sobriety. No longer the roistering squire of Sir Jonah Barrington's *Recollections* or Maria Edgeworth's *Castle Rackrent*, the better-off Church of Ireland layman came to be perceived by some of his Roman Catholic contemporaries as what D. P. Moran of *The Leader* was to call a 'sourface.'[70] a far cry indeed from Oliver Goldsmith's 'men of a thousand pound a year in Ireland' who 'spend their whole lives in running after a hare, drinking to be drunk, and getting every Girl with Child, that will let them . . .!'[71] As for the clergy, long before Disestablishment abolished their absenteeism and pluralism while making part of their income dependent on voluntary subscriptions from the laity, the Established Church Home Mission (founded by Mathias and others in 1828) had sent its volunteers from parish to parish, setting new standards of preaching and pastoral care for lax or lazy incumbents.[72]

As Annan reminds us,

> The intellectual heritage of Evangelicalism has been too readily forgotten . . . it is too often assumed to be a religion with a theology simplified to the point of banality which calls men to action rather than strengthens their minds – the enemy of intelligence and learning. It is true that no outstanding intellect emerges among the Anglican and Nonconformist clergy of the Evangelical

persuasion, but the histories of the movement, perhaps naturally, do not follow the sheep who stray from the fold. Half the men and much of the enthusiasm of Tractarianism were of Evangelical origin; the most fervent recruits to rationalism came from Evangelical homes. And how many of the middle-class intellectual aristocracy are reared in Evangelical families![73]

What he says of England here was at least equally true of Ireland: we cannot perhaps be sure how evangelical the homes of those famous rationalists John Tyndall and W. E. H. Lecky were, but J. B. Bury was born the eldest son of the curate of Monaghan, later rector of Clontibret and a canon of Clogher. Two of the great scholar's younger brothers became Anglican clergymen: one died young, but it would be interesting to know the other's opinion of, say, *A History of Freedom of Thought* or some of his eldest brother's work on the early history of Christianity.[74]

Sir John Pentland Mahaffy, though not the intellectual equal of Bury, had a world reputation in his day for both classical scholarship and *haute vulgarisation*. The son of a clergyman, he received an impeccably evangelical training from both father and mother; having taken orders himself, he remained a Church of Ireland clergyman all his life, though perhaps veering, as we have seen, towards a broad-church attitude in later years.[75] Another son of an evangelical clergyman who played a distinguished part in the intellectual life of his time was the Rev. Stopford Augustus Brooke, son of the Rev. R. S. Brooke. His mother was the daughter of the Rev. Joseph Stopford, who as a Fellow of Trinity (1790–1809) took part in 'weekly meetings for prayer or reading the Scriptures' and was revered as a pioneer Evangelical; as he had the largest class of pupils in college, his influence was widely felt.[76] Stopford Brooke is now remembered, if at all, for his anthologies and somewhat uncritical studies of English literature, but in his day he was a famous London preacher and a model for the Rev. James Mavor Morell in Shaw's *Candida*.[77] Shaw received some of his early lessons in Socialism at the Bedford Chapel Debating Society, founded by Brooke in connection with his ministry at the chapel.[78] Alice Stopford, a cousin of Brooke, was the daughter and granddaughter of evangelical clergymen, her grandfather being Edward Stopford, bishop of Meath and a brother of Joseph Stopford. She married J. R. Green, the once-famous historian, who was himself for a time an Anglican clergyman but, like his friend Stopford Brooke, eventually left the

Church.[79] Mrs. Green, a passionate Irish nationalist, also won fame as a historian.[80]

One important fact must never be forgotten: unlike their Non-conformist counterparts, Anglican evangelical clergymen almost without exception had earned university degrees, and some were truly learned men. A wit who knew Bury's father (was it Mahaffy?) said that the historian's mother must have been a very clever woman; in fact, she was, but the Rev. Edward John Bury had been a prizeman in divinity and Hebrew.[81] Mahaffy had learned all the Latin and Greek he knew when he entered Trinity from his father, 'a good classic.'[82] As the nineteenth century advanced, a broader range of learning and culture could be expected from the Irish clergy. The Rev. Charles William Benson, founder and headmaster of Rathmines School, 1859–99, taught Chaucer, Shakespeare, philology and astronomy, as well as Scripture and Greek Testament. His pupils included, besides many future Anglican clergymen, the poet 'A.E.' (George Russell), the painter Walter Osborne, and the most famous convert to Catholicism from an Irish evangelical family – George Tyrrell, destined to be expelled from the Jesuits and to undergo minor excommunication for the heresy of Modernism.[83]

Tyrrell's tribute to Benson ('Dearest and best of men!' he called him) is worth reading in full; the following passage, however, deserves special attention:

Dr. Benson was an exceedingly religious man, and, although Evangelical, had a taste for liturgical observance. Thus we opened school by an abbreviated Choral matins; *i.e.* the *Venite*, the Psalms for the day, a chapter, a hymn, then a lecture on the Scriptures and finally some collects – the whole taking about three-quarters of an hour. To this I owe my acquaintance, not only with the text, but with the sense of the Scriptures, and also my liturgical taste, which, later, helped me on towards Catholicism. These lectures were fairly critical, and were interspersed with many terse, practical and devotional comments from the Doctor's well-stored mind and ready wit.[84]

George Tyrrell's father was a journalist, but two uncles were Church of Ireland clergymen. Robert Yelverton Tyrrell, the great classical scholar, was the son of perhaps the more evangelical of these; he himself became a rationalist. George's ill-fated elder brother, William (1851–1876), also was both a fine classical scholar and a sceptic. Thus within a single family the two opposite ways of leaving the evangelical fold were strikingly exemplified, to the bitter regret of George:

> Willie lies in Tipperary Churchyard under two pagan epitaphs, in Greek and Latin. Except for a memorial medal for classical literature . . ., no trace of him remains, beyond a handful of epigrams and translations in a book published by my cousin [R. Y. Tyrrell].[85]

George Tyrrell's progress into the Roman Catholic Church and then, in a sense, out of it again underlines an evangelical tendency described by Annan as 'following the inner light wherever it shines.'[86] A passage from Stopford Brooke's diary about the pain he had caused his father by seceding from Anglicanism drives home Annan's point:

> I sat down on the grass of [my father's] grave, and read the inscription I wrote for him. And I remembered all he had been, and how I had disappointed him . . . I was not vext, even then. I knew he would feel in that way. But I was deeply moved and sorry. I did not regret what I had done; I did regret that he had suffered for it. But what else could I have done? A man must do what he must do.[87]

Had Stopford broken with the church of his ancestors – many of them clerical – on any ground other than his denial of the divinity of Jesus Christ, Richard might have been less afflicted. The elder Brooke was a man of broad human sympathy, widely read, and a lover of poetry, however narrow he may appear in politics and theology. Here is a characteristic comment by him:

> The Rev. Charles Bayly . . . perhaps had more culture and reading than most Evangelical ministers – the weak point in the body being, more or less, an inclination to ignore literature and despise art, forgetting that these are the good Lord's gifts to refine and adorn our poor fallen nature . . .[88]

This remark, implying that culture is good for the righteous, is reinforced by one from *Christ in Shadow* implying that the converse is also true:

On the other hand, a cultivated understanding, into which grace has descended, will lose nothing of true taste or appreciation of the beautiful, while it will gain much in refinement and spiritualized judgment.[89]

If all Evangelicals had shared R. S. Brooke's views on literature and art, fewer of the Revival writers might have felt the need to reject the religion in which they were brought up.

The readiness of Irish Evangelicals to change or abandon their beliefs has been the subject of puzzled or even admiring comment. We are told of A.E. that

He delighted George Moore once by relating how, while staying with his aunt in Armagh, he left the house one day to 'think the whole thing out,' and in five minutes had decided to defy a God who threatened him for 'doing things which he had never promised not to do.'[90]

Though not a clergyman, A.E.'s father, Thomas Elias Russell, was 'gentle and cultured, and of deep religious convictions, attending the Parish Church in the mornings and the Primitive Methodist Church in the afternoons . . .'[91] The son of so evangelical a father must have been fully aware of the necessity of conversion, which, as Mahaffy reminds us, was always sudden. A.E.'s sudden conversion *from* evangelical Christianity as he understood it was soon followed by a conversion *to* Theosophy.

Beyond the evangelical emphasis on conversion one has to recognise a broader Protestant tendency to secession and sectarianism, for which the justification offered is nearly always a greater simplicity, a greater naturalness, a supposedly more universal human appeal – often most passionately claimed by the very smallest splinter groups. Protestantism, after all, was born of secession, and its logical conclusion might seem to be 'one man, one church.' In the early days of Church of Ireland Evangelicalism, first Walkerites and then Kellyites followed the Rev. John Walker and the Rev. Thomas Kelly out of the Established Church.[92] Somewhat later, in 1827, the Rev. John Nelson Darby joined A. N. Groves in forming a sect in Dublin called 'The Brethren'. Darby's missionary activities led to the founding in Plymouth of the Plymouth Brethren; after the seemingly inevitable schism, one section of the Brethren came to be known as Darbyites.[93]

Perhaps not fully aware of this Protestant tradition, Augustine Martin has nevertheless some perceptive pages contrasting the agonisings over their loss of faith revealed by Irish Catholic writers such as James Joyce and Austin Clarke with the cooler Protestant reactions to similar experiences:

> Synge takes two paragraphs in his fragmentary *Autobiography* to record the 'terrible experience' of his apostasy; Yeats describes his break with 'the simple-minded religion of my childhood' in a sentence of *Autobiographies*; the work of Shaw shows little evidence of anguish or remorse at the loss of his Anglicanism . . .[94]

It was the morality of evangelicalism rather than its theology that Shaw found difficulty in casting off. His frugality and abstemiousness were life-long, but the bourgeois evangelical morality of his first important prose work is reflected in far later works which profess to be socialist. *My Dear Dorothea* (written in 1878, when he was 22, but first published, posthumously, in 1956), 'A Practical System of Moral Education for Females . . .,' professes to give a five-year-old girl 'directions quite opposite to those you are accustomed to receive,' but Shaw often smuggles in a morality acceptable to Aunt Tabitha, who seeks to improve Dorothea by tracts, though he disguises Duty in the garb of Utilitarianism.[95] The following passage is the most revealing in the entire work:

> Nothing is more important to your happiness than the habit, which you must try to form, of never wishing for anything that you cannot either buy or make for yourself. Everybody in this world is expected to take care of himself, and live without asking help from his fellow creatures . . .
>
> Therefore, never ask anything as a favor, but only those things which you are entitled to have, or which you have deserved by your conduct. If this should sometimes prove hard to abide by, remember that the world is an unhappy place, and that it is only made bearable by each person agreeing to bear some share of trouble. No matter how heavy a load is, its weight is scarcely felt when it is divided among many persons.
>
> Every person must bravely take his share, and you must take yours. When you see others wanting to escape their little portion of the great burden, by begging from others or refusing to repay their politeness, you may despise them, and feel that you have a greater claim to respect than they.[96]

Except for the idea of sharing the load, there is no room for socialism – and precious little for Christianity – in this quintessence of middle-class morality, reinforced by the evangelical view of this world as a vale of tears. Even when Shaw had adopted socialism, he still felt free to despise the poor and the idle. Both *Major Barbara* and its preface teach that 'the worst of our crimes is poverty, and that our first duty, to which every other consideration should be sacrificed, is not to be poor.'[97] This should not be mistaken for irony: in the preface to *Androcles and the Lion*, where the context is Jesus himself and not merely the Salvation Army, Shaw calls poor people 'cancers in the commonwealth.' As for the idler, rich or poor,

> Since it is evident that the first condition on which he can be kept alive without enslaving somebody else is that he shall produce an equivalent for what it costs to keep him alive, we may quite rationally compel him to abstain from idling by whatever means we employ to compel him to abstain from murder, arson, forgery, or any other crime.[98]

These words, published in 1916, reveal Shaw as a totalitarian socialist even before the existence of Soviet Russia. His pharisaical attitude to the poor and the idle rich is very similar to that of the Dublin Evangelicals among whom he grew up in the third quarter of the last century.

For in Dublin, as in Cork and occasionally elsewhere, the Evangelicals came to form a middle-class enclave, a church within a church, with their own ministers and their own places of worship. How this happened is partly explained by that gifted amateur sociologist James Godkin, writing in 1866–67:

> In Dublin more than half the Episcopal population attend non-parochial churches, sometimes called free churches or proprietary churches, founded chiefly by the laity from time to time, in order that they might have their spiritual wants supplied by ministers whom they considered more evangelical, more spiritually minded, more earnest and active than the parochial clergy. In the course of time, the rapid increase of population in the southern suburbs rendered it necessary to erect new buildings, in order to meet the demand for church accommodation.[99]

Some of these new suburban churches had districts assigned them within the wide boundaries of the old parishes, so that the incumbents could marry, baptise and bury members of their flocks, but the rectors of the parishes sometimes 'disputed their legal right to use the Sunday collections for the poor, arguing that they were robbing the poor of the parish churches by alienating from them the wealthy parishioners.'[100]

Godkin's account, however, is not fair to the pioneer Evangelicals: they too ministered in proprietary chapels, but only because the Archbishops of Dublin prior to Magee, who removed the ban on Mathias in 1828, would not license them to preach in the parish churches.[101] These chapels were attached to charitable institutions such as the Magdalene Asylum and the Molyneux Asylum for the Blind; Mathias's Bethesda Chapel was part of an institution first founded as a female orphanage but later incorporating 'a Lock Penitentiary, for the reception and employment of women leaving the Lock hospital [for venereal diseases], and wishing to return . . . to the pursuits of industry and virtue.' One may guess that Evangelicals were first welcomed into these institutional chapels because the fervour of their extemporary preaching encouraged subscriptions, gifts and bequests, especially at the annual charity sermon. 'The chapel of the Bethesda,' says an account published in 1818, 'is unusually crowded during divine service, either because it is supposed the service is performed with more solemnity, the preaching more impressive, or the doctrine more pure.' The same writer attributes much of the appeal of the service to the contrast between the penitents, who have passed 'through the extremes of misery and vice,' and the orphans, 'as yet pure and unacquainted with sin and wretchedness.' The two groups sing at opposite sides of the chapel:

> The impression of this is very affecting, and the voice of one penitent in particular has been long celebrated for its pensive sweetness.[102]

The principle established by such institutions, founded by private charity and administered by trustees, was soon extended to include churches not attached to charitable institutions: for instance, Trinity Church was built in the centre of Dublin for the great evangelical preacher John Gregg, afterwards bishop of Cork, whose pulpit eloquence is scathingly described in Thackeray's *Irish Sketch Book*.[103] R. S. Brooke's Mariners' Church provides another example.

Not all Irish Evangelicals, of course, belonged to the middle classes. The small minority of evangelical bishops who were also aristocrats happen to have been named already: Archbishop Trench of Tuam, second son of the first Earl of Clancarty; Bishop Daly, grandson of the Earl of Farnham; and the second and fourth Barons Plunket. Lord Farnham, Lady Powerscourt, and her brother the third Earl of Roden (made notorious by the affair at Dolly's Brae) were prominent among the evangelical laity.[104] Members of the lower classes were viewed as proper objects of charity or proselytism, but Church of Ireland Evangelicalism lacked the democratic spirit of English Nonconformism: in fact, its political affiliations were chiefly Tory. The Rev. R. S. Brooke describes his Sunday school at Kingstown about 1840 as strictly segregated on class lines:

> . . . nearly 500 scholars, and upward of 40 unpaid teachers . . . large classes for the children of the gentry; a class of beggars; one of converts from Romanism; one for servants, men and women; one for young men preparing for the ministry; one for pauper old women; a great class of young ladies . . .; but the most prized was our adult seamen's class.[105]

These seamen must have been mainly English or Welsh, for they were all Wesleyan Methodists.[106] Among the few descriptions of rousing prayer-meetings under Church of Ireland auspices are those given by Lennox Robinson and his brother and sister while recalling their father's curacy at Kinsale, 1892–1900. There, the chief lay participants were Manx and Cornish fishermen, again 'Methodists almost to a man.' No Church of Ireland layman of their class would have dared to behave with the self-assurance described by Tom Robinson:

> Besides singing, the men spoke at great length and prayed at even greater. It was their prayers, I am afraid, which chiefly amused us . . . the quaintness of their phraseology and their occasional assumption of familiarity – even of patronage – towards the Almighty were at times too much for our gravity.
>
> The meetings ran themselves. After an opening hymn and probably a short prayer and a very few words of exhortation and encouragement from the Rector ('Don't be backward in coming forward'), the men took control, and address, prayer and hymn followed one another without pause . . .[107]

The amusement of the curate's children serves to underline how undemocratic the Church of Ireland still was after a century of Evangelicalism: and yet the Rev. Andrew Robinson had given up a flourishing business as a stockbroker in Cork to 'answer the call,' at the age of fifty, as a humble curate.[108]

It was against the laity rather than the clergy of the Dublin proprietary churches that Godkin directed his irony:

It is a fact that the free church congregations are for the greater part far the most select, respectable, and fashionable, for they consist generally of those who are able to pay their way, and who prefer paying liberally for pews which they can call their own, and into which no strangers may intrude. And it sometimes happens that the gradations of wealth and respectability are marked by the position occupied by certain families in the church. Some gentlemen are trustees, or have been large contributors, or choose to pay a high figure for the best places, where they can hear and see and be seen to the greatest advantage; and no doubt one cause of the success of these churches is that the worshippers may avoid unpleasant contact with people of inferior positions, some of whom may not be very well dressed, perhaps not over clean; or they may be offensive by the vulgarity of their manners . . .[109]

Shaw insists that he gave up going to church at about the age of ten, perhaps while Godkin was writing the words just quoted, and stayed away for twenty years: 'To this day, my flesh creeps when I recall that genteel suburban Irish Protestant church, built by Roman Catholic workmen who would have considered themselves damned had they crossed its threshold afterwards.'[110] This was none other than Christ Church, Leeson Park, described by Godkin as 'the most splendid monument about Dublin of the power of the voluntary principle in the Establishment – a church built in the Gothic style, light, commodious, and elegant in all its internal arrangements, and affording accommodation to 1,300 people . . .'[111] It replaced the old chapel of the Molyneux Asylum for the Blind, situated in a decaying area of the inner city; the Asylum itself was also moved to the new site in the suburbs, south of the Grand Canal. Faith can move mountains: it was the faith of the Rev. Dr. Charles Marlay Fleury, chaplain to the Asylum and a famous evangelical preacher, that brought about this unprecedented move; more tangible assistance was provided by Henry Shaw, the dramatist's only wealthy uncle, one of whose daughters married a son of Dr. Fleury.[112] Few people, it might seem, had a better right to worship in the new church than the boy Shaw, but many years later he summed up Godkin's charges in one devastating sentence:

> What helped to make 'church' a hot-bed of all the social vices was that no working folk ever came there.[113]

IV

Clearly, by the late 1860s Irish Evangelicalism had ceased to be a revolutionary, prophetic movement; like many such renewals of the spirit it had solidified into a church: specifically, the post-disestablishment Church of Ireland, in which for a variety of reasons middle-class laymen not only controlled the economic organisation but seemed at first likely to change the Prayer Book radically in the direction of evangelical orthodoxy.[114] If the old energy and idealism were to survive, they must find new channels in the minds and hearts of the young.

And find them they did. Nobody has given a better account of the intellectual ferment in Protestant Dublin during the 1870's than the Rev. Charles E. Osborne, brother of the painter, in his essay on 'George Tyrrell's Dublin Period.'

> The truth is that, just when Tyrrell was a youth in Dublin, various groups of thinking young men, whose parents were nearly always orthodox Protestants of the old-fashioned Low Church variety, were experiencing . . . disengagement of their minds from Puritan moorings. The direction taken was not the same in each case, but the liberating process was experienced, whatever the ultimate goal of the soul's barque might be.[115]

The most obvious direction to take led towards some other form of religion, the nearest to hand being high-church Anglicanism:

> The excesses of St. Bartholomew's Dublin (mild indeed compared to English ritualism), and similar features, a little more pronounced, at Grangegorman [parish church], attracted small knots of young people, some from genuine interest and earnest-

ness, some from affectation and a desire to shock Protestant parents.[116]

Puseyism, however, could not flourish in the Irish capital at that time, when – as in Northern Ireland to this day – everyone had to be either a Protestant or a Catholic, and any holder of an intermediate position was despised or feared as a double agent. Of the young rebels who took this direction, Osborne says, 'some changed their minds or ceased to trouble about such matters, others left the country, generally to serve in the Anglican ministry in England or the Colonies; while a very few acknowledged Rome as the true end of their wanderings . . .'[117] Notable among the last were George Tyrrell and Oscar Wilde, but the conversion of both to Roman Catholicism took place after they had left Ireland for good.

Christianity, in whatever form, was not to be the only religious option: by 1886, a Dublin Lodge of the Theosophical Society had been founded by Charles Johnston, friend of both Yeats and A.E.[118] Given the peculiar religious sociology of Ireland, the fact that Theosophy was non-Christian did not prevent it from attaining almost exactly the status of a tiny Protestant sect. The principle of 'following the inner light wherever it shines' inhibited Protestants from objecting too strongly to what often seemed more like a debating society than a church; official Catholicism rarely felt obliged to notice a group which in practice attracted few Roman Catholics. 'John Eglinton' (William Kirkpatrick Magee), A.E.'s first biographer, claimed a greater role for Theosophy in the Irish Literary Revival than seems justifiable, though the present article is partly based on his premise that 'Probably there has never been in any country a period of literary activity which has not been preceded or accompanied by some stimulation of the religous interest.' Eglinton denies that this stimulation was to be found 'in either the Catholic or the various Protestant religious bodies'; instead one must look to 'the ferment caused in the minds of a group of young men by the early activities of the Theosophical Movement in Dublin.'[119] What this theory fails to explain is why Protestants, and – with one or two exceptions –*only* Protestants (mainly from evangelical Church of Ireland families), became Theosophists.[120] As I see it, both the interest in Theosophy and the 'period of literary activity' were among the consequences of Evangelicalism.

Osborne does not suggest that all the young Dubliners of the seventies turned towards religion: many of the 'thinking students' at

Trinity 'were much more influenced by the rationalism of John Stuart Mill's writings . . . than by the mental attitude usual in the well-to-do Evangelical churches of the city . . .' Mill's *Logic,* as Osborne points out, had already been adopted as a textbook in philosophy at Trinity. He mentions Lecky as 'the most perfected specimen of the Dublin disciples of John Stuart Mill and his school . . .' The connection between Evangelicalism and rationalism has already been noted, but it may be harder to trace, in a religious movement seemingly committed to the Union of Ireland with Great Britain, that 'distinct vein of national sentiment and aspiration, never entirely quenched among Protestant young men,' which Osborne recognised among his Trinity contemporaries.[121]

I am not writing political history, so it is no part of my task to explain why Irish Evangelicals, at every stage of the nineteenth-century party struggles, were Tories, Conservatives, Unionists. The reader must simply learn to accept it as one of the paradoxical facts of Irish life. In England, High Churchmen were Tories; Evangelicals and Nonconformists generally were Whigs, Radicals, or Liberals; but in Ireland the Whigs and later the Liberals tended to favour a conciliatory policy towards the Catholics, including, of course, Catholic Emancipation. It seemed as if only Tory governments would promote Evangelicals to Irish bishoprics. Finally, it was Gladstone and the Liberals who committed the ultimate atrocity – Disestablishment.

Nevertheless, support of the Union did not preclude a sturdy pride in one's Irishness: Lady Gregory described Standish James O'Grady as 'a Fenian Unionist,'[122] but long before him there were Tories who were as proud of being Irish as Sir Walter Scott was of being Scottish. Over and over again, the *Dublin University Magazine* sings a paean to what it loves to call 'Irish genius'. In an 1847 article attacking the O'Connellites' choice of parliamentary candidates, for instance, we read the following:

> Comparisons in this as in other cases, will prove odious. They will, however, establish the fact, that Ireland has, within the last twenty years, retrograded in parliamentary talent.
> This fact is the more remarkable, because in other pursuits Irish genius has burned with increased splendour. We have not retrograded in the fine arts, in science, or in literature.

After supplying a list of writers, artists, and scientists, the article continues – unexpectedly but by no means unjustifiably – by praising 'our leading medical men':

> It is impossible for young men of ingenuous minds to frequent the classes of some of these truly illustrious teachers, without learning to love what is morally, as well as to know what is physically true; and, among the many virtues so inculcated and developed, not the least, and, doubtless, not the rarest, has been a temperate nationality and self-respecting pride, as Irishmen and gentlemen.[123]

The evangelical tone of this passage is unmistakable: observe the stress laid on moral teaching. One is pleasantly surprised to learn that 'a temperate nationality' can rank among the evangelical virtues.

More significant for literature, however, than a merely political nationalism were two patriotic tendencies peculiar to the Irish version of Evangelicalism: its interest, however narrow and utilitarian, in the Irish language, and its determined efforts to link the post-Reformation Church of Ireland with the pre-Norman Celtic Church of St. Patrick and his successors. The notion that the Reformed Church in Ireland had merely pruned away Roman corruptions, accretions and excrescences, thus restoring the Celtic Church to its primitive purity, was by no means an invention of the nineteenth century. It goes back to the great James Ussher, Anglican Archbishop of Armagh from 1625, who stated it most succinctly in *A Discourse of the Religion Anciently Professed by the Irish and British*[124] and supported it by his tremendous scholarly efforts to collect, edit and publish early ecclesiastical documents.[125] Like much else, this idea was neglected by the Irish clergy in the eighteenth century, but it returned to prominence in the nineteenth. The last work published by the Rev. William Hales (1747–1831), an Irish clergyman best known for his *New Analysis of Chronology,* was an *Essay on the Origin and Purity of the Primitive Church of the British Isles* (1819).[126]

One might suppose that publications which followed the line laid down by Ussher and Hales would be the work of High Churchmen rather than Evangelicals, but in 1836 Henry Joseph Monck Mason, an evangelical layman who had helped to found the Irish Society and was its secretary for many years, published *Primitive Christianity in Ireland: A Letter to Thomas Moore, Esq.* In the first volume of his *History of Ireland,* the poet had summarily dismissed Ussher's argument that the early Irish Church, 'on most of the leading points of Christian doctrine, professed the opinions at present entertained by Protestants.'[127] Monck Mason, however, denied that the Celtic Church taught any of the following doctrines: the supremacy of the Roman See; transsubstantiation and the real presence of Christ in the Eucharist; the offering of prayers for the dead and the related belief in Purgatory; the invocation of saints; the sacramental nature of penance; and the celibacy of the clergy.[128] On the other hand, he insists that the Celtic Church did agree with the Church of Ireland – and especially, of course, with the Evangelicals, though he does not say so – on 'the two grand points now alluded to – the great standard of faith, and the great doctrine of justification . . .' He continues:

> It is certainly the fact, that the great standard of faith referred to by the early Irish Christians was the Bible itself.[129]

Monck Mason then goes on to quote texts which prove, to his satisfaction at least, that 'in the primitive Christian Church of Ireland the Bible was read, . . . by all, in their vulgar tongue . . .'[130] On the other 'grand point', justification by faith alone, he bases his argument chiefly on quotations from St. Patrick's *Epistle to Coroticus*: for example, 'but what shall I say, or what shall I promise unto my Lord? because I see nothing that he has not bestowed on me.'[131] Monck Mason ends his long 'letter' by reproaching Moore for having 'fanned the dying embers of national and religious jealousy to a devastating flame.' However, the poet can still make amends in 'the later centuries' of his history

> . . . by assuring the poor Irishman of the fact – that it is not to the Saxon invasion that he is to attribute the establishment of Protestantism in this island; that with the British conquest first came a full acquiescence in a subjection to the see of Rome; and that it was not until about the period of Henry the Second's invasion, that the Pope sent over his palls, and his legates, or assumed anything like the authority which he has since laid claim to.[132]

From this period onwards, virtually every major history of the Church of Ireland – J. T. Ball's *The Reformed Church of Ireland* being the notable exception – has either repeated Monck Mason's claim or, more usually, actually begun with the arrival of St. Patrick in 432. First in point of time is the celebrated *History of the Church of Ireland* (1840) by Richard Mant, Bishop of Down and Connor, which mainly deals with the period from the Reformation to the Union; the full title of the first of Mant's two volumes shows a polemical thrust, however: *History of the Church of Ireland, from the Reformation to the Revolution, with a Preliminary Survey from the Papal Usurpation, in the Twelfth Century, to Its Legal Abolition in the Seventeenth.* Not long afterwards, the Rev. Robert King complemented Mant's study with his *Primer of the History of the Holy Catholic Church in Ireland,* a lucid but far from elementary work, written from a somewhat high-church point of view and covering the period from the introduction of Christianity to 1603. One-volume histories of the Church of Ireland by the Rev. Thomas Olden (1892) and the Rev. Thomas J. Johnston and others (1953) begin at the same point as King and continue the narrative almost to the moment of writing. It is, however, somewhat disturbing that a professional historian not in holy orders, Professor W. Alison Phillips, should have accepted the same limits for a 'standard' three-volume history of the Church of Ireland published as recently as 1933. Hardly any of Monck Mason's propositions about the Early Irish Church could have been safely accepted after about 1900, even by scholars familiar only with the Latin sources,* let alone those who could read Old and Middle Irish. Certainly, after the publication of James F. Kenney's *Sources for the Early History of Ireland* in 1929, it seems undignified to continue the controversy.[133]

From the point of view of the Revival writers, this harking back to a period antedating both religious and ethnic divisions in Ireland had positive merit: they were trying to create in the cultural domain a national unity that had become more and more elusive in the political arena. Standish O'Grady summed up their aims unforgettably: 'I have not come out from my own camp to join any other. I stand between the camps and call.'[134] For various reasons, including the influence of theosophical ideas, the literary movement finally sought common ground not in any Christian century but in the pagan era, which Celtic scholars of many nationalities were rapidly bringing to light; the folklorists and language revivalists were uncovering contemporary Irish survivals of paganism with equal rapidity.

*The sceptical Bury was one of these, and he concluded that 'the Roman Catholic conception of St. Patrick's work is, generally, nearer to historical fact than the views of some anti-Papal divines.' *The Life of St. Patrick and His Place in History* (London: Macmillan, 1905), pp. vii–viii.

As we have seen, the preservation of the Irish language was aided, though not exactly in good faith, by the evangelically inspired Irish Society. Because of pressure from that body, under the guidance of Monck Mason, Trinity College was induced to found a Professorship of Irish in 1838, 'its endowment being at first provided largely by a fund raised for the purpose by public subscription.' As late as 1951, the power of nomination to the Professorship was vested in the trustees of the fund, 'subject to the approval of the Board of Trinity College.'[135] It is not surprising, then, that the first four holders of the Chair were Church of Ireland clergymen, at least one, the Rev. Daniel Foley, being a convert from Roman Catholicism.[136] It was the fourth in line, the Rev. James Goodman, who gave Synge his first lessons in Irish,

> . . . an amiable old clergyman who made [me] read a crabbed version of the New Testament, and seemed to know nothing, or at least to care nothing, about the old literature of Ireland or the fine folk-tales and folk-poetry of Munster and Connaught.[137]

In April 1843, thanks to the energy of an English Tractarian, the Rev. William Sewell, St. Columba's College opened at Stackallan, Co. Meath. The founders, being High Churchmen rather than Evangelicals, intended to give the Irish people '*squires and parsons speaking their own tongue.*'[138] Irish scholarships were endowed at Trinity under the same auspices. Despite the resignations in 1846 of Sewell and the first Warden along with several Fellows, the College survived, moving to its present site near Rathfarnham in 1849.[139] Two Irish textbooks for the use of its students were issued in 1845: one a primer by Denis Coffey and the Rev. Robert King; the other, for the senior classes, John O'Donovan's monumental *Grammar of the Irish Language*.[140] Sewell and his original supporters had refused to allow the Irish Society representation on the governing body of St. Columba's, clearly because they disliked its evangelical orientation: the Rev. James Henthorn Todd, F.T.C.D., later professor of Hebrew and a notable Celtic scholar, used to write to Sewell in disparaging terms of 'the Singers and Dalys,' 'the Monck Masons and Singers.'[141] Nevertheless, as Monck Mason was quick to point out in his history of the Irish Society, Sewell acknowledged in his address at the opening of St. Columba's:

It was at Kingscourt that, as an Englishman, I myself was first amazed by the power of the Irish language. – It was in the well known centres of the operation of the Irish Society, that we carried on personal inquiries on the subject . . .[142]

These and most of the other consequences of Evangelicalism discussed in this article must in the last analysis be viewed as accidental products of a particular historical situation. The essential point is that evangelical renewal, though it may have encouraged some philistinism among the laity, brought to the clergy of the Church of Ireland spiritual gains far outweighing any putative intellectual loss. James Anthony Froude became disillusioned with Tractarianism during a stay of 'some months in Ireland in the family of an Evangelical clergyman.' Part of his tribute to them deserves to be quoted here:

There was a quiet good sense, an intellectual breadth of feeling in this household, which to me, who had been bred up to despise Evangelicals as unreal and affected, was a startling surprise . . . here were persons whose creed differed little from that of the Calvinistic Methodists, yet they were easy, natural, and dignified . . . Christianity at – – was part of the atmosphere which we breathed; it was the great fact of our existence, to which everything else was subordinated . . .

Evangelicalism had been represented to me as weak and illiterate. I had found it in harmony with reason and experience, and recommended as it was by personal holiness in its professors, and general beauty of mind and character, I concluded that Protestantism had more to say for itself than my Oxford teachers had allowed.[143]

The literary descendants of such clergymen were not always conspicuous by their quiet good sense, but their intellectual breadth of feeling cannot be denied. It was no accident that the movement they initiated proved to be idealistic in the highest degree, a last towering wave of the great Romantic surge, for the beginnings of Romanticism in English literature had been intimately bound up with the revival of 'enthusiasm' in religion led by George Whitefield and John Wesley, and continued by the Anglican Evangelicals. Works once again gave way to faith, facts to myth, the truths of the head to the truths of the heart:

A nation's history is made for it by circumstances, and the irresistible progress of events; but their legends, they make for themselves. In that dim twilight region, where day meets night, the intellect of man, tired by contact with the vulgarity of actual things, goes back for rest and recuperation, and there sleeping, projects its dreams against the waning night and before the rising of the sun.

The legends represent the imagination of the country; they are that kind of history which a nation desires to possess. They betray the ambition and ideals of the people, and, in this respect, have a value far beyond the tale of events and duly recorded deeds, which are no more history than a skeleton is a man.[144]

No doubt Standish O'Grady saw the bourgeois evangelical orthodoxy of his day as part of 'the vulgarity of actual things,' with which he contrasts the ideal world of the imagination. One common form taken by the reaction against Evangelicalism is completely overlooked in Charles Osborne's essay: the substitution for it of the religion of Art. It is a strange omission on the part of a son and brother of painters; W. B. Yeats, with a similar family background, could not have been guilty of it:

I am very religious, and deprived by Huxley and Tyndall, whom I detested, of the simple-minded religion of my childhood, I had made a new religion, almost an infallible Church of poetic tradition, of a fardel of stories, and of personages, and of emotions, inseparable from their first expression, passed on from generation to generation by poets and painters with some help from philosophers and theologians.[145]

Yeats's rapid conversion contrasts with that of Stopford Brooke, born a full generation (1832–1865) before him and raised in the far from simple-minded version of Evangelicalism taught by the Rev. R. S. Brooke. In L. P. Jacks's biography of the younger Brooke we can trace a slow, steady evolution from his youthful Evangelicalism to an old age more concerned with art than with religion. Yet one can agree with Jacks that Brooke,

. . . quite early in life, with little aid from others and in the face of much opposition, . . . had formed for himself an ideal of the Christian ministry which was to reconcile the two currents of his being in a deep synthesis of Art and Religion, of Nature and Spirit.[146]

Unfortunately, Brooke never created any important works of art, though the passages from his diary quoted by Jacks suggest that if it were published in whole or in part, it might become a late-Victorian classic.

The religion of Art, as understood in England in the 1890s, excluded morality: even of Stopford Brooke in his old age we read that 'Morality ceased to have any meaning for him save as the expression of love.'[147] Yeats, in an early letter, said of George Eliot that 'if she had more religion she would have less morals.'[148] Paradoxical as it sounds, this judgement could be approved by a believing Evangelical, for it stresses salvation by faith not works. Indeed, Irish churchmen of the old 'high-and-dry' school, who taught morality to the exclusion of almost everything else, were very suspicious of the morals of the early Evangelicals, who preached about nothing but faith. In fact, of course, the morals of the latter were excellent, and few of their literary progeny rebelled against their rules of conduct. The stereotype of the *fin-de-siècle* poet – drunkard, gambler, womaniser, suicide – simply did not exist in Protestant Ireland; among Irish exiles, the frugality – perhaps even asceticism – of a Shaw effectively counter-balanced the self-destructiveness of a Wilde. Neither greed of gain nor more amiable vices distracted the Revival writers from their self-imposed task. If they had a besetting sin, it was amateurism, a reluctance to learn their trade as artists, or even as scholars, that can be found in Hyde, O'Grady, Russell, and numerous minor figures. In part, it was due to the anti-intellectualism threatening every movement that values emotion more than thought: to prefer the one does not require us to hate the other – something the Evangelicals too often forgot. Mainly, though, this amateurism suggests a belief in salvation by faith: so long as one's heart is in the right place, why be anxious about one's collected works? Synge never subscribed to this attitude, nor did Lady Gregory, but in *The Countess Cathleen* Yeats seems to suggest that the road to Heaven is paved with good intentions:

The Light of Lights
Looks always on the motive, not the deed,
The Shadow of Shadows on the deed alone.[149]

In maturity he took a different view, stating the alternatives with a starkness reminiscent of Bishop O'Brien on the choice between faith and works:

The intellect of man is forced to choose
Perfection of the life, or of the work,
And if it take the second must refuse
A heavenly mansion, raging in the dark.[150]

Perhaps both these quotations affirm the same truth: salvation by works alone is impossible; in the second, therefore, Yeats accepts his own damnation. The doctrine is purely evangelical.

NOTES

1 George Malcolm Young, *Victorian England: Portrait of an Age* (London: Oxford Univ. Press, 1936), p. 5.

2 For the Synge genealogy and much information about other persons mentioned in this article, see *Burke's Irish Family Records,* ed. H. J. Montgomery-Massingberd (London: Burke's Peerage, 1976).

3 Joseph Hone, *W. B. Yeats 1865–1939* (New York: Macmillan, 1943), p. 5. But see Michael Sadleir, *Dublin University Magazine: Its History, Contents and Bibliography* (Dublin: Bibliographical Society of Ireland, 1938), p. 64. Sadleir says that Butt edited the magazine from August 1834 'until some time in 1838,' but does not mention any 'co-editor' – Hone's description of Yeats.

4 On Traill, see David H. Greene and Edward M. Stephens, *J. M. Synge 1871–1909* (New York: Macmillan, 1959), p. 4. For Hyde's education, see Dominic Daly, *The Young Douglas Hyde . . . 1874–1893* (Dublin: Irish Univ. Press, 1974), pp. 1–2. On Thomas O'Grady, see Hugh Art O'Grady, *Standish James O'Grady: The Man and the Writer* (Dublin: Talbot Press, 1929), pp. 23–29.

5 Donald Harman Akenson, *The Church of Ireland: Ecclesiastical Reform and Revolution, 1800–1885* (New Haven: Yale Univ. Press, 1971), p. 132.

6 O'Grady, p. 23.

7 O'Grady, p. 28.

8 O'Grady, p. 34.

9 O'Grady, pp. 28–29.

10 Richard Sinclair Brooke, *Recollections of the Irish Church* (London: Macmillan, 1877), pp. 34–35. The 'second series' with the same title (Dublin: Hodges, Foster, and Figgis, 1878) is hastily compiled and has not been quoted in this article.

11 This and the three following quotations are from Greene, p. 75.

12 Greene, p. 3.

13 Greene, p. 4.

14 See his fragmentary 'Autobiography', in *Collected Works,* II, ed. Alan Price (London: Oxford Univ. Press, 1966), 3–15, esp. 4–5, 11.

15 Samuel believed, I think, that his youngest brother had undergone the conversion thought necessary by Evangelicals when they both attended 'the Mission held by Rev. Marcus Rainsford in Zion Church,' Rathgar, apparently in 1881. The church was built (and, obviously, named) under evangelical auspices, so it was appropriate that missions should be held there periodically. See *Letters to My Daughter: Memories of John Millington Synge* (Dublin: Talbot Press, n.d. [1931]), pp. 20, 50.

16 S. Synge, p. 104.

17 S. Synge, p. 76.

18 S. Synge, p. 131.

19 J. M. Synge, *Letters to Molly,* ed. Ann Saddlemyer (Cambridge, Mass.: Belknap-Harvard Univ. Press, 1971), p. 43.

20 S. Synge, pp. 139, 122.

21 John Butler Yeats, *Letters to His Son W. B. Yeats and Others*, ed. Joseph Hone (New York: Dutton, 1946), p. 214.

22 William Michael Murphy, *Prodigal Father: The Life of John Butler Yeats* (Ithaca, N.Y.: Cornell Univ. Press, 1978), p. 549, n. 15.

23 Sadleir, pp. 61–63, 68–70. For Stanford's proselytising, see James Godkin, *Ireland and Her Churches* (London: Chapman & Hall, 1867), pp. 199, 204. Brooke pays tribute to Stanford's culture, *Recollections,* p. 128.

24 Murphy, p. 21.

25 Murphy, p. 19.

26 Thomas S. W. Lewis, 'Some New Letters of John Butler Yeats,' in *Modern Irish Literature: Essays in Honor of William York Tindall,* ed. Raymond J. Porter and James D. Brophy (New York: Iona College Press-Twayne, 1972), p. 343.

27 Lewis, pp. 350–51.

28 Lewis, p. 343.

29 Daly, p. 15. For a brief summary of Hyde's Trinity career, see Daly, pp. xiv–xv.

30 Daly, p. 14.

31 Daly, p. 20. Hyde's diary was written mostly in Irish, which Daly translates: hence peculiarities like the spelling of Ezekiel and the references to Hyde's father as 'the Master', the name used by Irish-speaking peasants and servants in referring to him.

32 Daly, p. 51.

33 Daly, p. 52.

34 Daly, p. 82.

35 Daly, p. 55.

36 J. P. Mahaffy, 'The Drifting of Doctrine,' *Hibbert Journal,* 1 (1902–3), 503.

37 Mahaffy, p. 503.

38 J. T. Ball states that in the teaching of the Irish Evangelicals 'no doctrine had more prominence than the doctrine of Justification by faith only. Some of them connected this doctrine with the Calvinistic tenets as to predestination; but the others, and probably the larger number, held it not in association with these opinions, and it was in very many instances accompanied by even decided opposition to them'. *The Reformed Church of Ireland (1537–1886)* (London: Longmans, Green, 1886), p. 241. John Thomas Ball (1815–1898), a former Lord Chancellor of Ireland, seems to be offering here, in noticeably judicial language, a summing-up based on his wide personal knowledge of the Church of Ireland community.

39 Mahaffy, p. 504.
40 Mahaffy, pp. 504–05.
41 Brooke, pp. 28–29.
42 *Christ in Shadow* (Dublin: Robert T. White, 1858), p. 49.
43 'The Bishop of Ossory's Charge,' *Dublin University Magazine*, 29, (1847), 736.
44 'The Bishop of Ossory's Charge,' p. 735.
45 *Brief Memorials of the Rev. B. W. Mathias, Late Chaplain of Bethesda Chapel* (Dublin: William Curry, Jun. 1842), p. 70. The preface to this work is signed with the initials of the Rev. Joseph Henderson Singer (1786–1866), a leading Evangelical, later Regius Professor of Divinity at T.C.D., 1850–52, and Bishop of Meath, 1852–66.
46 'Evangelical,' *Everyman's Encyclopaedia*, 4th ed. (1958).
47 Akenson, p. 136.
48 *Brief Memorials*, p. 164. Among the Church of Ireland members consulted by Mathias were Bernard Shaw, Esq., grandfather of the dramatist, and the Rev. Walter Stephens. One of G.B.S.'s uncles was named Walter Stephens Shaw, just as another was named Edward Carr Shaw after his own grandfather on his mother's side – and therefore a great-grandfather of the dramatist – the Rev. Edward Carr, rector of Kilmacow. Further evidence of Shaw's evangelical antecedents will be presented later.
49 Akenson, pp. 134–35.
50 For the controversies stirred up by the Hibernian Bible Society and some of its local branches, see Desmond Bowen, *The Protestant Crusade in Ireland, 1800–70* (Dublin: Gill & Macmillan, 1978), pp. 71–73, 98–103. The society was multi-denominational from its inception, as the quotation from *Brief Memorials* indicates. In 1821 the Protestant Archbishops of Armagh and Dublin resigned from their posts in the society, though Church of Ireland Evangelicals continued to work with it (Akenson, p. 135).
51 See Henry Joseph Monck Mason, *History of the Origin and Progress of the Irish Society* (Dublin: Goodwin, Son & Nethercroft, 1844).
52 Lionel James, *A Forgotten Genius: Sewell of St. Columba's and Radley* (London: Faber & Faber, 1945), p. 99.
53 Akenson, pp. 146–85.
54 Akenson, pp. 201–06.
55 The centres in Dublin in the 1830's were Swift's Alley Church, under the chaplaincy of the Rev. Tresham Dames Gregg, and St. Michan's Parish, of which Stanford, formerly of the *Dublin University Magazine*, was rector. See Bowen, pp. 108–09; also pp. 109–13 for the further exploits of the preposterous Gregg – not to be confused with John, the future Bishop of Cork. For St. Michan's see Godkin, pp. 198–200.
56 On Nangle, see Desmond Bowen, *Souperism: Myth or Reality?* (Cork: Mercier Press, 1970), pp. 88–104; also Henry Seddall, *Edward Nangle: The Apostle of Achill* (London: Hatchards, 1884). Nangle learned the Irish language and reprinted Irish textbooks in Achill.
57 Bowen, *Souperism*, pp. 83–88. The Rev. Thomas Moriarty began his ministry in 1839, at the invitation of Gayer. The Rev. William Sewell and his friends Viscount Adare and William Monsell believed that Moriarty was more of a High Churchman than an Evangelical. According to Monsell, 'The difference between Ventry and other places consisted in the Irish-speaking minister there

and the Church principles which he advocated' (James, p. 82).

58   Bowen, *Protestant Crusade,* pp. 208–46; Bowen, *Souperism,* pp. 125–35.
59   Bowen, *Souperism,* pp. 153–77 (Trench and the Plunkets); pp. 135–36
     (D'Arcy). Godkin, pp. 365–92, gives a vivid picture of Trench based on the
     biography by Joseph D'Arcy Sirr. On the emigration of converts to Protestant-
     ism, see Bowen, *Souperism,* pp. 88, 103; *Protestant Crusade,* p. 185.
60   Akenson, p. 210 (table 36). The same statistics are quoted by many historians
     of the period.
61   Bowen, *Protestant Crusade,* pp. 259–73.
62   Bowen, *Souperism,* pp. 139–44. See also *Missions in Ireland . . . by One of the
     Missioners* (Dublin: James Duffy, 1855) for a lively account of the adventures
     of some Fathers of Charity sent to Ireland from Rugby, especially Fr. A. M.
     Rinolfi and Fr. W. Lockhart (a Tractarian convert to Roman Catholicism).
63   Godkin, pp. 420–25, quotes tellingly from a pamphlet entitled *Proselytism* by
     'An Irish Peer' (Dublin: Hodges & Smith, 1865): 'The chapels are everywhere
     better attended upon holidays, and the lower orders, at all events, are far more
     strict in their confessions, fasts, and other religious observances, than they
     used to be . . . An Irish layman who can look back thirty or forty years, will
     have no difficulty in recognising that the antagonism between the creeds is
     greatly increased, and that the Roman Catholics have received a stronger and
     more exclusive organization under the priesthood . . . In the matter of relative
     morality, they have cut the ground from under our feet, and deprived us of the
     best argument in our mouths by showing that the assumed superiority of
     Protestants might be denied.'
64   Bowen, *Souperism,* p. 84.
65   See Vivian Mercier, *The Irish Comic Tradition* (Oxford: Clarendon Press,
     1962), pp. 171–73 and, for the sixteenth century, pp. 138–39.
66   Bowen, *Souperism,* p. 124.
67   Bowen, *Souperism,* p. 125.
68   W. B. Yeats, *Autobiographies* (London: Macmillan, 1955), pp. 414–16. See
     also George Moore, *Hail and Farewell: Ave* (New York: Appleton, 1911), pp.
     127–28, 133–37.
69   Noel Gilroy Annan, *Leslie Stephen: His Thought and Character in Relation to
     His Time* (London: MacGibbon & Kee, 1951), p. 110.
70   Conor Cruise O'Brien, '1891–1916', in *The Shaping of Modern Ireland,* ed.
     Conor Cruise O'Brien (London: Routledge & Kegan Paul, 1960), p. 18.
71   Oliver Goldsmith, *Collected Letters,* ed. Katharine C. Balderston (Cambridge:
     Univ. Press, 1928), p. 10.
72   Walter Alison Phillips, ed., *History of the Church of Ireland from the Earliest
     Times to the Present Day,* III (London: Oxford Univ. Press, 1934), 349, 351;
     Brooke, *Recollections,* 123–25.
73   Annan, p. 110.
74   James B. Leslie, *Clogher Clergy and Parishes* (Enniskillen: Printed for the
     Author, 1929), pp. 82–83.
75   See William Bedell Stanford and Robert Brendan McDowell, *Mahaffy: A
     Biography of an Anglo-Irishman* (London: Routledge & Kegan Paul, 1971).
76   Brooke, *Recollections,* p. 16.
77   Robert Fleming Rattray, *Bernard Shaw: A Chronicle* (London: Dennis Dob-
     son, 1951), p. 102.
78   Lawrence Pearsall Jacks, *Life and Letters of Stopford Brooke* (London: John

Murray, 1917), II, 359–60; Bernard Shaw, *Sixteen Self Sketches* (New York: Dodd, Mead, 1949), p. 96.

79 Jacks, I, 287, 327–28; for the friendship between Green and Brooke, see esp. Jacks, II, 374.

80 See Bowen, *Protestant Crusade,* pp. 277; 380, n. 82, for Alice Stopford Green's ancestry and evangelical upbringing.

81 Leslie, p. 83.

82 Stanford, pp. 9–10.

83 Maud Dominica Mary Petre, *Autobiography and Life of George Tyrrell* (London: Arnold, 1912), I, 58–63.

84 Petre, I, 60.

85 Petre, I, 115.

86 Annan, p. 110.

87 Jacks, I, 321.

88 Brooke, *Recollections,* p. 165.

89 *Christ in Shadow,* p. 76.

90 John Eglinton (pseud. of William Kirkpatrick Magee), *A Memoir of AE, George William Russell* (London: Macmillan, 1937), p. 7. Moore, pp. 162–63.

91 Eglinton, p. 2.

92 Edward Irving Carlyle, 'Walker, John (1768–1833),' *DNB* (1899). *Brief Memorials* gives a detailed account of how Mathias came to succeed Walker at Bethesda Chapel. On Kelly, see Brooke, *Recollections,* pp. 16–17, 193. Godkin, p. 106, mentions 'the Walkerites, the Kellyites, and others.'

93 George Clement Boase, 'Darby, John Nelson,' *DNB* (1888).

94 Augustine Martin, 'Anglo-Irish Literature,' in *Irish Anglicanism 1869–1969,* ed. Michael Hurley (Dublin: Allen Figgis, 1970), p. 120.

95 Bernard Shaw, *My Dear Dorothea* (New York: Vanguard, 1956), p. 25 et passim.

96 Shaw, *Dorothea,* pp. 38–39.

97 Bernard Shaw, *Prefaces* (London: Odhams, 1938), p. 118.

98 Shaw, *Prefaces,* p. 578.

99 Godkin, p. 207.

100 Godkin, p. 207.

101 Phillips, III, 331.

102 John Warburton, J. Whitelaw, and Robert Walsh, *History of the City of Dublin* (London: Cadell & Davies, 1818), II, 773–75.

103 *The Irish Sketch Book* . . ., Vol. V of *The Oxford Thackeray,* ed. George Saintsbury (London: Oxford Univ. Press, 1908), pp. 263–65. For another view of Gregg's preaching, see Robert Samuel Gregg, *'Faithful unto Death': Memorials of the Life of John Gregg, D.D.* (Dublin: George Herbert, 1879), pp. 73–82. Gregg could also preach effectively in Irish, though told by a native speaker that he 'could not play near so many variations in Irish as in English' (p. 28).

104 Bowen, *Protestant Crusade,* pp. 74–75. Thomas Hamilton, 'Jocelyn, Robert, third Earl of Roden,' *DNB* (1891–2). A number of Catholics were killed by Orangemen at Dolly's Brae, near Lord Roden's seat at Castlewellan, County Down, on 12 July, 1849.

105 Brooke, *Recollections,* p. 108.

106 Brooke tells of their rebellion against a temporary teacher who tried to indoctrinate them with Calvinism. Note that their regular teacher used to visit

them on Saturdays and 'constrained them to bank their savings' – a good example of evangelical prudence and thrift.

107 Lennox Robinson, Tom Robinson and Nora Dorman, *Three Homes* (London: Michael Joseph, 1938), p. 142.

108 Robinson, pp. 48–51.

109 Godkin, p. 207.

110 'On Going to Church,' in *Selected Non-Dramatic Writings of Bernard Shaw*, ed. Dan H. Laurence (Boston: Houghton Mifflin, 1965), p. 386.

111 Godkin, p. 213.

112 Charles MacMahon Shaw, *Bernard's Brethren* (New York: Henry Holt, n.d. [1939]), pp. 47–48. On Dr. Fleury, descendant of a long line of Huguenot *pasteurs*, see Brooke, *Recollections*, pp. 43–44.

113 Shaw, *Self Sketches*, p. 76; note the reference to 'the Molyneux in Upper Leeson Street' on the same page.

114 Akenson, pp. 302–09; Ball, pp. 294–303.

115 Petre, I, 145.

116 Petre, I, 145.

117 Petre, I, 146–47.

118 Henry Summerfield, *That Myriad-Minded Man: A Biography of George William Russell, 'A.E.'* (Gerrards Cross, Bucks.: Colin Smythe, 1975), p. 16.

119 Eglinton, p. 11.

120 Edward Corbett, a Roman Catholic acquaintance of A.E.'s, became a Theosophist, at least for a time (Summerfield, p. 11). I know of no other Catholic converts in Ireland.

121 Petre, I, 145.

122 Ernest A. Boyd, 'Introduction,' in Standish O'Grady, *Selected Essays and Passages* (Dublin: Talbot Press, n.d. [1918]), p. 17.

123 'The Irish Representatives,' *Dublin University Magazine*, 29 (1847), 389.

124 So described on the title page (London: Printed by R.Y. for the Partners of the Irish Stocke, 1631), but on the first page of the text and the running heads it is more correctly titled 'Of the Religion Professed by the Ancient Irish.'

125 *The Whole Works of the Most Rev. James Ussher*, ed. Charles Richard Elrington, 17 vols. (Dublin: Hodges & Smith, 1847–64). Vols. XIV and XVII were edited by James Henthorn Todd.

126 Warwick William Wroth, 'Hales, William,' *DNB* (1890).

127 Henry J. Monck Mason, *Primitive Christianity in Ireland: A Letter to Thomas Moore, Esq.* (Dublin: William Curry, Jun., 1836), p. 24. Bowen, *Protestant Crusade*, p. 51, mentions a pamphlet in similar vein by Edward Nangle, published in 1834.

128 *Primitive Christianity*, pp. 24–106.

129 *Primitive Christianity*, pp. 107–08.

130 *Primitive Christianity*, p. 115.

131 *Primitive Christianity*, p. 116.

132 *Primitive Christianity*, pp. 138–39.

133 Richard Mant, *History of the Church of Ireland*, 2 vols. (London: John W. Parker, 1840); Robert King, *A Primer of the History of the Holy Catholic Church in Ireland*, 3rd ed., 2 vols. (Dublin: William Curry, Jun., 1845–46); Thomas Olden, *The Church of Ireland* (London: Wells Gardner, Darton, 1892); Thomas J. Johnston, John L. Robinson, and Robert Wyse Jackson, *A History of the Church of Ireland* (Dublin: A.P.C.K., 1953): Walter Alison

Phillips, ed., *History of the Church of Ireland from the Earliest Times to the Present Day*, 3 vols. (London: Oxford Univ. Press, 1933–34); James F. Kenney, *The Sources for the Early History of Ireland: An Introduction and Guide*, vol. I, *Ecclesiastical* [all pub.] (New York: Columbia Univ. Press, 1929).

134   *All Ireland Review*, 4 (1903), 340. For a rather similar attitude, see Yeats, *Autobiographies*, pp. 101–02.

135   *Trinity College Record Volume* (Dublin: Hodges, Figgis, 1951), p. 72.

136   Brooke, *Recollections*, p. 55. The first holder of the chair, the Rev. Thomas De Vere Coneys, had been Nangle's assistant at the Achill Mission, 1838–40 (Seddall, p. 117).

137   J. M. Synge, *Works*, II, 384.

138   James, p. 80.

139   James, pp. 118, 120.

140   National Library of Ireland, *Bibliography of Irish Philology and of Printed Irish Literature* (Dublin: Browne & Nolan, 1913), p. 46. Hyde owned a version in Irish of Robert King's primer of Church history, *Ceachtanna sóthuigsiona air stair eagluise na h-Éirionn* (Dublin: Goodwin, 1850); see Daly, p. 182.

141   James, pp. 101–02. For Singer, see n. 45 above.

142   Monck Mason, *History*, p. 73.

143   James Anthony Froude, 'The Oxford Counter-Reformation: Letter IV,' in *Short Studies on Great Subjects*, IV (New York: Schribner's, 1888), 193, 194, 197. The family was that of the Rev. William Cleaver, rector of Delgany, to whose two elder sons Froude acted as tutor. One of the boys, Euseby, 'spent his life as a clergyman in England,' but 'was an enthusiast for the Irish language, a hobby that brought him into friendship with Douglas Hyde . . .' Waldo Hilary Dunn, *James Anthony Froude: A Biography*, I (Oxford: Clarendon Press, 1961), 62–63.

144   Standish O'Grady, *History of Ireland: Critical and Philosophical*, I [all pub.] (London: Sampson Low, 1881), 41.

145   Yeats, *Autobiographies*, pp. 115–16.

146   Jacks, I, 57–58. See also II, 454: 'In later life he would quote with approval the saying of Blake "Art and Christianity are one." '

147   Jacks, II, 454.

148   *The Letters of W. B. Yeats*, ed. Allan Wade (New York: Macmillan, 1955), p. 31.

149   *The Collected Plays of W. B. Yeats*, 2nd ed. (London: Macmillan, 1952), p. 50.

150   'The Choice,' in *The Collected Poems of W. B. Yeats*, 2nd ed. (London: Macmillan, 1950), p. 278.

IMAGES OF A CHANGING IRELAND IN THE WORKS OF W. B. YEATS

SUHEIL B. BUSHRUI

I

'Yeats' real hope for Ireland was not a politician's platform, it was the poet's dream'[1] – this was the view of one delineator of Yeats's attitude towards Ireland in his works: R. J. Loftus. I hope to add in this paper one more assessment of the poet's lifelong, intense, and ambivalent pre-occupation with the land that contributed so much to the shaping of his poetic genius, from 'The Madness of King Goll' to 'Under Ben Bulben'.

Yeats's poetic dream was always uppermost in his outlook on Ireland. That dream was not petrified, but possessed the living quality of change. As Ireland changed and Yeats matured his attitudes towards Ireland varied. The pyramid of these changing outlooks nevertheless had for its pinnacle Yeats's poetic vision of an ideal Irish nation – one founded on the aristocratic, heroic and peasant ideals intrinsic in his poet's creed. This he, in his turn, developed from Irish models; from traditional myth, imagined values inherent in sections of the Irish people, and the pride he drew from his own Irishness.

All of the efforts of Yeats's celebrations of Irish nationality were directed toward the spiritual ennoblement of Ireland, and to make the Irish people aware and proud of their nobility. In order to envisage Ireland as it might become Yeats created a national myth, not loosely fabricated, but deeply rooted in heritage and history of Ireland. Thus he writes in 1888:

> To the greater poets everything they see has its relation to the national life, and through that to the universal and divine life: nothing is an isolated artistic moment; there is unity everywhere . . . But to this universalism, this seeing of unity everywhere, you can only attain through what is near you, your nation, or, if you be no traveller, your village and the cobwebs on your walls. You can

no more have the greatest poetry without a nation than religion without symbols. One can only reach out to the universe with a gloved hand – that glove is one's nation, the only thing one knows even a little of.[2]

First of all then, the poet needed the landscape of his own nation. In Professor Ellmann's words:

> By drawing his native landscape inside him, he has at hand a group of symbols to which he feels related by personal experience and, because of legendary and historical associations, by the experience of his race.[3]

Fit subject implies fit audience; the poet is bound to his brethren by national symbols: 'Nations, races, and individual men,' Yeats maintained, 'are unified by an image, or bundle of related images.'[4] The poet is thus furnished with the means to create or re-inforce a national myth:

> Might I not, with health and good luck to aid me, create some new *Prometheus Unbound*; Patrick or Columcille, Oisin or Finn, in Prometheus' stead; and, instead of Caucasus, Cro-Patrick or Ben Bulben? Have not all races had their first unity from a mythology, that marries them to rock and hill?[5]

Most central to Yeats's mythopoeic process – of creating a national myth for Ireland – were themes such as pride, individualism and passion; ideals of aristocracy, peasantry and heroism. Yeats would endeavour to make Irishmen appreciate these values and experience these emotions in their hearts. He would seek, in R. J. Loftus's words, to 'invest the Irish race with a deep-rooted sense of the spiritual passion that permits men to live in harmony with Nature's grand design.'[6]

It would seem that circumstances favoured Yeats, for in the last two decades of the nineteenth century Ireland was developing from a crude nascent nationalism in politics to a rich cultural self-awareness. However, Yeats was later to experience the bitterness of political violence and fanaticism intruding upon his poet's dream. His literary career with regard to the impact of variant cultural and political nationalisms on his verse can be divided into six major phases. The periods to be dealt with in this discussion shall be:

Yeats's early years before the turn of the century; his middle years in the first decade or so of the twentieth century; his reaction to the Easter Rising; his verse at the time of the Black and Tans; Yeats as a Free State Senator; and his later years as an old man.

II

The Ireland of Yeats's early manhood was to a great degree overshadowed by the legacy of Charles Stewart Parnell, whilst it was being transformed materially and socially by the effects of industrialisation. The ghost of Parnell might haunt Irish political life until 1916, but the impact of Ireland's social and economic transformation was more ubiquitous and far more tangible. It was fateful that Ireland's cultural renaissance should coincide with this fundamental change in her environment. It was particularly influential in the career of Ireland's greatest poet.

Yeats's whole life as a poet was profoundly affected by the conflict of an ideal rooted in agrarian society suffering from the realities of an advancing, alien order. As one of the 'last romantics' he was destined to experience a conflict of artistic and spiritual values already impressed upon Victorians like Carlyle, Arnold, Ruskin and Morris. Yet the issue was made exceedingly more complicated by the passionate, violent or potentially violent element of Irish nationalism. The national ideals of the poet and those of the politicians and the masses they levered were inevitably destined for variance. But nationalism was perhaps partly the immediate factor of stress covering the many points of stress existing in the relationship between idealistic artist and industrial society. When Yeats spoke of 'an imaginary Ireland' for which he and his dead poet-friends labored[7], his image entailed ideals of nobility, spiritual effort and sacrifice, and a piquant intangibility, that found small reciprocity in the minds of the men who followed Parnell's death in the cause of nationalism. In 1907 Yeats wrote:

> I could not foresee that a new class, which had begun to rise to power under the shadow of Parnell, would change the nature of the Irish movement, which, needing no longer great sacrifices, nor bringing any great risk to individuals, could do without exceptional men and those activities of the mind that are founded on the exceptional moment.[8]

It is thus that one finds that beneath the surface of the nationalist issues, more fundamental values are at stake. 'Immediate victory, immediate utility,' Yeats wrote again in 1907, 'became everything', and the ideals of the earlier inspired nationalists like Mazzini, 'that life is greater than the cause, withered, and we artists, who are the servants not of any cause but of mere naked life, and above all of that life in its nobler forms, where joy and sorrow are one . . . became as elsewhere in Europe protesting individual voices.'[9]

For Yeats at least, the protesting voice was to be raised in the name of universal ideals which he held to tenaciously as Irish values. Thus he would champion Irish characteristics against those who claimed to speak for the soul of Ireland:

> Forms of emotion and thought which the future will recognise as peculiarly Irish, for no other country has had the like, are looked upon as un-Irish because of their novelty in a land that is so nearly conquered that it has all but nothing of its own.[10]

The very proponents of Irish patriotism uttered commonplace opinions which savoured more of provincial England than of an Irish tradition.

Yeats had little doubt that the majority of Irishmen needed educating, and that his mission, as well as that of the writers and patrons with whom he collaborated, was to help achieve this through his art. His own personal commitment to Ireland as the land of his poet's inheritance was unrelenting. Within his lifetime his eminence as an inspirer of Irish culture was generally recognized. Yet while he set out on this task with hopes and enthusiasm, the journey led him in his mature years into a position of embittered alienation.

Yeats was both prime mover and the driving force of 'the men who helped to shape the Irish cultural revival in the eighteen-nineties, in the years following the death of Charles Steward Parnell, and dedicated themselves to the regeneration of their race and nation.'[11] During this period his dominant theme was Ireland's ancient myths and legends to which he alluded in the hope of instilling national pride into the Irish. His aim as early as the 1890s was to realise in his compatriots a sense of what he later called 'the unity of being'. But he found himself – either through desire to win Maud Gonne's admiration or, as Dr. Conor Cruise O'Brien has suggested, to make his name – enmeshed in political activities. His quarrel with the narrow nationalism propounded by members of The Young Ireland Society was not really fought out until the battles of the 1900s over the Irish Theatre. However, through The Young Ireland Society, Yeats was able to work with John O'Leary. O'Leary's speeches of 1866 on 'What Irishmen Should Know' and 'How Irishmen Should Feel' greatly influenced Yeats. 'As to how an Irishman should feel, O'Leary declared that he should feel first of all that he was an Irishman; second, that Irish unity must be secured; and finally, that he should make some sacrifice for Ireland. These simple, unpolitical precepts, with O'Leary's moral force and revolutionary record behind them, had considerable effect upon Yeats, who up to that time had thought of the nationalist movement as an affair for politicians.'[12] O'Leary 'sent Yeats to read Eugene O'Curry on the ancient Celts',[13] and Yeats was cognisant of the debt he owed the older man:

It was through the old Fenian leader John O'Leary I found my theme. His long imprisonment, his longer banishment, his magnificent head, his scholarship, his pride, his integrity, all that aristocratic dream nourished amid little shops and little farms, had drawn around him a group of young men; I was but eighteen or nineteen and had already, under the influence of *The Faerie Queene* and *The Sad Shepherd*, written a pastoral play, and under that of Shelley's *Prometheus Unbound* two plays, one staged somewhere in the Caucasus, the other in a crater of the moon; and I knew myself to be vague and incoherent.[14]

Until meeting O'Leary, Yeats had 'preferred to all other countries Arcadia and the India of romance, but presently [he] convinced [himself] . . . that [he] should never go for the scenery of a poem to any country but [his] own.'[15]

Through O'Leary's inspiration, Yeats founded in London the Irish Literary Society (1891), and in Dublin the Irish National Literary Society (1892) with O'Leary as President. Already, Yeats had proclaimed his belief in the value of Irish legend, made accessible to the ordinary reader after the scholars and antiquarians, by Samuel Ferguson's heroic metres and Standish O'Grady's imaginative narrations. Yeats proclaimed in the *Dublin University Review* in 1886:

Of all the many things the past bequeaths to the future, the greatest are great legends; they are the mother of nations. I hold it the duty of every Irish reader to study those of his own country till they are familiar as his own hands, for in them is the Celtic heart.[16]

In *The Wanderings of Oisin* he exemplified his belief in legend, and at the same time inaugurated the Irish Literary Renaissance.[17] But as Ellmann observes, the poem, with its dense symbols and Pre-Raphaelite setting, is perhaps only Irish in name and in its suggestion of England's oppression of Ireland in Part Two.[18] At all events, Sligo now replaced the Arcadian and Indian scenery in his poems. Eastern mystical ideas that he was absorbing in his theosophical and esoteric studies are transferred to an Irish setting. 'Fergus and the Druid' includes the concept of reincarnation found elsewhere in Yeats's poems on fantastic themes. Stories from the sagas were, in addition, re-told through apparently peasant sources. Moll Magee and other imaginary Irish peasants seemed to give credence to Yeats's settings of Irish ballads.

In his early poetry, Yeats aspires to a deeper and emotional representation of Ireland in his use of symbol. In the 'Rose of Battle', the individuality of Ireland is invoked in the line 'Rose of all Roses, Rose of all the World'. In another of his romantic allusions, Yeats refers to Ireland's historical heritage:

> Know, that I would accounted be
> True brother of a company
> That sang, to sweeten Ireland's wrong,
> Ballad and story, rann and song;
> Nor be I any less of them,
> Because the red-rose-bordered hem
> Of her, whose history began
> Before God made the angelic clan,
> Trails all about the written page.
> When Time began to rant and rage[19]

The use of image and symbol in reference to Ireland would be a developing feature in Yeats's verse.

Nor was it just symbol that Yeats began to develop in his early verse. 'He had an intricate searching mind that reached deeply into the legends and superstitions of Ireland and was capable of penetrating below the surface of human ambiguity.'[20] Out of his research emerged Yeats's own image of Cuchulain – one of those characters he saw as the cornerstones of the heroic age of Ireland and the tradition it preserved.

However, in this early period, local Irish features, occult ideas and symbols, and the beginnings of an heroic ideal all blur into the Celtic Twilight background. The Cuchulain of 'Cuchulain's Fight with the Sea' is not yet the wild, passionate hero who does battle in *On Baile's Strand*. The 'flight into fairyland from the real world' which he told Katharine Tynan was summed up in the Chorus to 'The Stolen Child'[21] was not eradicated from Yeats's early works by adopting Irish models. Most of the symbols of *The Shadowy Waters* of 1900 are drawn from Irish legendary and mythological material,[22] but this eclecticism still serves to create the overall dream-world ambience which Yeats later deprecated in *The Land of Heart's Desire*. Yeats's 'mystical Order', which was to combine the symbols of both pagan and Christian Ireland, was still envisaged in terms of retreat: the empty castle on the Castle Rock in Lough Key where he and Maud Gonne were to preside. Yeats's order of Celtic Mysteries was for him a means of escaping from politics as well as a means of gaining Maud Gonne's love.[23] *The Countess Cathleen*, written for her benefit, was a symbol of Maud Gonne's 'soul that seemed incapable of rest'.

The influence of Maud Gonne upon Yeats the Irish poet was most apparent at this period – on her behalf he engaged in political organization, culminating in the Wolfe Tone centennial celebrations of 1898. For her he wrote *Cathleen Ni Houlihan*, his most obvious contribution to the swelling tide of nationalism.[24] Its apparent political effect was summed up in Stephen Gwynn's well-known comment: 'I went home asking myself if such plays should be produced unless one was prepared for people to go out to shoot and be shot'.[25] Later events would prove the irony of Gwynn's words – and the irony was not in the least lost on the older Yeats. Cathleen Ni Houlihan in Yeats's verse became a symbol of Ireland's nobility and passion; an image in which Irish people could find consolation in their struggle for self-identity:

Under a bitter black wind that blows from the left hand;
Our courage breaks like an old tree in a black wind and dies,
But we have hidden in our hearts the flame of the eyes
Of Kathleen, the daughter of Houlihan.[26]

In a letter to Lady Gregory in 1903 Yeats wrote: 'My work has got more masculine, it has more salt in it.'[27] The statement illustrates the general quality of Yeats's verse in his middle years of the first decade or so of the twentieth century. Far more than in the so-called 'Celtic Twilight Period', contemporary events now influenced him; whilst the distant past was concentrated into a few potent myth-symbols which served to emphasize the new heroic qualities he was advocating. Passionate involvement in public affairs drew out a sardonic tone and a more conversational style. Against a deep developing dissatisfaction with contemporary Irish politics, Yeats evolved his heroic and aristocratic ideals that projected a different vision of Ireland to the rabid quarrels of the hour.

In his revisions of *The Shadowy Waters*, Yeats conceived Forgael standing alone, proud and aloof, his personality set towards its moment of 'passionate intensity' which it gains in the final scene.[28] This passionate, potentially tragic nature of the hero was embodied more fully in the Cuchulain of *On Baile's Strand*, who declares:

> I'll not be bound
> I'll dance or hunt, or quarrel or make love,
> Wherever and whenever I've a mind to.[29]

The intensity of life suggested here was meant to hold out a noble image to which Irishmen might aspire. More than willing to make public display of their nationality, they were not prepared to engage in any soul-searching or to question seriously their own values.[30] By introducing the heroic type, Yeats in a sense was encouraging the Irish to do this soul-searching and so follow a higher ideal.

Looking back on his earlier friends of the 'Cheshire Cheese' – men like Dowson and Johnson – Yeats concluded: '. . . so many of the greatest talents were to live such passionate lives and die such tragic deaths . . .'[31] In his plays written for the Abbey Theatre, Yeats creates heroic figures from Irish myth – Cuchulain, Seanchan and Deirdre – who represents the heroic vision of his middle period in their espousal of that 'passion' and 'tragedy', and that 'passionate life' and 'tragic death'.[32] These characters – especially Cuchulain and Seanchan – stand for higher aims than those around them. Seanchan, in his heroic passivity, is as passionate and untameable as the unrestrained Cuchulain.

In *The King's Threshold*, moreover, the hero's intensity creates a situation fraught with an element of social satire new to Yeats.

There is magnificent satire in his treatment of the Monk and his idea of God, the Soldier and his slavish obedience to the King, and the Chamberlain in his narrow-mindedness. Above all, in the grovelling stupidity of the Mayor, Yeats's satire looks sardonically askance at a materialist ethos not far to be sought in the Irish community of his own day. The Mayor is bemused by Seanchan:

> What is he saying? I never understood a poet's talk more than the baa of a sheep![33]

In contrast, Brian, the honest, uncorrupted peasant servant, has not succumbed to reason and material values. Representing the spontaneity and imagination of the peasantry, Brian's criticism of the Mayor reveals a realism and alertness on Yeats's part to the peasantry's hardships fully marking his emergence from the 'Celtic Twilight' into the daylight of modern Ireland:

> Then show the people what a king is like:
> Pull down old merings and root custom up,
> Whitewash the dung-hills, fatten hogs and geese,
> Hang your gold chain upon an ass's neck,
> And burn the blessed thorn trees out of the fields,
> And drive what's comely away![34]

This powerful new note of satire, seen elsewhere in *The Green Helmet*, whose satirization of the quarrelsome political sects of modern Ireland came after the Playboy riots, shows the influence of John Synge. Synge not only taught Yeats a lot stylistically, he also showed him a new approach to art in its relation to Irish life:

> When I was twenty-five or twenty-six I planned a *Legende des Siècles* of Ireland that was to set out with my *Wanderings of Oisin*, and show something of every century. Lionel Johnson's work and, later, Lady Gregory's, carried on the dream in a different form; and I did not see, until Synge began to write, that we must renounce the deliberate creation of a kind of Holy City in the imagination, and express the individual.[35]

Synge brought Yeats into a closer contact with Ireland at the simple level of ordinary life. In *Discoveries*, Yeats revealed a new concern with 'human personality' and those regions 'where there is visible beauty or mirth, where life is exciting, at high tide as it were.'[36] This concern with the richness of life is reflected in *The Green Helmet*, where Cuchulain's noble, individual stand against the petty jealousies of those around him is expressed in a racy, boisterous Irish idiom:

> Townland may rail at townland till all have gone to wrack,
> The very straws may wrangle till they've thrown down the stack;
> The very door-posts bicker till they've pulled in the door,
> The very ale-jars jostle till the ale is on the floor,
> But this shall help no further.[37]

In his defence of *The Playboy*, Yeats insisted: '. . . Irish life contains, like all vigorous life, the seeds of all good and evil, and a writer must be free here as elsewhere to watch where leek or flower ripens.'[38] The Ireland that Yeats and Synge fought to create was a 'romantic Ireland'. They were fighting against the Ireland of Thomas Davis, which 'was artificial, an idea built up in a couple of generations by a few commonplace men.'[39]

Yeats's attempt to create a living Irish culture through the theatre movement – one which was at once unifying through the use of national symbols but autonomous as real art must be – saw him move away from a simple nationalism toward complexity.[40] The battles fought at the Abbey Theatre fixed in Yeats's work an aristocratic contempt for the mob, and for the nationalist politics that invoked its support. He remembered O'Leary had told him: 'There are things a man must not do to save a nation',[41] and forged out of his bitter experiences a nationalism fitted to his personal myth:

> Romantic Ireland's dead and gone
> It's with O'Leary in the grave.[42]

In 'A Coat', Yeats expressed overtly the change from glorification of Ireland's past to a cynical awareness of its present philistinism:

> I made my song a coat
> Covered with embroideries
> Out of old mythologies
> From heel to throat;
> But the fools caught it

112

> Wore it in the world's eyes
> As though they's wrought it.
> Song, let them take it,
> For there's more enterprise
> In walking naked.[43]

This was a confession of the failure of his earlier romantic verse to effect the desired nobility in Irishmen. No longer looking at his country through coloured glasses, Yeats would now publicly express his dissatisfaction.

III

In his middle period Yeats learned the meaning of mob violence and that 'to be counted one with Davis, Mangan, Ferguson' was not likely to be understood or appreciated by the philistines whose influence was as strong as the power of the nationalist politicians was weak. In his personal myth of Irish nationalism, 'holy' men like Parnell became the defenders of that holy cause. Yeats also came to regard mob force as a negative influence on this: 'the shades of holy men' were 'plagued by crowds'.[44] His discontent with Irish politicians was founded on the opinion that they espoused hollow reason and practised hypocrisy:

> You say, as I have often given tongue
> In praise of what another's said or sung'
> 'Twere politic to do the like by these;
> But was there ever dog that praised his fleas?[45]

Against the specious rationalism and commonplace eloquence of the politicians, Yeats juxtaposed the spontaneous actions of his imagined peasantry:

> 'Though logic-choppers rule the town,
> And every man and maid and boy
> Has marked a distant object down,
> An aimless joy is a pure joy.'[46]

113

In Yeats's national myth, where passion was dominant, the peasantry found a favored place; the politicians, with their use of rationality alone, were antithetical to the poet's ideal.

Yeats's ideal nationality was thus founded on unsullied attributes – for such real traits of Irish society as mercantilist materialism he had nothing but bitter denunciation:

> What need you, being come to sense,
> But fumble in a greasy till
> And add the halfpence to the pence
> And prayer to shivering prayer, until
> You have dried the marrow from the bone?[47]

Yeats would have no truck with the naive political nationalism that made Ireland prim and holy, and England the embodiment of Satan: 'When his colleagues in the national movement spoke . . . of their hatred of England, Yeats tried to transmute it into a hatred of the materialism that was associated with England.'[48]

The public controversies that stirred Yeats's imagination in his middle years rouses him to wage a personal attack on the middle class in Ireland. It was this class that supplied Ireland's Paudeens. They had destroyed Parnell, and later Synge. Yeats tells the ghost of Parnell apropos of the Hugh Lane picture controversy:

> A man
> Of your own passionate serving kind who had brought
> In his full hands what, had they only known,
> Had given their children's children loftier thought
> Sweeter emotion, working in their veins
> Like gentle blood, has been driven from the place,
> And insult heaped upon him for his pains,
> And for his open-handedness, disgrace;
> Your enemy, an old foul mouth, had set
> The pack upon him.[49]

It was this same element in Irish society that he later named the force of 'Whiggery'. In his notes to the poems dealing with these issues, Yeats wrote: 'These controversies, political, literary, and artistic, have showed that neither religion nor politics can of itself create minds with enough receptivity to become wise, or just and generous enough to make a nation.'[50] The middle class religiously thought of divine things as a round of duties separate from life, and politically saw the good citizen as a man who held to certain opinions rather than one who possessed good will. Worse, when attached to the formula of political nationalism, this class developed a stultifying hatred:

> The root of it all is that the political class in Ireland – the lower-middle class from whom the patriotic associations have drawn their journalists and their leaders for the last ten years – have suffered through the cultivation of hatred as the one energy of their movement, a deprivation which is the intellectual equivalent to a certain surgical operation. Hence the shrillness of their voices. They contemplate all creative power as the eunuchs contemplate Don Juan as he passes through Hell on the white horse.'[51]

Yet his differences with the nationalist movement only served to strengthen Yeats's own personal ideal of Ireland. His poetic sarcasms were tempered by a sense of aristocratic dignity. In the middle period of Yeats's verse the aristocratic ideal came to be fully developed. As with his heroic ideal, the attribute of passionate intensity marked the ideal aristocrat. 'The aristocrat, in the context of Yeats's verse, is the embodiment of human passion; he becomes a symbol of human perfection.'[52] Major Robert Gregory was Yeats's symbol of that aristocratic perfection:

> Soldier, scholar, horseman he
> And all he did done perfectly
> As though he had but that one trade alone.[53]

And Robert Gregory, the Irish Airman, displayed the same exultant, lonely intensity as Cuchulain:

> Nor law, nor duty bade me fight,
> Nor public men, nor cheering crowds,
> A lonely impulse of delight
> Drove to this tumult in the clouds.[54]

115

Coole Park, where Robert Gregory was born and raised and where he learnt the aristocratic qualities of pride and independence, courtesy and ceremoniousness, became a symbol of dignity and perfection:

> How should the world be luckier if this house,
> Where passion and precision have been one
> Time out of mind, became too ruinous
> To breed the lidless eye that loves the sun?[55]

The ideal aristocrat was one of the fundamental constituents of Yeats's personal-mythical Irish nation.

Yeats's defence of Parnell, Synge and Hugh Lane – personally, and through his voice as poet – contrasts his middle with his earlier period. In taking a definite stand he sought to unify – as in his attempt to heal the split between Parnellites and anti-Parnellites – but not through compromising his ideals and, in the last analysis, with no real chance of practical success. From henceforth the rift between Yeats and the bulk of the Irish audience was struck. Though the Black and Tan atrocities and more particularly, his defence of Roger Casement, would later bring him momentarily back to his audience, it seems inevitable that Yeats's ideals for Ireland should have grown increasingly isolated and personal as he grew older.

IV

The Easter Rebellion of 1916 had an effect upon Yeats commensurate in its profundity with the changes it wrought in the national destiny of Ireland. It could not but affect Yeats's established heroic ideal, and at this particular level he registered a deep response. The 'Rising Poets' 'found in Irish history a tradition of heroic gesture, of dedication and courage in the face of overwhelming odds'.[56] Yeats knew this heroic gesture well, for in essence it was the same as the heroic ideal he had developed for himself. It was natural for him, therefore, to take up the heroic theme again and glorify the central figures in the Easter Rising as true Irishmen making a selfless sacrifice for their country.

This theme of sacrifice is at the heart of 'The Rose Tree', where Pearse says to Connolly: 'There's nothing but our own red blood/

116

Can make a right Rose Tree.'[57] Thus, in Yeats's reaction in this poem, Pearse and Connolly 'are no longer political leaders but consecrated priests performing a mystic ritual, that of exorcising the Sacred Rose Tree of the Irish race and nation with a lustral liquid – in this instance their own blood.'[58] The heroism of Pearse and Connolly achieves still greater celebration in Yeats's poetry in that they are taken up into the poet's heroic symbolism of Ireland's greatness. They come to rank alongside men like Parnell and, most fitting tribute of all, alongside Cuchulain. The symbolic elevation is completed in one of his finest public and political poems 'Easter 1916':

> Hearts with one purpose alone
> Through summer and winter seem
> Enchanted to a stone
> To trouble the living stream.
> The horse that comes from the road,
> The rider, the birds that range
> From cloud to tumbling cloud,
> Minute by minute they change;
> A shadow of cloud on the stream
> Changes minute by minute;
> A horse-hoof slides on the brim,
> And a horse plashes within it;
> The long-legged moor-hens dive,
> And hens to moor-cocks call;
> Minute by minute they live:
> The stone's in the midst of all.

*   *   *

> Too long a sacrifice
> Can make a stone of the heart.
> O when may it suffice?
> That is Heaven's part, our part
> To murmur name upon name,
> As a mother names her child
> When sleep at last has come
> On limbs that had run wild.
> What is it but nightfall?
> No, no, not night but death;

Was it needless death after all?
For England may keep faith
For all that is done and said.
We know their dream; enough
To know they dreamed and are dead;
And what if excess of love
Bewildered them till they died?
I write it out in a verse –
MacDonagh and MacBride
And Connolly and Pearse
Now and in time to be,
Wherever green is worn,
And changed, changed utterly:
A terrible beauty is born.[59]

At one level – the heroic personal one – Yeats appears to accept
the act of the leaders of the rebellion in terms similar to those they
themselves intended. Yeats canonizes Pearse alongside Pearse's
redeemer, Cuchulain. Yet the last line of each strophe is the refrain:
'A terrible beauty is born', and it suggests an intended ambiguity
that reflects Yeats's persisting sense of the imponderability of the
Rebellion. Both an ominous and a joyous reaction is implied. Each
correlates with a personal feeling in Yeats: he held in awe the
martyrdom of the sixteen leaders, but inclined to condemn the
hatred to which their action gave birth.

For Yeats realized, as he wrote to Augusta Gregory after the
rebellion, 'that all the work of years has been overturned, all the
bringing together of classes, all the freeing of Irish literature and
criticism from politics.'[60] The years of war unleashed by 1916 – the
war against the British and the Civil War that followed – wrought in
Yeats's mind an even more complex response. Though in his last
period he continued to glorify the martyrs – 'the longer Yeats
thought of the men of 1916, the more their deaths took on the tragic
joy that Yeats esteemed as the highest wisdom man could embody
in action'[61] – still the wars forced themselves forward in images of
Armageddon.

V

T. R. Henn has suggested that the period of the Black and Tans
awoke Yeats's nationalist feelings. Yeats at this time published, in

Michael Roberts and The Dancer, what Henn calls the 'first fruits' of Yeats's reaction to the earlier Rebellion. These include the poems 'An Irish Airman Foresees His Death', 'Easter 1916', 'Sixteen Dead Men' and 'The Rose Tree'.[62] It is certainly true that Yeats was enraged by the deeds of the British soldiery, and his verse reflects the extreme to which his cynical bitterness could reach:

> Now days are dragon-ridden, the nightmare
> Rides upon sleep: a drunken soldiery
> Can leave the mother, murdered at her door,
> To crawl in her own blood, and go scot-free.[63]

In 'Reprisals', the Black and Tans and their fearful atrocities are roundly denounced:

> Half-drunk or whole-mad soldiery
> Are murdering your tenants there.
> Men that revere your father yet
> Are shot at on the open plain.
> Where may new-married women sit
> And suckle children now? Armed men
> May murder them in passing by
> Nor law nor parliament take heed.[64]

First reading might suggest Yeats was seeking to stir up anti-British hatred. That this was not his aim is indicated by the deeper level at which his images of destruction and atrocity work. Yeats's objective was that 'passionate nationalism was a good, but not if it became mere impotent Anglophobia'.[65] Rather he was concerned to express in a cogent manner the events resulting from a wider phenomenon of disruption.

T. R. Henn is surely right to suggest that Yeats saw in the Black and Tan period and that of Civil War which followed, the microcosmic expression of conflagrations of macrocosmic proportions. Yeats did not experience the First World War at first hand, but saw enough in the Ireland of the 'troubles' to appreciate the forces threatening the collapse of civilization. The theme appears most notably in 'The Second Coming':

Mere anarchy is loosed upon the world,
The blood-dimmed tide is loosed, and everywhere
The ceremony of innocence is drowned;
The best lack all conviction, while the worst
Are full of passionate intensity.[66]

Perhaps he now remembered MacGregor Mather's prophecy of the 1890s of great wars to come. Disillusioned by the Irish Free State, Yeats must live to see the onset in Ireland of 'the filthy modern tide'.[67] The 'casual comedy' that preceded Easter 1916 had passed through a 'terrible beauty', to become embodied in a government that was the antithesis of all that he valued.'[68] And in the back of his mind, Yeats could not discount his own contribution to these violent results:

Did that play of mine send out
Certain men the English shot?[69]

Still, from 1922 to 1928, Yeats served as a senator in the new Irish Free State, and during this period strove to put into practice some of his poetic ideas. During his term of office he still carried on the struggle of promoting national feeling and endeavoured to improve the conditions of education in Ireland in order to make her people more culturally receptive. He was not just a politician, 'a sixty-year-old smiling public man'[70] making a periodic inspection of Irish schools. In his Senate speeches his aim was 'the development of national excellence by the best modern education available'.[71] He even proposed a revision of educational practice in these terms:

. . . begin geography with your native fields, arithmetic by counting the school chairs and measuring the walls, history with local monuments, religion with local saints, and then to pass on from that to the nation itself.[72]

Here was his old feeling that any national pride should be deeply-rooted in the culture, tradition and history of the Irish nation itself. He maintained that his revision of the educational system was both a modern method and that it would promote that desired deep-rootedness. 'If your education therefore is efficient in the modern sense, it will be more national than the dreams of politicians.'[73] For Yeats the principle of education was the same as his concept of

120

nationality: it should be as intuitive and as close to the development of the self as possible. And, in accordance with his perpetual vitalist belief, it should never be rigidly controlled by means of logic or science.

In his essay 'Compulsory Gaelic', Yeats spoke out once more for freedom and spontaneity:

> I am not sure that I like the idea of a state with a definite purpose, and there are moments, impractical moments, perhaps, when I think that the State should leave the mind free to create. I think Aristotle defined the soul as that which moves itself, and how can it move itself if everything is arranged beforehand?[74]

Clearly, this was of a piece with the glorification of the attributes of spontaneity, individualism and nobility to be observed in his previous verse. Yeats notionally considered education as a necessary institution, but also, above all, it was a noble one.

Nevertheless, Yeats's period as a Senator did not see him satisfy his desire for the regeneration of Ireland. It was obvious that one potent source of his Utopian Ireland was passing. In 'Meditations in Time of Civil War', he voiced his awareness that the Anglo-Irish aristocracy was dispersed, its achievement lost:

> Surely among a rich man's flowering lawns,
> Amid the rustle of his planted hills,
> Life overflows without ambitious pains;
> And rains down life until the basin spills,
> And mounts more dizzy high the more it rains
> As though to choose whatever shape it wills
> And never stoop to a mechanical
> Or servile shape, at others' beck and call.[75]

The free, uncramped environment that had produced a Robert Gregory was giving way to the 'mechanical', 'servile' shapes wrought by the force of 'Whiggery', that 'levelling, rancorous, rational sort of mind/That never looked out of the eye of a saint/Or out of drunkard's eye'.[76] Passion must give way to materialist calculation. The heritage of Locke and the Age of Reason was being forced home.

However, Yeats still had a proud, fanatic heart. He spoke in the

Senate in 1925 in the Divorce debate with the pride of a member of the Protestant minority:

> I am proud to consider myself a typical man of that minority. We against whom you have done this thing are no petty people. We are one of the great stocks of Europe. We are the people of Burke; we are the people of Grattan; we are the people of Swift, the people of Emmet, the people of Parnell. We have created the most of the modern literature of this country. We have created the best of its political intelligence.[77]

This was no empty claim, but given the character of the new Irish state it was a forlorn one. Yeats's aristocratic ideal could have no place here: later . . . [he] grew into a Swiftian contempt for popery and the Irish masses and delighted in saying outrageous things to an incensed Senate of Catholic business men.[78]

> Out of Ireland have we come
> Great hatred, little room,
> Maimed us at the start.
> I carry from my mother's womb
> A fanatic heart.[79]

VII

Yeats's final years following his Senatorial term marked a period in which many of his attitudes towards Ireland are characterized by this fanaticism. Some of his earlier feelings were developed: disillusionment and realism from his middle period sharpened still further. Glorification of Ireland's past and modern heroes persisted. He could express himself in just as biting a fashion as in his middle verse where he waged 'the day's war with every knave and dolt.'[80] In his final period, Yeats grew frustrated by the hollowness of the people in general, and their failure to respond to his previous ideals.

In his seclusion, Yeats seemed to feel the futility of his hopes for Ireland. In 1921, in his note to *Four Plays for Dancers*, he presaged his final isolation:

In writing these little plays I knew that I was creating something which could only fully succeed in a civilization very unlike ours. I think they should be written for some country where all classes share in a half-mythological, half-philosophical folk-belief which the writer and his small audience lift into a new subtlety. All my life I have longed for such a country, and always found it quite impossible to write without having as much belief in its real existence as a child has in that of the wooden birds, beasts, and persons of his toy Noah's Ark. I have now found all the mythology and philosophy I need in the papers of my old friend and rival, Robartes.[81]

The private, mythical Ireland that he had developed in his early period had not materialized – as indeed it never could have done. But still Yeats reproved the churlishness of compatriots who, he believed, could not even live up to the example of other nations:

Poland is a Catholic nation and some ten years ago inflicted upon the national enemy an overwhelming, world-famous defeat, but its fanaticism, if it has any, thwarts neither science, nor art, nor letters. Sometimes as the representative of the Abbey Theatre I have called upon some member of Mr. Cosgrave's or Mr. de Valera's government to explain some fanatical attack – we are a State Theatre though our small subsidy has been lately reduced – once as a member of the Irish Academy to complain of the illegal suppression of a book, and upon each occasion I came away with the conviction that the Minister felt exactly as I felt but was helpless: the mob reigned.[82]

To those people who did not make the effort to change, his reproachful reply was: 'Fail, and that history turns into rubbish.'[83] To voice his opinion of his hollowness, he wrote 'Three Songs to the same Tune':

> Soldiers take pride in saluting their Captain,
> Where are the captains that govern mankind?
> What happens a tree that has nothing within it?[84]

Still, this lack of response to his life-long-preoccupation of stimulating national ideals did not force Yeats to yield, even though through it his mythopoeic vision became more intensely personal, mirroring his disillusionment:

123

> I ranted to the knave and fool,
> But outgrew that school,
> Would transform the part,
> Fit audience found, but cannot rule
> My fanatic heart.[85]

For his own benefit, Yeats developed a vibrant sense of nationality strengthening his valuation of heroic personality, aristocracy – especially Anglo-Irish aristocracy – and also his peasant myth.

In *The Tower*, Yeats discovered his Anglo-Irish ancestry; that, as he told the Irish Senate, he was from 'The people of Burke and of Grattan.'[85] Long since, in his middle period, he had been proud to state his blood 'has not passed through any huckster's loin'.[87] Now he conceived of his ancestry as people:

> Bound neither to Cause nor to State,
> Neither to slaves that were spat on,
> Nor to the tyrants that spat.[88]

They were of the community that produced 'God-appointed Berkeley that proved all things a dream', and 'haughtier-headed Burke that proved the State a tree.'[89] Yeats was deeply interested in philosophy and discovered in those great Anglo-Irishmen opposition to the modern trend of materialism fostered by the Englishman Locke and the Scotsman Hume. Berkeley's idealist philosophy was a denial of Hume's sceptic materialism and Burke's organic metaphor for the state opposed Locke's society of component mechanism. In his verse, Yeats invested his heroes with aristocratic nobility and proud individuality. But Yeats probably felt closest kin with Swift, whom he portrays 'beating on his breast in sibylline frenzy blind/because the heart in his blood-sodden breast had dragged him down into mankind.'[90] What united them all with Yeats was: 'All hated Whiggery.'[91]

Yeats had not given up by any means the controversies of his middle period. He returned to the heroic personality in 'Parnell's Funeral', where a procession of Yeats's national heroes is rehearsed, re-iterating that in modern times Ireland had traduced her own heroic heritage:

> Come, fix upon me that accusing eye.
> I thirst for accusation. All that was sung,
> All that was said in Ireland is a lie.[92]

Parnell himself is conceived of by Yeats as repudiating the mob with an aristocratic contempt:

> Parnell came down the road, he said to a cheering man: 'Ireland shall get her freedom and you still break stone.'[93]

Indeed the last poems show Yeats synthesizing his aristocratic and heroic ideals in the world of passionately conceived private myth. There were in this realm god-like heroes: Parnell, Casement, O'Rahilly, Pearse, Connolly, and O'Higgins. They had served Ireland as active, heroic martyrs, their actions always tempered by an abandon that was its own, passionate, *raison d'etre*:

> Sing of the O'Rahilly
> That had such little sense
> He told Pearse and Connolly
> He'd gone to great expense
> Keeping all the Kerry men
> Out of that crazy fight;
> That he might be there himself
> Had travelled half the night.[97]

These heroes managed both devotion to the national cause, and personal fulfilment:

> And Parnell loved his country,
> And Parnell loved his lass.[98]

That they could do both was axiomatic for their rank as heroes: it meant they had attained their unity of being, their personal completion which set them apart from the hollowness of the collective mass.

Besides these active aristocratic heroes were the sainted figures of modern Irish culture. These had sacrificed themselves in the same cause; they too had done all they did for reasons that defied calculation. Thus he wrote of Lady Gregory:

> ... where is the brush that could show anything
> Of all that pride and that humility?
> And I am in despair that time may bring
> Approved patterns of women or of men
> But not that selfsame excellence again.[99]

125

There was of course Synge as well: 'that rooted man/Forgetting human words; a grave deep face.' And Hugh Lane, ' "onlie begetter" of all these' – the man who made possible Yeats's visit to the Municipal Gallery. It was the gesture of a disillusioned, alienated man. With his retirement from the Senate, de Valera's regime, the death of Kevin O'Higgins and the failure of O'Duffy, there was no longer any room for Yeats and his friends. 'There was left for Yeats,' as Henn said, 'little but a proud and formal withdrawal'.[94]

Nevertheless, Yeats was true to his own myth of national heroism to the last. In 'The Statues', he showed once more intense poetic praise of a modern hero: 'When Pearse summoned Cuchulain to his side/What stalked through the Post Office?'[95] Two years before, he gained his last gleam of popularity in defending Roger Casement. Yeats's two poems on Casement exemplified the fanaticism of his later years, and fanned into flames embers of anti-English feeling in Ireland. Yet in a sense, Yeats was only being true to his own ideal again: as he defended Parnell's memory and turned full blame on his Irish accusers, so he now condemned those who 'turned a trick by forgery/ And blackened his [Casement's] good name.'[96] Again, in 'The Ghost of Roger Casement', the refrain: 'The Ghost of Roger Casement/Is beating on the door' was potentially explosive, and reminds us of the young nationalistic poet who wrote *Cathleen Ni Houlihan*. But Yeats does not use a loosely-found propagandist device. Once more he invokes the culture, tradition and heredity of the Irish which from the beginning had been the source of his mythopoeic vision.

In these last years, Yeats's verse showed the completion of his mythopoeic process with the development of the peasant ideal. This had always been an integral part of his ideal of the nation, and had been strengthened by his collaboration with John Synge. It was in fact a part of his earliest love of Ireland, imbibed through his mother and the local people and scenery in Sligo. Writing in 1909, Yeats distinguished between his love of the nation and the artificial one of Young Ireland:

Allingham and Davis have two different kinds of love of Ireland. In Allingham I find the entire emotion for the place one grew up in which I felt as a child. Davis on the other hand was concerned with ideas of Ireland, with conscious patriotism. His Ireland was artificial, an idea built up in a couple of generations by a few commonplace men. This artificial idea has done me as much harm as the other has helped me . . . The beauty of peasant thought is partly from a spontaneity unspoiled by the artificial town-made thought. One cannot sum up a nation intellectually, and when the summing-up is made by half-educated men the idea fills one with alarm.[100]

Yeats's creation of the character of Crazy Jane is both rejection of an intellectually-shaped nationalism and affirmation of his earlier concern for passionate intensity. She becomes the major symbol of the peasant ideal of Yeats's last phase; at once physical and anti-clerical, the lyrics in which she features achieve Yeats's desire for the 'rooting of mythology in the earth.'[101] Having had her dead lover denounced as a 'coxcomb' by the Bishop, Crazy Jane pits the vigour of her Jack in his prime against the deformity of the cleric:

> Nor can he hide in holy black
> The heron's hunch upon his back,
> But a birch-tree stood my Jack;
> The solid man and the coxcomb.[102]

And thus the meaning is reversed and the Bishop is made the coxcomb and Jack the solid man. Through Crazy Jane's sensuality a knowledge is gained which is a total antithesis to the abstract, being instead passionate and vitalistic:

> My friends are gone, but that's a truth
> Nor grave nor bed denied,
> Learned in bodily lowliness
> And in the heart's pride.[103]

The earthy knowledge of the peasant, the intense abandon of the hero, and the perfected passion of the aristocrat – all are woven into the one unified national myth in which pride, individuality and passion are the constituent elements. 'For Yeats, passion was at the centre of all, and love was but one of its manifestations; passion was 'the universal principle' by which unity of being could be achieved.'[104]

It was this unity of being, long and hard sought for in his works, which gave meaning to Yeats's national myth. Yeats strove to achieve such a unity of being despite the inexorable progression of 'the filthy modern tide' brought on by the changing of the gyres. '. . .

In the inevitable flow of history the ideal would someday re-emerge and flourish and then again disappear as an antithetical epoch gained ascendancy.'[105] Yeats insisted on proclaiming his ideal undaunted, exhorting young Irish poets to:

> Sing whatever is well made,
> Scorn the sort now growing up
> All out of shape from toe to top,
> Their unremembering hearts and heads
> Base-born products of base beds.
> Sing the peasantry, and then
> Hard-riding country gentlemen,
> The holiness of monks, and after
> Porter-drinkers' randy laughter;
> Sing the lords and ladies gay
> That were beaten into the clay
> Through seven heroic centuries;
> Cast your minds on other days
> That we in coming days may be
> Still the indomitable Irishry.[106]

Thus through a lifetime during which Ireland underwent profound metamorphosis, Yeats retained a personal dedication to 'the cause that never dies'.[107] It was a concern that changed as his verse matured and as outside events registered their impact. At times the component parts of Yeats's Utopian Ireland – heroic, aristocratic and peasant – received greater or lesser accent according to mood and situation. Ireland's heroic past, the influence of Maud Gonne, disillusionment with the narrowness and materialism in Irish politics and society, the Easter Rising, the flood of violence following upon it, and after his period as Senator the final years of estrangement – all were sources of stimulation shaping Yeats's ideal. Common to all was the central, unifying image of passionate intensity: amidst the changes that transformed Ireland, and in the images in Yeats's works forged in response, this passionate intensity remained the chief attribute of Yeats's national myth and also the unattainable goal of life itself. As he expressed it in 'A Prayer for Old Age':

God guard me from those thoughts men think
In the mind alone;
He that sings a lasting song
Thinks in a marrow-bone;

From all that makes a wise old man
That can be praised of all;
O what am I that I should not seem
For the song's sake a fool?

I pray – for fashion's word is out
And prayer comes round again –
That I may seem, though I am old,
A foolish, passionate man.[108]

VIII

Yeats remained true to his ideal nationalism in spite of the wounds
given and received in its espousal. He lived up to O'Leary's three
standards enunciated in 'How Irishmen Should Feel.' First, Irishmen must feel they were Irish. This Yeats especially sought to
realize in his early period by revitalizing the rightful cultural heritage of Irishmen. As he told the Royal Academy of Sweden: 'Synge's
work, the work of Lady Gregory, my own *Cathleen ni Houlihan* and
my *Hour-Glass* . . . are characteristic of our first ambition. They
bring the imagination and speech of the country, all that poetical
tradition descended from the Middle Ages, to the people of the
town.'[109] Second, an Irishman must try to secure Irish unity. Even in
the bitter sectarian days of his time at the Abbey in the early 1900s,
Yeats's aim was to cleanse the Irish nation of disruptive, divisive
forces. Finally, an Irishman must make some sacrifice for Ireland.
Yeats, who as Ellmann concluded,[110] never eschewed asking the
same, fundamental questions, also did not shirk the responsibility
he felt as an artist towards Ireland. With regard to O'Leary's third
precept, throughout his lifetime, Yeats made the greatest sacrifice
he could for Ireland – his life, not as a political martyr, but as a poet
dedicated, in spite of all vicissitudes, to the spiritual ennoblement of
Ireland; to make the Irish aware and proud of their nobility.

NOTES

1　R. J. Loftus, *Nationalism in Modern Anglo-Irish Poetry* (Madison: University of Wisconsin Press, 1964), p. 41.
2　W. B. Yeats, *Letters To A New Ireland* (London: Oxford University Press, 1970), p. 174.
3　R. Ellmann, *The Identity of Yeats* (London: Faber and Faber, 1964), p. 16.
4　W. B. Yeats, *Autobiographies* (London: Macmillan, 1966), p. 194.
5　Ibid., pp. 193–94.
6　Loftus, op. cit., p. 95.
7　W. B. Yeats, *Essays and Introductions* (London: Macmillan, 1961), p. 246.
8　Ibid., p. 259.
9　Ibid., p. 260.
10　W. B. Yeats, *Explorations* (New York: Macmillan, 1962), p. 232.
11　Loftus, op. cit., p. 4.
12　R. Ellmann, *Yeats: The Man and The Masks* (New York: Macmillan, 1948), p. 46.
13　P. Costollo, *The Heart Grown Brutal: The Irish Revolution In Liberature, From Parnell To The Death of Yeats 1891–1939* (Dublin: Gill and MacMillan, 1977), p. 22.
14　Yeats, *Essays and Introductions*, p. 510.
15　Quoted in Ellmann, *The Identity of Yeats*, p. 13.
16　W. B. Yeats, 'The Poetry of Sir Samuel Ferguson,' *Dublin University Review*, 11 (1886), 941.
17　W. I. Thompson, *The Imagination Of An Insurrection* (New York: Oxford University Press, 1967), p. 44.
18　Ellmann, *Yeats: The Man and The Masks*, pp. 51–52.
19　W. B. Yeats, *Collected Poems* (London: Macmillan, 1958), p. 56.
20　L. Edel, 'No More Opinions . . . No More Politics, *'The New Republic'*, 132 (14 March, 1955), p. 21.
21　*The Letters of W. B. Yeats*, ed. Allan Wade (London: Rupert Hart-Davis, 1954), p. 63 (Letter to Katharine Tynan, 14 March [1888]).
22　S. B. Bushrui, *Yeats's Verse-Plays: The Revisions 1900–1910* (Oxford: Clarendon Press, 1965), p. 4.
23　Ellmann, *Yeats: The Man and The Masks*, pp. 124–27.
24　Loftus, op. cit., p. 41.
25　Quoted by A. N. Jeffares in *W.B. Yeats: The Critical Heritage* (London & Boston: Routledge Kegan and Paul, 1977), p. 376.
26　Yeats, *Collected Poems*, p. 90.
27　J. A. Byars, 'Yeats's Introduction Of The Heroic Type,' *Modern Drama*, 8 (Feb. 1966), p. 410.
28　Bushrui, *Yeats's Verse-Plays: The Revisions 1900–1910*, p. 16.
29　W. B. Yeats, *Collected Plays* (London: Macmillan, 1966), p. 255.
30　Loftus, op. cit., p. 12.
31　Yeats, *Autobiographies*, p. 170.
32　Bushrui, *Yeats's Verse-Plays: The Revisions 1900–1910*, p. 44.
33　Yeats, *Collected Plays*, p. 119.
34　W. B. Yeats, Poems, 1988–1905 (London: Bullen, 1906), p. 218.
35　Yeats, *Autobiographies*, pp. 493–94.
36　Yeats, *Essays and Introductions*, p. 276.

37 Yeats, *Collected Plays*, p. 240.
38 Bushrui, *Yeats's Verse-Plays: The Revisions 1900–1910*, p. 217.
39 Yeats, *Autobiographies*, p. 472.
40 Thompson, op. cit., p. 48.
41 Yeats, *Autobiographies*, p. 96.
42 Yeats, *Collected Poems*, p. 121.
43 Ibid., p. 142.
44 Ibid., p. 127.
45 Ibid., p. 105.
46 Ibid., p. 158.
47 Ibid., pp. 120–21.
48 Ellmann, *Yeats: The Man and The Masks*, p. 111.
49 Yeats, *Collected Poems*, p. 123.
50 P. Allt and R. K. Alsprach, eds., *The Variorum Edition Of The Poems Of W.B. Yeats*, (New York: Macmillan, 1957), p. 818.
51 Yeats, *Autobiographies*, p. 486.
52 Loftus, op. cit., p. 57.
53 Yeats, *Collected Poems*, p. 151.
54 Ibid., p. 152.
55 Ibid., p. 106.
56 Loftus, op. cit., pp. 151–52.
57 Yeats, *Collected Poems*, p. 206.
58 Loftus, op. cit., pp. 82–83.
59 Yeats, *Collected Poems*, p. 204.
60 *The Letters of W. B. Yeats*, p. 13.
61 Thompson, op. cit., pp. 163–64.
62 T. R. Henn, 'W. B. Yeats and The Poetry of War,' *From The Proceedings Of The British Academy* (London: Oxford University Press, 1965), p. 51, p. 311.
63 Yeats, *Collected Poems*, p. 233.
64 Allt and Alsprach, *The Variorum Edition Of The Poems of W. B. Yeats*, p. 791.
65 Ellmann, *Yeats: The Man and The Masks*, p. 288.
66 Yeats, *Collected Poems*, p. 211.
67 Ibid., p. 376.
68 Henn. loc. cit., p. 314.
69 Yeats, *Collected Poems*, p. 393.
70 Ibid., p. 243.
71 Jeffares & Cross (eds.), *In Excited Reverie* (New York: St. Martins Press, 1965), p. 127.
72 *The Senate Speeches Of W. B. Yeats*, ed. D. R. Pearce (London: Faber and Faber, 1961), pp. 170–71.
73 Ibid., p. 171.
74 From Yeats's article 'Compulsory Gaelic: A Dialogue', *The Irish Statesman* (2 August, 1924) quoted by Jeffares in *In Excited Reverie*, pp. 127–28.
75 Yeats, *Collected Poems*, p. 225.
76 Ibid., p. 272.
77 *The Senate Speeches of W. B. Yeats*, p. 99.
78 Thompson, op. cit., p. 131.
79 Yeats, *Collected Poems*, p. 288.
80 Ibid., p. 104.

81 P. Allt and C. C. Alsprach, *The Variorum Edition Of The Plays of W. B. Yeats* (New York: Macmillan, 1966), p. 566.
82 A. N. Jeffares, *A Commentary On The Collected Poems of W. B. Yeats* (London: Macmillan, 1968), p. 416.
83 Yeats, *Collected Poems*, p. 322.
84 Ibid., pp. 323–24.
85 Ibid., pp. 287–88.
86 Ibid., p. 223.
87 Ibid., p. 113.
88 Ibid., p. 223.
89 Ibid., p. 268.
90 Ibid., p. 268.
91 Ibid., p. 272.
92 Ibid., p. 320.
93 Ibid., p. 359.
94 Henn, loc. cit., p. 314.
95 Yeats, *Collected Poems*, p. 375.
96 Ibid., p. 351.
97 Ibid., p. 354.
98 Ibid., p. 356.
99 Ibid., p. 369.
100 Yeats, *Autobiographies*, pp. 471–72.
101 Ellman, *Yeats: The Man and The Masks*, p. 267.
102 Yeats, *Collected Poems*, p. 290.
103 Ibid., p. 294.
104 Loftus, op. cit., p. 226.
105 Ibid., p. 85.
106 Yeats, *Collected Poems*, p. 400.
107 'Dedication,' *Representative Irish Tales Compiled, with an introduction and Notes by W. B. Yeats* (New York and London: G. P. Putman's Sons, 1891).
108 Yeats, *Collected Poems*, p. 326.
109 Yeats, *Autobiographies*, p. 570.
110 Ellmann, *Yeats: The Man and The Masks*, p. 295.

HISTORIANS AND MAGICIANS: IRELAND BETWEEN FANTASY AND HISTORY

STAN SMITH

Near the beginning of Act II of *Waiting for Godot* there's a moment of recapitulation which sharply distinguishes Vladimir's and Estragon's attitudes towards history. Vladimir, the ideologist, insists on holding on to memory: for him, it's the foundation of identity, the continuity which sustains the self. It's important that 'things have changed since yesterday', it's important that Estragon remember their shared experience in the Macon country, that he should recall Lucky and Pozzo and the suicide attempt. All these are unreal for Estragon: the past lives on in his present only as bruised shins, and the rest Vladimir has dreamt ('Another of your night-mares'). For Estragon, the self is a momentary being, its past and future fictional ('You can start from anything,' he notes in passing). For Vladimir, finding something to start from means returning to where you left off:

    V.:   What was I saying, we could go on from there.
    E.:   What were you saying when?
    V.:   At the very beginning.
    E.:   The beginning of WHAT?
    V.:   This evening . . . I was saying . . . I was saying . . .

And Estragon cuts him short: 'I'm not a historian.'

For Vladimir the future can be constituted only by reclaiming the past, which tells us who we are. But for Estragon the past is supposi-tional – primarily a figment invented to keep others happy – 'I suppose we blathered' – which, once invented, takes on a spurious certainty: 'Blathering about nothing in particular. That's been going on now for half a century.' Trying on unrecognized boots then becomes a new and original experience:

133

E.:   We always find something, eh Didi, to give us the impression we exist?

V.:   (*impatiently*) Yes, yes, we're magicians. But let us persevere in what we have resolved, before we forget.

Beckett sets in opposition here not only two personalities but also two modes of historical perception. If Estragon in annoyance disclaims the name of historian, Vladimir with equally impatient sarcasm defines the improvisatory, existential approach as that of the magician, inventing something out of nothing, without recourse to or knowledge of any determining precedents. Yet both these definitions have a common factor: the fact of *discourse*, as Vladimir indicates later, when a fallen Pozzo calls for help:

E.:   And suppose he –

V.:   Let us not waste time in idle discourse! Let us do something, while we have the chance! It is not every day that we are needed. Not indeed that we personally are needed. Others would meet the case equally well, if not better. To all mankind they were addressed, those cries for help still ringing in our ears! But at this place, at this moment of time, all mankind is us, whether we like it or not ...

Like any history-conscious intellectual, Vladimir goes on, sententiously proclaiming his gospel of action as the words drift further and further away from the deeds they contemplate.

What's at issue here is of course an old ambiguity in the word 'history' itself, an ambiguity obscured in English by the evolution of two words and concepts from the same root, but one preserved in the French 'histoire.' For 'history' is both events and the narrative in which we inscribe them, simultaneously the discourses of action and of language, and the whole problematic of the play derives from the fact that we cannot separate out, except for brief moments, 'history' as event from 'story' as interpretation. Beckett in a sense is exploring the roots of the *ideological* – that rich, elusive, opaque, mystifying medium in which we misperceive and misrepresent to ourselves the significance and texture of our being-in-the-world. It's something he's indicated already, in the opening song of Act II, with its receding, never completed narrative which recurrently embeds within itself its own repetition and therefore like history never reaches any conclusion:

Then all the dogs came running
And dug the dog a tomb
And wrote upon the tombstone
For the eyes of dogs to come:

A dog came in the kitchen . . .

This multiple embedding, like Zeno's paradox, always puts an uncrossable and infinite distance between start and finish, writing and event. Similarly, 'All the dead voices' the two hear 'talk about their lives. To have lived is not enough for them. They have to talk about it. To be dead is not enough for them. It is not sufficient.' The same process occurs towards the end of the play when Vladimir, watching over a sleeping Estragon, envisages a similar regression in space:

At me too someone is looking, of me too someone is saying, he is sleeping, he knows nothing, let him sleep on. I can't go on. What have I said?

The sense of an infinite recession of interpretations, of 'sayings', in which authentic action drowns, is related very specifically to the anxiety of history, that polysemic discourse which is both events and narrative:

Was I sleeping, while the others suffered? Am I sleeping now? Tomorrow, when I wake, or think I do, what shall I say of today? That with Estragon my friend, at this place, until the fall of night, I waited for Godot? That Pozzo passed, with his carrier, and that he spoke to us? Probably. But in all that, what truth will there be?

This question – what stories do we tell about the events that may have happened? – is intimately related to that other question, to which the opening line of the play is a (somewhat belated) answer. The words 'Nothing to be done', which Beckett scrupulously insisted on retaining as the translation when others preferred 'Nothing doing', are not without historical precedent. They evoke that momentous question, first asked in 1902 (almost exactly half a century of blathering earlier) by another Vladimir, Vladimir Ilyich Lenin, in a pamphlet whose very title spelt out the central question of twentieth-century history for the bourgeois intellectual whose figure Vladimir is: *What is to be done*? And Beckett here intimates

135

that 'what is to be done?' is a question that cannot be dissociated from those other questions, questions of historical interpretation: 'What have I said?' and 'what shall I say?'

The end of *Molloy* takes this whole procedure further, separating, by a deliberate change of tense and person, and the negative mode, these two dimensions of 'history'. In the retelling of experience, or in its simultaneous telling and acting, we are at once 'historians' and 'magicians,' spinning our ideological rationales out of the very stuff of language and event. Significantly, Beckett does not simply dissociate the past tense of the written from the living present of the writer. In the run-up to the final sentence he relates this to a larger process of acculturation, that learning of a language in which the child is appropriated to history, made a party to its terms, learning to reproduce in his own life the experiential paradigms of his forebears:

> I have spoken of a voice telling me things. I was getting to know it better now, to understand what it wanted. It did not use the words that Moran had been taught when he was little and that he in his turn had taught to his little one . . . But in the end I understood this language. I understood it, I understand it, all wrong perhaps. That is not what matters. It told me to write the report. Does that mean I am freer now than I was? I do not know. I shall learn. Then I went back into the house and wrote. It is midnight. The rain is beating on the windows. It was not midnight. It was not raining.

Writing the report turns the present tense of events and voice into the past tense of print. But the story is apparently present, and the 'real' events apparently past; and the relation between them is one of direct contradiction. 'I speak in the present tense,' says Molloy at the beginning of the book, 'it is so easy to speak in the present tense, when speaking of the past. It is the mythological present, don't mind it.' We are at sea in a fabular confusion of times. History as events is here turned into a magical story, to be taken with a pinch of salt.

* * *

It is perhaps one of the most repeated motifs in modern Irish literature, signalled in the opening sentence of *A Portrait of the Artist as a Young Man* by a cunning textual duplicity. For this most sophisticated of *avant-garde* novels, with all its elaborate aesthetics, chooses to introduce itself, and gives away the secret of all narrative, with that most primitive and fundamental of formulae: 'Once upon a time and a very good time it was . . .' Joyce indicates here the doubleness of any literary text. At the end of *Molloy*, the text tells us not to believe it just as it solicits our credence. So, here, Joyce warns us that this is a *story*, at the moment that he announces the opening of Stephen Dedalus's *history*. We can, as naive realists, hear these words simply as the *content* of this history (this is Simon Dedalus, dramatically caught in the act of telling his son a tale). At the same time, as subtle formalists, or as even more naive readers, we can hear these words as the formulaic opening of the whole story we are about to read (for how else do all good stories begin but 'Once upon a time . . .'?). The formula, that is, is both form *and* content, signifier *and* signified. The close of *Portrait* points towards a time beyond the bounds of Stephen's present life while simultaneously indicating a real world beyond the book's frontiers, speaking of 'the *spell* of arms and voices' and the tall ships' *'tale* of distant nations.' But the ending also points back to the beginning of the book, in a circular movement which makes it precisely the *product* of the future time only imputed, not yet realized, in those closing paragraphs. (The same temporal paradox lies behind Stephen's inversions of the parent/child relation, here and in *Ulysses*). The opening of *Portrait* similarly initiates a structuring analogy between the articulation of characters in a story and a society's articulation of its subjects: we are witnesses, in these paragraphs, to the simultaneous genesis of child and text, 'young man' and 'portrait'. Stephen is constructed as a *subject*, a conscious ego, by learning to recognize his place in a story: the story his father tells him about himself, the story through which 'his' family, 'his' church and 'his' nation donate him a role and an identity. The text here enacts, in appropriate nursery-tale terms, what Jacques Lacan has called the 'mirror-phase' in the construction of the human subject.[1] The child learns who he is by seeing himself as an object of the other's gaze, an image in his parents' eyes which he then learns to identify with the 'me' in the mirror. Just as, in the story his father tells him, the moocow coming down the road is grammatical subject, and the 'nicens little boy named baby tuckoo' initially only the object of the sentence, so in Stephen's life the father precedes and names the son, assigns him his place in an already constituted tale. Stephen's role is simply to confirm this role, recognizing himself in the mirror of the tale, and thereby learning that trick by which, happily ever after, he remains

137

that person he has recognized himself to be: 'His father told him
that story; his father looked at him through a glass . . . He [Stephen]
was baby tuckoo.' Identity is then simply a matter of acknowledging
the properties and appurtenances that go with the role ('He sang
that song. That was his song').

It's significant, then, that the narrative moves on, from
impromptu nursery-tale, through rhyme and the child's familiar
landscape, to the larger history implied in the names of Michael
Davitt and Parnell. In acquiring a language the child is simultaneously acquired by it. History is a mode of discourse in which we
simultaneously discover and lose ourselves. For it is at the very
moment that we acknowledge, 'yes, we are baby tuckoo', that we
enter into that closed ideological universe where we will forever
remain that which we have indisputably established ourselves to be.
This is what Stephen puzzles over when he speaks, vaguely, of the
soul's birth, 'a slow and dark birth, more mysterious than the birth
of the body'. Nationality, religion, language, may be for *Stephen* the
nets which the self has to evade; but *Joyce* presents us with an image
of Stephen forever trammelled in the language which has constituted him. He may revolt against allegiance in a language not his
own ('Non serviam'); but those words are at the same time a sign of
the potency they strive to renounce: the very possibility of rebellion
has been instilled in Stephen's soul by the tales his culture tells him.
He may refuse the linguistic nationalism of Davin; he may, forced
by the verbal puzzlings of the old English dean, come to feel that the
English language is, first and foremost, the agency of an alien
oppression. But that language is inscribed in his own soul: it would
be more accurate to say, *his soul is inscribed in that language*:

> The language in which we are speaking is his before it is mine.
> How different are the words *home, Christ, ale, master*, on his lips
> and on mine! I cannot speak or write these words without unrest
> of spirit. His language, so familiar and so foreign, will always be
> for me an acquired speech. I have not made or accepted its words.
> My voice holds them at bay. My soul frets in the shadow of his
> language.

Stephen's mistake (not shared by Joyce, as the pun on 'familiar'
indicates) is to assume that language is ever anything else. English is
Stephen's *family* tongue: the whole book demonstrates how, in
passing through the changing idioms of infancy, school, church,

138

politics, art, the 'young man' is also being recruited. The 'unrest of spirit', the 'fretting' of the soul, is not that of an Irishman in the shadow of English; it is that of any man in the shadow of the language which has made him what he is. Always, as in the parent/child relation, there is an oedipal struggle against as well as attraction to the language which tells one what to think, an obscure intuition that one is *being thought*, that one is a *vehicle* for meaning, rather than their instigator. Language is not just form and not just content in *Portrait*. It is the real hero of the book. Language utters Stephen in the very moment that Stephen struggles to master and transcend language. No man 'makes' or 'accepts' its words: they make and accept him.

Thinking of the quarrel at the Christmas dinner, the young Stephen obscurely senses that this is something to do with language. The whole episode opens with his awareness that words can mean quite different things, are not to be relied upon ('Why did Mr. Barrett in Clongowes call his pandybat a turkey?'). Throughout the squabble, which focusses so many Irish contradictions, history is lived as a discord of discourses: election addresses and pulpit sermons, oaths and prayers, 'The language of the Holy Ghost', 'and very bad language if you ask me', 'the language he heard against God and religion and priests in his own home', 'the language with which the priests and the priests' pawns broke Parnell's heart', and so on. For the boy, such conflicts can be resolved to simple confusions of metaphor and metonymy, as for example in his puzzling over the Protestant gibes:

> *Tower of Ivory* they used to say, *House of Gold*! How could a woman be a tower of ivory or a house of gold? . . . Eileen had long white hands . . . That was ivory: a cold white thing. That was the meaning of *Tower of Ivory*.

The correlation of language and power is recurrent. When, listening to the hellfire sermon, Stephen feels the particular target of its rhetoric ('Every word for him') he sees consciously a process that has been happening unconsciously throughout the formation of his identity – what Louis Althusser has named the 'interpellation' or *calling* of the subject to be that being history has assigned to him ('God could call him now . . .').[2] This at once for Stephen moves on to the larger recognition, the acceptance of his place in history, along with all the others who had been called, named, and judged:

The English lesson began with the hearing of history. Royal persons, favourites, intriguers, bishops, passed like mute phantoms behind their veil of names. All had died, all had been judged. What did it profit a man to gain the whole world if he lost his soul? At last he had understood: . . . and when he spoke to answer a question of his master he heard his own voice full of the quietude of humility and contrition.

The 'hearing of history' is a significant phrase, describing a process which is never complete but has repeatedly to be ratified by its counterpart, the subject's self-estranging hearing of his own voice, as if another's, joining in the liturgy. And such a contracting-in leaves the soul, finally, not its own, but a 'mute' creature, appropriated to some exterior discourse.

Althusser has written brilliantly of this process of interpellation, in terms which are apposite both to the theological context here, and to Stephen's larger dilemma:

As St Paul admirably put it, it is in the 'Logos', meaning in ideology, that we 'live, move and have our being'. It follows that for you and for me, the category of the subject is a primary 'obviousness': . . . it is clear that you and I are subjects (free, ethical, etc. . .). Like all obviousnesses, including those that make a word 'name a thing' or 'have a meaning' (therefore including the obviousness of the 'transparency' of language), the 'obviousness' that you and I are subjects – and that that does not cause any problems – is an ideological effect, the elementary ideological effect. It is indeed a peculiarity of ideology that it imposes . . . obviousnesses as obviousnesses, which we cannot *fail to recognize* and before which we have the inevitable and natural reaction of crying out (aloud or in the 'still, small voice of conscience'): 'That's obvious! That's right! That's true!'

If such a cry is that which Stephen utters here, Althusser also has a description of the wider rituals which incorporate the child, even before its birth, into a particular history: 'Before its birth, the child is always-already a subject, appointed as a subject in and by the specific familial ideological configuration in which it is "expected" once it has been conceived,' and by 'all the rituals of rearing and then education in the family'.

There are two complementary extremes to language in *Portrait*, each of which is a snare that may threaten the integrity of the constituted subject. The one is the *cry*, brutal, inarticulate, falling below the human. The other is the *inscription*, as a crudely physical presence. Speech at its most spontaneous and inarticulate, disjunctive, interruptive (the exclamatory moment in which Estragon lives) is one threat: 'From the foul laneways he heard bursts of hoarse riot and wrangling and the drawling of drunken singers.' But there is also *script* at its most brutal, incised by clumsy and brutish labour in the desk tops at Belvedere (Vladimir's residual, oppressive past, telling us nothing is ever new): 'The letters cut in the stained wood of the desk stared upon him, mocking his bodily weakness and futile enthusiasms.' At times, the two extremes meet in hostile conspiracy, as when he hears 'A cry which was but the echo of an obscene scrawl which he had read on the oozing wall of a urinal.' In between, is the prison-house of articulate discourse, where his father endlessly spins an imaginary, self-aggrandizing present out of imaginatively embroidered memories, retold tales of 'heroism':

> Stephen walked at his father's side, listening to stories he had heard before, hearing again the names of the scattered and dead revellers who had been the companions of his father's youth. And a faint sickness sighed in his heart . . .

Even revolt, such as Stephen's at Clongowes, is second-hand in such a world, an already-written story, only made real for the new subject when it is taken up into the printed schedule: 'A thing like that had been done before by somebody in history, by some person whose head was in the books of history.' The translation here of 'history' into 'the books of history' is so subtle as to be barely noticeable, but it brings us back to the central issue. The final irony of *Portrait* lies in that unexpected shift, in the last pages, from the cool translucent narrative to the fragmentary, disjunctive items of Stephen's diary. The crude fragmentariness of his written text reproduces as script the lyric fragmentariness of speech, chant and song in the opening pages. The openness of the *voice* has been sealed off into the closure of *writing*: at the moment the subject writes of escape, the book closes and imprisons him in the text. As a model of the way in which the subject relates to the discourse of history, it is a complex and subtle account.

In *Ulysses*, Stephen finds himself trapped in the classroom, still transmitting this double inheritance to others, himself the teller of

141

history in an hour when, for him, history is a nightmare from which he is trying to wake up. A nightmare, not because, in some archly aesthetic way, he is contemptuous of the world's demands, but because, as in a nightmare, one is lived, as if without volition, by the story which constitutes one's consciousness. It's for this reason that apocalyptic wishes lurk just below the surface of Stephen's (as of Bloom's) mind. History is again a double field: 'fabled by the daughters of memory. And yet it was in some way if not as memory fabled it'. On the one hand, it is the deadly reality of a 'corpsestrewn plain', and, on the other, a 'phrase the world had remembered'.

For Stephen, it's this doubleness which makes the nightmare: 'for them too history was a tale like any other too often heard, their land a pawnshop'. Infinite possibility is fossilized into finished event, in the text of the history-book, and the text of the past:

Had Pyrrhus not fallen to a beldam's hand in Argus or Julius Caesar not been knifed to death? They are not to be thought away. Time has branded them and fettered they are lodged in the room of the infinite possibilities they have ousted. But can those have been possible seeing that they never were? Or was that only possible which came to pass? Weave, weaver of the wind.

Tell us a story, sir.

Oh, do, sir. A ghoststory . . .

The movement in this sequence between history and story now contains a larger contradiction, between necessity and freedom, determinism and possibility: the story-teller magician deals with the realm of speech, where each next word is as yet unuttered and therefore unpredictable. In the classroom, however, Stephen's memories are of the prison of *print*, recalling, for example, 'the studious silence of the library of St Genevieve where he had read, sheltered from the sin of Paris', his brain 'impaled' like those around him. And it's a characteristic rhythm of the book, in which the script of libraries, newspaper files, schoolbooks, sandwich-men, letters, documents, tracts, bills, accounts, alphabets all *conscript* (literally) the future. That process is here signalled by the slavish dependence of teacher and pupils on the brute fact of the book from which the poem 'Lycidas' is being recited: the spoken (but pre-ordained) words are interrupted by the pause required actually to turn over the page; speech and print are reunited by a brief, mute action. The final collocation of a weary tyranny and the 'mummery' of script is contained in the sums, 'writ[ten] out all again' which Stephen has to correct.

The gamut of language which runs from cry to hieroglyph is the primary matrix of *Ulysses*. The book, like the city it transcribes, is an interpenetrating flux of discourses, none of them privileged. And these discourses are not coterminous with individual subjects, but cut across them, so that, for example, Gerty MacDowell's identity is the nexus where the discourses of True Romance and Mariolatry converge. The same words and phrases are repeated by different individuals; Bloom has a knowledge of matters too arcane to be typical of his particular consciousness. Joyce is not setting out to depict a world of autonomous subjects: rather to reveal the extent to which our common experience is constructed out of language, so that, in a sense, we do not utter it – it utters us. Equally, he is not simply engaged in a series of parodies of linguistic forms: rather the text spells out the multiplicity of ideological forms through which history is articulated.

The fissure between history and story accounts, in fact, for the most remarkable absence in the book, ostensibly simply a matter of dates. By pitching the events of *Ulysses* ten years before its writing began, Joyce omits the central historic fact which determines its whole shape. This is a day like any other, and it is lived by its actors as if it will go on forever. But the writer and every reader know what none of these characters can: the fact of world war, of insurrection and fratricidal struggle in Europe and at home. In this context, the apocalyptic fantasies of Stephen and Bloom, the violence of the Citizen and the rumpus with the British soldiers, all take on a new and ominous significance, one denied to the people trapped in the text. Written out as stories, they are forever denied knowledge of that real world which brutally negates their (in retrospect) paradisal innocence. *Ulysses* is, finally, a presentation of the world before the Fall. The last words of the book embed the fabled Dublin of 1904 in the context of the historic Trieste, Zurich, Paris of 1914–21, as another casualty of that long record which reaches back through Tarentum, Asculum, Carthage to Troy itself. When we consider that it was Ulysses himself who designed the Wooden Horse that betrayed Troy, we have to ask again how innocent is Leopold Bloom, as the average man, of the guilt of history? Do the sado-masochistic, *Uebermensch* fantasies, the daydreams of revenge and the 'horse-play' of the brothel (all unfulfilled 'stories') not have something to do with the real *nightmare* of history? Is innocence not, perhaps, history's Trojan horse? The violence of that real future, if we look closely, is everywhere predicted, spoken in advance and not heard, in the body of the text.

*   *   *

Contrasting Joyce and Yeats, Richard Ellmann remarks, before going on to discuss their respective views of history:

Yeats has no barrier about subjects, but in responding to unexalted occasions he guards a verbal formality. Even at his wildest, he maintains the poise, the authority of language. It is just this poise and authority which Joyce seems always to be disturbing, as if he were mounting a revolution against that worst of tyrannies, the lexical.[3]

In Yeats's poetry the ego arrives fully formed on the stage of history. He may, in 'A Dialogue of Self and Soul,' speak of 'that toil of growing up;/The ignominy of boyhood; the distress/Of boyhood changing into man', but the starting-point of his poetry is always the already-constituted subject, 'The finished man among his enemies'. Childhood hardly exists for the poet as a stage in his own being. He can look at children from the outside, 'A sixty year old smiling public man', and even, in imaginative sympathy, respond to the recovery of another's childhood, as story:

> I dream of a Ledaean body, bent
> Above a sinking fire, a tale that she
> Told of a harsh reproof, or trivial event
> That changed some childish day to tragedy –
> Told . . .

For Yeats, the child is almost always an external object, taken up into the fluent medium of the poet's own subjectivity, as in 'A Prayer for my Daughter', where he walks and prays, evoking a possible future out of his own magical imagination. 'A Prayer for my Son' indicates why he shies away from acknowledging infancy as a state through which he himself has passed. The child, like God, 'can fashion everything/From nothing every day, and teach the morning stars to sing'; but its essential vulnerability, as object and dependant

144

of others, undermines this naive solipsism, even when the child is Christ:

> You have lacked articulate speech
> To tell your simplest want, and known,
> Wailing upon a woman's knee,
> All of that worst ignominy
> Of flesh and bone . . .

Lack of articulate speech places one at risk among one's enemies, exposes one to 'ignominy.' When, occasionally, Yeats does advert to his own childhood, as in the first section of 'The Tower', it is mediated through a literary filter – here, the Wordsworthian mode and shrewd use of the disowning negative:

> . . . Never had I more
> Excited, passionate, fantastical
> Imagination. . . .
> No, not in boyhood when with rod and fly,
> Or the humbler worm, I climbed Ben Bulben's back.

The autonomy of the subject, its freedom from history, lies in its power of 'articulate speech' – a power which, spinning a cocoon of imaginary selfhood out of the 'fantastical/Imagination,' insulates the self against the world.

In his study of 'the fantastic' in literature,[4] Tzvetan Todorov argues that it 'can subsist only within fiction; poetry cannot be fantastic', because, unlike fiction, poetry does not have a referent in the external world against which the deviations of fantasy can be measured. This works as a definition of lyric and symbolist poetry; but it hardly bears up against a poetry such as Yeats's which again and again takes as its theme and locus the major events of a familiar, verifiable history. What Yeats in fact does is to appropriate the realm of history to poetry precisely by converting it into story, transforming it into that literary mode which Todorov calls the 'fantastic'.

According to Todorov, the fantastic has, at its centre, a deliberate 'transgression' of what the text had previously imputed to be reality:

> The reader and hero . . . must decide if a certain event or phenomenon belongs to reality or imagination, that is, must

determine whether or not it is real. It is therefore the category of the real which has furnished a basis for our definition of the fantastic . . . By the hesitation it engenders, the fantastic questions precisely the existence of an irreducible opposition between real and unreal . . . If a certain apparition is only the fruit of an overexcited imagination, then everything around it is real.

'Easter 1916' is a poem centrally concerned with the process by which an everyday world undergoes this 'transgression' by a force it cannot interpret. Unequivocally posited on 'real' events, it takes the *real*, the discourse of history, and encloses it within the text, not as some external referent of the words, but as an *interior perspective* of the poem, against which the *transgressions* of the imagination, of magic, have to be set. The more we examine the text, the more this interiorization of 'history' becomes apparent.

Like *A Portrait*, 'Easter 1916' signals its literariness: it opens, for example, on a close: 'I have met them at close of day'. This closure seals out the discourse that preceded the poem as the ending opens anew on that discourse: 'A terrible beauty is born.' Throughout the poem there is an insistence on its status as a linguistic artefact. Language, as recurring motif, calls attention to the fact that the poem itself is made up only of those events which we call words. From the start, the variety of forms language takes in the world of history offer alternative versions of the function this poem might be fulfilling, and the functions it's resisting: 'polite meaningless words', 'a mocking tale or a gibe', political 'argument' that makes the voice grow shrill, even the 'call' of hens to moor-cock, and the mother's 'naming' of her child, England's 'keeping faith' 'For all that is done and said', and so on. Only halfway through the poem does it declare itself for what it is, at precisely the moment that the most intractable aspect of the real, the loutishness of history's 'casual comedy', is transformed into the purity of 'song', and reality itself is retrospectively reduced to the unreality of 'dream' ('This other man I had dreamed/A drunken vainglorious lout . . ./Yet I number him in the song'). But it's only at the end that this transubstantiation is completed, and it's signalled, noticeably, by a shift from the open, fluid spontaneities of speech and action to the finality of *script*, in that elegiac listing with which the poem concludes ('I write it out in a verse . . .').

The 'transgression' in this poem is a purely verbal event: the assertive repetition of those words, 'changed, changed utterly:/A terrible beauty is born'. We, of course, locked in our guilty historicity, know exactly what is meant. That which is not spoken, the absent centre of the poem, we can supply, from our knowledge of a history in which we are all involved. Yet it's a remarkable operation, when we think about it. As in 'All Soul's Night', the poet/magician is conjuring with our connivance. There too, nothing is actually summoned up except words, names, stories, yet we are left feeling that we have participated in some mysterious séance, that the fantastic has invaded the realm of the quotidian.

Todorov speaks of the process by which, in fantastic literature, the reader becomes a character in the text. The text, he says, 'must oblige the reader to consider the world of the characters as a world of living persons and to hesitate between a natural and supernatural explanation of the events described . . . [T]his hesitation must also be experienced by a character; thus the reader's role is so to speak entrusted to a character, and at the same time the hesitation is *represented*, it becomes one of the themes of the work.' Yeats achieves this identification by moving from the opening 'I' of the poet to the implicating 'we' of the final section ('We know their dream'). Both poet and reader alike are faced with the problem of interpretation: is this 'transgression' an imaginary or an actual event? But the reader, unlike the 'hero', has a further problem; for he has to ask: are we reading a history of events external to the poem, does the text have a referent? Or are we reading a story, something which exists in its own right, without reference to anything external even when it is appropriating that externality to its own interior discourse?

Yeats allows for this doubleness by the sequence of unanswered questions around which the text is constructed, questions which bring the 'I' of poem and of reader into an uneasy identity before the incomprehensible order of things. Each of these questions in turn is closely bound up with the motif of language, either directly ('What voice more sweet than hers?') or because it is at once answered by a changing of the subject, away from deeds to the words into which we have to displace them ('O when may it suffice?/That is heaven's part, our part/To murmur name upon name'; 'What is it but nightfall? . . . Was it needless death after all? . . ./For England may keep faith/For all that is done and said'). The final strategic withdrawal from the historical question to the unequivocal affirmations of story is also that transit from speech to script already noted: 'And what if excess of love/Bewildered them till they died?/I write it out in a verse . . .' The date which concludes the poem, unlike the title, pointedly refers to the time of that writing out, and not to the time of the events described.

Wherever story touches history in Yeats's poetry, the rhetorical question is not far away. And this is not simply a matter of Yeats's liberal uncertainties. Rather it's the very function of poetry to articulate this hesitation, this stuttering in language, within which its meanings are located, parentheses which willingly suspend not belief but disbelief, bracketting a textual reality with hints and rumours of a real world where questions have to be answered. In this world, fantasy is not just a literary mode but a political reality on which the heart feeds and grows brutal, a world where images are not contemplative but efficacious ('And yet they too break hearts'), and 'fanatics invent . . ./Fantasy or incident/Not worth thinking of' ('Quarrel in Old Age') that disturb the living stream.

Yeats asks this question, about the relation of fantasy to history, in 'The Statues', again without providing an answer:

> When Pearse summoned Cuchulain to his side
> What stalked through the Post Office?

The poem's meaning lies precisely in this unanswerableness. Did Cuchulain, a 'real' supernatural force, stalk through the Post Office? Did Pearse merely 'summon' something out of his own dark, and was it a phantasm, an imaginary thing? *What* did stalk? Nothing, perhaps; but the sentence is posed in such a way that, though it affirms nothing, the interrogative pronoun, in taking a verb, presupposes that *something* did the stalking. The historian would ask a different question: 'Did anything stalk?' or, even more sceptically, 'What on earth did Pearse think he was up to?' Yeats's sentence describes a pseudo-event, like all the events of literature. The question functions in exactly the same way, for example, in 'The Second Coming': 'And what rough beast . . .', where the concreteness of the verb 'slouches' disguises the fact that this is a fantasy evoked by words ('The Second Coming! Hardly are those words out . . .'). 'A Stick of Incense' likewise juxtaposes two questions ('Whence did all that fury come?/From empty tomb or Virgin womb?') which imply a supernatural transgression of the natural, with a subversive and yet strangely innocent statement of secular scepticism which is *not* an answer to the questions but merely a counterposing assertion ('Saint Joseph thought the world would

148

melt/But liked the way his finger smelt'). The answer lies in the silence between the couplets: the *meaning* of the poem is the juxtaposition of these incompatibles. Again, those famous and harrowing lines in 'The Man and the Echo' where Yeats agonizes over his political responsibility, lines apparently raw with uncertainty and remorse, asking 'What have I done?' actually perform the same, *literary* function:

> Did that play of mine send out
> Certain men the English shot?

The question seems to point backwards, towards an anterior, historical world, in which art has its effect directly, as propaganda and provocation. But in fact the lines constitute only themselves. Whether *Cathleen ni Houlihan* provoked men to die for Ireland is beside the point. Now and in time to be, *in this poem*, the conjunction has occurred: in the *story* of this particular poem, a play may have sent men out to die. This throws a critical light back upon that earlier statement:

> All that I have said and done
> Now that I am old and ill,
> Turns into a question till
> I lie awake night after night
> And never get the answers right.

The formulaic couplings here indicate the fabular nature of this questioning, which becomes more explicit in that last aggressive interrogation of the oracle:

> O Rocky Voice
> Shall we in that great night rejoice?
> What do we know but that we face
> One another in this place?

'That' and 'this' have no real location outside the text. 'That great night' is simply the 'fabulous formless dark' which encloses 'this place', the circumscribed text. Art itself becomes the echo which gives us back our own words, strangely transformed, turning the historic conditional/subjunctive, 'Sleepless would lie down and die', into a fictional imperative, in the mythological present: 'Lie down and die'.

149

It's for this reason that, having raised the problem, Yeats can drop it, with a cunning changing of the subject which masquerades as an aesthetic muffing of his lines: 'But hush, for I have lost the theme,/Its joy or might seem but a dream.' We are then distracted away from the text by a cry which seems to come from beyond but which is really only its final invention, distracting the poem into closure: 'A stricken rabbit is crying out,/And its cry distracts my thought.' For the (historical) men sent out to die *in this poem*, Yeats cares as little as for the legendary Oisin in 'The Circus Animals' Desertion': 'But what cared I that set him on to ride?' They are simply 'themes/ . . . That might adorn old songs.'

Having warned us that history is only a set of themes, metaphors for his poetry, Yeats's stories always leave us with a sense of the fatuousness of historical action. Like Beckett, but with confidence and joy, he shouts: Nothing to be done; everything to be written out.' And this itself is an ideological strategy, a way of coming to terms with the paralysis of an Ireland that, having almost destroyed itself in inconclusive civil war, seemed to have nowhere anymore to go. An urgent and imperative history is thus transformed into an image out of *Spiritus Mundi*, a theme in the Great Memory. In the last words Yeats wrote for *A Vision*, in 1925, he confessed this with his usual gnomic insistence:

I can recognise that the limit itself has become a new dimension, that this ever hidden thing which makes us fold our hands has begun to press down upon multitudes. Having bruised their hands upon that limit, men, for the first time since the seventeenth century, see the world as an object of contemplation, not as something to be remade.

Words become the lonely tower in which the subject confronts history, a world yet to be remade. In the words added in 1934–36, in even more pressing times, this is spelt out with greater candour: 'How far can I accept socialistic or communistic prophecies?' he asks, and, without answering, replies, climbing to his 'proper dark' – out of history, into the 'fabulous dark' of story – 'Then I draw myself up into the symbol and it seems as if I should know all if I could but banish such memories and find everything in the symbol.' Yet the mythological present of the symbol can in the end offer no solace for the victim of history's memories, as he ruefully concedes: 'But nothing comes'.

   The linking of language and history is remarkably persistent in
the literature of the subsequent generation. The deliberately contrived naivety of Padraic Fallon's poetry,[5] for example, allows for a
constant elision between story and history. Fallon describes a world
which has 'exhausted history', confined within the 'Eternal pre-
cincts/Of a huge present tense'. In 'Curragh, November Meeting',
distance and time are both 'threaded over' with a spider's web of
legend (the image itself recalls the Sleeping Beauty). Time con-
denses into a moment without any beyond, where all is compacted,
unmoving, as in a tale:

>   Distances are
>   Threaded over, a web. And the same spider
>   Spins the tale of
>   The dying sun

>   Caught on his last legs. Bleaching too
>   Are the bright horses: Jackets
>   And jockeys run
>   Out of pigment, are

>   A caveman's scratches, a jostling script.
>   There's some time left
>   To use your magic on it, wish
>   The winner home . . .

'It means nothing, nor should,' he concludes. Precisely this movement beyond the realm of signifying (and therefore of sequence,
causality, transit) takes up Fallon's world into the magician's realm
of the spun tale, event turned into jostling script. But like Yeats
Fallon acknowledges the prestidigitation involved in this 'magic.' In
'Fin de Siècle' he identifies an aesthetic which is also a vision of
reality. The tradition of narrative which compresses time into co-
presence, making the 'He' of the poem contemporary with Homer
(as in Eliot's famous axiom), is a particular way of living history, not
an escape from it – an outdated attitudinizing which has its own
ideological function:

Out on the periphery he put in the time;
  Achilles dead, and Hector, Ulysses flown . . .
Who makes the rhyme
Will have the resonance. Carefully
He lived to tell the tale;
Homer is he who survives the crumbling wall.

Thomas MacGreevy's 'Homage to Vercingetorix'[6] makes the same point about the ideological uses of history and story. The poem opens with a piece of contemporary speech which, in its mundanity, places the opinion, literally, in inverted commas:

'For me,' said my host –
An o, so Norman, Norman-Irishman in England –
'For me, Julius Caesar is,
'Divine personages apart of course,
'The greatest man who ever lived.'

The poem is pre-occupied with the strain between event and interpretation, the ideological strain of distinguishing one from the other. The poet admits that he has no 'unanswerable repudiation' of his host's inanities. He persists in inward speculation:

It is perhaps debatable
Whether Caesar was a renegade
To the radiant gods
Of sympathetic understanding . . .
What is self-evident
Is that Caesar's book is special pleading.

'History' is always *someone*'s story: the victor's account of his achievement. Vercingetorix doesn't get a word in, and the poem's 'homage' becomes, not an attempt to redress the balance, but a placing of one set of words within another, embedding recessive depths of history within a collapsed time-scale where all are equally present, in the language of the poem, so as to test the validity of each against the others. As the poem opened with an assertion, within quotation marks, of one prejudice, so it closes with a deliberate declaration of interest, an admission of partiality which subverts the claim to universal objectivity, and restores the text to history:

> But the answer
> Which,
> Especially if timed fortunately
> Out of silence,
> Has universal validity
> And for an Irishman,
> Particular significance
> Is the generalisation
> That a Black-and-Tan,
> Even one who has reserves
> Of literary talent
> And polite manners,
> Is a Black-and-Tan.

A similar process takes place in Denis Devlin's 'At the Tomb of Michael Collins', where the news of Collins's death is embedded, for the twelve-year-old Devlin, within other story/histories ('Those of the past were heroes in my mind . . .'). Whitman's poem on the assassination of Lincoln, that day's lesson at school, is the primary filter through which the event is simultaneously interpreted and controlled. History in Devlin's work is always this recurrence of the same stories in new forms. He speaks, in *The Heavenly Foreigner*, of time 'volumed round me, thick with echoes' (where 'volumed' has a double meaning). His 'Old Jacobin' himself grasps the way in which our participation in history is ideologically pre-determined by the words we inherit, the histories we acquire, seeing 'the hero-selves that my imperium/Summoned from the *Odes*, the Roman *Lives*' as, finally, 'the antique stuff I wrapt my virtues in'.[7]

'All poetry, as discriminated from the various paradigms of prosody, is prayer,' Beckett wrote in a review[8] of MacGreevy in 1934, adding that prayer is 'the only way out of the tongue-tied profanity'. In the poetry of Austin Clarke,[9] the interdependence of language and history is most originally and clearly grasped, through the metaphor not only of prayer but of all the other modes of language we create and endure. 'Pilgrimage', the title poem of his 1929 volume, adds a new dimension to that opposition of speech and script considered here.

'Pilgrimage' opens with a perception of a historic landscape which slips quietly, through metaphor, into language. This is a subtle reworking of the old concept of the Book of Nature, and fitting for the ancient Irish world it envisages. It suggests that there is no such

thing as a 'clean' perception of things, that all our awareness is
pre-structured by the history that has deposited us here, in this
moment. The beaching of the pilgrim's boat is a metaphor of an
entry into history, as 'tying a wish on thorn' turns language into fact,
tying the self down to an imagined future. In the same movement,
we enter into closure:

> There by dim wells the women tied
> A wish on thorn, while rainfall
> Was quiet as the turning of books
> In the holy schools at dawn.

The cloistered scholars of the second stanza, 'Whose knowledge
of the gospel/Is cast as metal in pure voices', are agencies through
which the provisional realm of speech becomes solidly material, not
just as script but as gilt illumination. The third stanza again sees
intangible speech already structured into ritual ('The chanting of
the hours,/White clergy saying High Mass,/A fasting crowd at
prayer,/A choir that sang before them'). Beyond this lies the
materialization of story into solid, abiding forms, which make even
the mythical actual, as stained glass and carved dragons. At this
point the solidifying of language into matter becomes explicit; the
'Great annals in the shrine' are not evanescent words, but embodied
script, which trace

> The noble forms of language –
> Brighter than green or blue enamels
> Burned in white bronze – embodied
> The wings and fiery animals
> Which veil the chair of God.

Speech then becomes a desperate insurrection out of the enclosed
world created from these fossilized embodiments, 'a sound/Of wild
confession' rising from praying congregations. Prayer, in the last
stanza, is equated with sailing away from material encumbrance,
but not with *flight*. It involves a passage through the world, not a
rising above it:

> We heard white Culdees pray
> Until our hollow ship was kneeling
> Over the long waves.

Language recruits the subject to an engrossing material history – not to something impalpable, but to something as tangible as embossing, woven handicraft, lines on a page, or, when speech, to a material vibration in real air. But language is also pilgrimage, an active movement beyond the constricting givenness of things, the creation of new vibrations which leave the ship itself praying as it journeys: *laborare est orare*, action itself becomes a form of discourse.

What Clarke suggests here, and it's a repeated theme in his poetry, is that the opposition between words and deeds, story and history, is not a valid one, but a stratagem of despair. Speech, print, script, are not only ways of distorting the world in our perception, but also ways of disturbing it, getting a purchase on it. There is always 'something to be done', and that doing cannot be simply separated from Beckett's questions, 'What have I said?' and 'what shall I say?', the interpretations we make of things. We are both historians and magicians, audiences and actors, collaborators in the storied histories we produce and reproduce. 'Inscription for a Headstone' seems initially to equate script with elegy and obituary, with the last word on a lost world of action and agitation. But it ends by stressing a new point, that language is a form and means of action.

The speech and writings of men such as James Larkin, it suggests, raucous, rabble-rousing, may seem to have been absorbed into the complacent murmur of the study. But, as the final internal rhyme of 'page' with 'rage' suggests, inscription is not necessarily burial. The 'bawled' of the first line can be translated into the 'scrawled' of the last without loss of intensity. And the poem itself, apparently an inscription, can be not just epitaph, but incitement. Language is never finally dead, whether spoken or written. It is never just history, story, record, but also polemic, invective, critique, open, pointed at the future, struggling to grasp the present, in a world where speech turns into deeds and batons into blessings:

> What Larkin bawled to hungry crowds
> Is murmured now in dining-hall
> And study. Faith bestirs itself
> Lest infidels in their impatience
> Leave it behind. Who could have guessed
> Batons were blessings in disguise,
> When every ambulance was filled

With half-killed men and Sunday trampled
Upon unrest? Such fear can harden
Or soften heart, knowing too clearly
His name endures on our holiest page,
Scrawled in a rage by Dublin's poor.

NOTES

1   Jacques Lacan, 'The Mirror-phase as formative of the Function of the I' (1949), trans. Jean Roussel, in *New Left Review*, 51, Sept–Oct 1968. See also the essays included in Lacan, *The Four Fundamental Concepts of Psycho-analysis*, ed. Jacques-Alain Miller, (London: The Hogarth Press, 1977).
2   Louis Althusser, 'Ideology and Ideological State Apparatuses', in *Lenin and Philosophy and Other Essays*, trans. Ben Brewster, (London: NLB, 1971).
3   Richard Ellmann, *Eminent Domain* (London: OUP, 1967).
4   Tzvetzvan Todorov, *The Fantastic: A Structural Approach to a Literary Genre*, trans. Richard Howard (Ithaca, N.Y.: Cornell UP, 1975).
5   Padraic Fallon, *Poems* (Dublin: The Dolmen Press, 1974).
6   Thomas MacGreevy, *Poems* (London: Chatto and Windus, 1934). *Collected Poems*, ed. Thomas Dillon Redshaw (Dublin: New Writers' Press, 1971). For more detailed discussions of MacGreevy's work, see my article, 'From a Great Distance: Thomas MacGreevy's Frames of Reference', and that by Anthony Cronin, 'Thomas MacGreevy: The First of the Few', both in *The Lace Curtain*, 6, Autumn 1978 (Dublin: New Writers' Press).
7   Denis Devlin, *Collected Poems*, ed. Brian Coffey (Dublin: The Dolmen Press, 1964). I have discussed these poems at greater length in 'Precarious Guest: The Poetry of Denis Devlin', *Irish University Review*, 8, i, 1978.
8   Samuel Beckett, 'Humanistic Quietism', *The Dublin Magazine*, 1934, usefully reprinted in the NWP edition of MacGreevy's poems cited above.
9   Austin Clarke, *Collected Poems*, ed. Liam Miller (Dublin: The Dolmen Press, 1974).

SEMANTIC SCRUPLES: A RHETORIC FOR POLITICS IN THE NORTH

D. E. S. MAXWELL

Here is one form of rhetoric:

> When I was a very small boy we used to sing at passing Protestants:
>
> Proddy, proddy dick
> Your ma can't knit
> And your da
> Won't go to bed
> Without a dummy tit.
>
> We might meet Protestants on the way to school because our school was outside the Bogside. No Protestant lived in the Bogside. The Unionist Party had seen to that. Not that the absence of Protestant neighbours was regarded by us as any deprivation. We came very early to our politics. One learned, quite literally at one's mother's knee, that Christ died for the human race and Patrick Pearse for the Irish section of it. The lessons were taught with dogmatic authority and were seemingly regarded as being of equal significance. Pearse ranked high in the teeming pantheon of Irish martyrdom. There were others. They had all died in the fight to free Ireland from British rule, a fight which had paused in partial victory in 1922 when twenty-six of our thirty-two counties won their independence. It was our task to finish the job, to cleanse the remaining traces of foreign rule from the face of Ireland.
>
> No one was explicit as to how this would be done.

That is an account of what is by way of being a private or domestic entrance into a public domain. The experience thus acquired later encounters the same sentiments in fully public utterance:

> At an election meeting in Cable Street once, Mr McAteer faced

157

opposition from a small group noisily urging a boycott of the Stormont Parliament. From the back of the flat-bed lorry which served as a platform Mr. McAteer surveyed them sadly and said: 'There are times when I weep for Mother Ireland,' which he then proceeded to do. Real tears coursed down his cheeks and, reaching up for the corner of the Tricolour which fluttered over the platform, he dried his eyes on the national flag. He won that election, of course. The Nationalist Party always did . . . Nationalist candidates were not selected; they were anointed.

Eamonn McCann, the author of these two quotations, is regarding a form of political rhetoric which did not have too many scruples, whether semantic or histrionic. Mr. McCann's own rhetoric, for all its wit, is not so far apart. It entertains a single attitude, a single intention, it has an ideological commitment in view. To set against it, here is a poem by Derek Mahon, 'Rage for Order':

> Somewhere beyond the scorched gable end and the
> > burnt-out buses
>
> > there is a poet indulging
> > > his wretched rage for order—
> > or not as the case may be; for his
> > > is a dying art,
> > an eddy of semantic scruples
> > > in an unstructurable sea.
>
> > He is far from people,
> > and the fitful glare of his high window is as
> > > nothing to our scattered glass.
>
> His posture is grandiloquent and deprecating, like this,
> > his diet ashes,
> his talk of justice and his mother
> > the rhetorical device
> of an etiolated emperor—
> Nero if you prefer, no mother there.
>
> > '. . . and this in the face of love,
> > death, and the wages of the poor . . .'

A Rhetoric for Politics in the North

If he is silent, it is the silence of enforced humility;
   if anxious to be heard, it is the anxiety
     of a last word
when the drums start; for his is a dying art.

Now watch me as I make history. Watch as I tear down
   to build up with a desperate love,
     Knowing it cannot be
long now till I have need of his
     desperate ironies

The voice of the poem comes from among the scorched gable ends, the burnt-out buses, the scattered glass, the drums. It is the voice not of the poet, but of the agitator, the activist, given voice by the poet, whose 'eddy of semantic scruples' remains visible, his desperate ironies' still a reference, in the 'unstructurable sea'. 'Rage for Order' is of course a poem about the troubles in the North. It is also a poem about the supposed irrelevance of poetry to such matters. And from its immediate circumstances it enacts a debate between two different sets of terminology, between the 'high window' and 'scattered glass', 'rhetorical device' and 'the wages of the poor', the drums and the dying art. One voice catches the inflections of another. The poet may at the end have his 'last word', but it is left to be inferred. Derek Mahon has written a poem about how one may admit a political content to poetry. 'Nero if you prefer' is a possible image; Nero both set fire to Rome and then fiddled while it burned. In the 1953 Berlin uprising, Brecht sat at his typewriter. Does the writer help to create events? If not, how should he express a commitment, or at least declare a presence?

II

Ireland is a notoriously political country. Mahon's poem has a national heredity. It includes W. B. Yeats and Louis MacNeice, though I suggest not influence or conscious imitation so much as concurrences of design.

One might begin with the speculation that Yeats wrote great political poems because he never, in a sense, wrote political poems at all, that is to say, poems operating within strictly political definitions – public occasions, public crisis, revolution; poems responsive to a choice of entirely political solutions or interpretations.

In some poems, political figures appear casually, or in order to be dismissed. 'The Statesman's Holiday' introduces de Valera, the King of Greece, and Henry Ford – as 'the man that made the motors' – only to conclude, 'Ach, call me what you please!'. 'Crazy Jane on the Mountain', more seriously but hardly reverentially, has the last Russian Tsar, who

> Had some beautiful cousins,
> But where are they gone?
> Battered to death in a cellar,
> And he stuck to his throne.

Elsewhere, Yeats often enough dismissed politics entirely as a possible subject. In 'Politics', a lovely poem of old age stirring to its past, a beautiful young girl dispossesses politics of any importance it might be supposed to have. 'A Model for the Laureate' tells us,

> The Muse is mute when public men
> Applaud a modern throne,

and asks rhetorically,

> For things like these what decent man
> Would keep his lover waiting . . .?

'Those Images' disparages its metonymical cities:

> I never bade you go
> To Moscow or to Rome
> Renounce that drudgery,
> Call the Muses home.

Yet despite that injunction, Yeats did not abandon the political
scene. In fact the next poem, 'The Municipal Gallery Revisited',
occupies it. The statements are true for the poems which make
them, not as generalities. When, as he frequently did, Yeats wrote
poems turning upon an identified political episode – 'Easter 1916'.
'Parnell's Funeral', 'Meditations in Time of Civil War' – he remarks
in it, for example, extensions into the fables which mythologise
human deaths and entrances. 'Parnell's Funeral' draws our attention by its title, but hardly at all by its opening stanzas, to a very
particular political event.

'Parnell's Funeral' is an enabling poem. It enables the historical
facts which are its genesis to become interrogative, not declarative.
The poem 'The Death of Parnell' in Joyce's 'Ivy Day in the Committee Room' is declarative:

> He would have had his Erin famed,
> The green flag gloriously unfurled,
> Her statesmen, bards and warriors raised
> Before the nations of the world.

After the audience's applause the immediate response, in Joyce's
narrative, is that the cork in a bottle of Guinness goes derisively,
'Pok!' The sentiments of Yeats's 'Parnell Funeral' are in fact not
dissimilar. But Yeats's poem achieves, by its obliqueness, the eleva-
tion to which the popular ballad only aspires.

'Parnell's Funeral' moves from the briefest glimpse of a crowd of
Dubliners under a stormy sky to a shooting star, to sacrificial death.
It then concerns the death of Balder, of Apollo, gods slain to be
re-born. Here, the cycle is interrupted. Parnell's death is without
succession or renewal. The lonely god surrenders to 'the contagion
of the throng'. The poem ends with an affirmation of sorts, but
questions it. The full rhymes of the previous stanzas modulate here
into distorted echoes:

> Had even O'Duffy – but I name no more –
> Their school a crowd, his master solitude;
> Through Jonathan Swift's dark grove he passed, and there
> Plucked bitter wisdom that enriched his blood.

The poem takes the immediate occasion up into both a personal
vision of guilt, reality, and illusion – 'None shared our guilt; nor did

we play a part/Upon a painted stage when we devoured his heart';
and a shadowing of ancient celebrations. It evokes a discouraging
past – 'Swift's dark grove' – a dire present; and no future.

In this poem and others like it Yeats has moved far from a manner
of which he was once at least indulgent, the sentimentalities and
noisy rhetoric of Davis, Mangan, and the rest. Their simplicities
were in fact uncongenial to Yeats. The poets, whom he described as
'the secret transformers of the world, needed 'a subtle, appropriate
language', and an 'impartial imagination, a furious impartiality . . .
to say all that people did not want to have said.' Mangan's Dark
Rosaleen – 'my saint of saints', 'my virgin flower' – is not unlike
Yeats's own Cathleen ni Houlihan – 'a young girl, and she had the
walk of a queen.' Both are comfortable among the platitudes that
people did want to have said. Neither would be comprehensible in
Yeats's darker vision, where 'There is no laughter too bitter, no
irony too harsh for utterance, no passion too terrible to be set before
the minds of men.' Neither Rosaleen nor Cathleen is at all kin to the
implied and enigmatic Medusa of 'Easter 1916, who 'enchanted to a
stone'.

'Meditations in Time of Civil War' similarly distances its declared
subject. It is of course a poem about the civil war in Ireland in the
nineteen-twenties. More important, it is a poem about exits, entrances, passages; about terraces, doors, chambers, galleries, stairs,
barricades. And in its ending, 'I turn away and shut the door.' Yeats
had abandoned 'the deliberate creation of a kind of Holy City in the
imagination, a Holy Sepulchre, as it were, or Holy Grail for the Irish
mind.' Those are prospects appropriate to theology or electioneer-
ing.

In his later political poems, Yeats is, so to speak, altering the
contours of Ireland by showing under their surface images which are
strange, but, once recognised, familiar. He is trafficking between
feelings, relationships, of his own, and public events in which they
find metaphors and an open stage. 'We are happy,' he wrote to
Olivia Shakespear, 'when for everything inside us there is an
equivalent something outside us.' The inhabitants of that inner
territory are often unsavoury, grotesque, frightening. Yeats considered Whitman and Emerson 'superficial precisely because they
lack the Vision of Evil.' Poe, to the contrary, he admired, because
Poe's sinister terrors – the necrophilia, the sadism, the consuming
lusts – are 'An image of our own secret thoughts'. Yeats, in fact,
acknowledged in himself the stir of desires that might make life

162

hateful – a phrase he used of Edward Martyn. In the political life of his later years he saw such perverted longings reach out into and control society at large. Thus at work, exploited and organized, they assumed an exterior form – 'an image of our own secret thoughts'.

Yeats spoke of the arts as 'an extension of the beatitudes', but admitted to contemplation much that was far from beatific. In his later poetry, a fairly limited set of images – the ditch, the sty, the harlot, for instance, the 'foul' images – links a large number of different themes: avarice, lust, mob politics, old age. And these generate their opposites – magnanimity, gaiety, innocence, the 'masterful images' of 'The Circus Animals' Desertion', all vulnerable, and all beginning, as 'The Circus Animals' Desertion' asserts, in 'the foul rag-and-bone shop of the heart'. And as that poem, like 'Lapis Lazuli', suggests, one of the positives is the act of poetic creation itself, seeking its metaphors to combine word and feeling.

Politics, for Yeats, was a source of metaphor indistinguishable from any other human activity, possessed by and manifesting the same passions, present and recognised in Yeats, as in the world around him. The political poems, whether ostensibly or indirectly political, achieve a fusion of public and private experience and utterance, of the various enigmas, mischiefs, and disciplines of the heart.

> 'Fair and foul are near of kin
> And fair needs foul',

cried Crazy Jane. Yeats's political poetry admits both, though it is true, especially in his vision of modern politics, that 'foul' is dominant, excresences of a corruptness from which no one is free. 'We must name,' Yeats said, 'and number the passions and motives of men . . . there is nothing uncommon, nothing unclean; every motive must be followed through all the obscure mystery of its logic . . . no irony too harsh for utterance, no passion too terrible to be set before the mind of men.'

III

Louis MacNeice was not in any strict sense an imitator of Yeats. But in his book about Yeats he said that the attraction of Yeats's poetry for him was the imaginative presence of personal events – whether 'historical' or 'casual and personal' – and the fusion of these which Yeats achieved. Like Yeats, MacNeice falls into that obscure category called Anglo-Irish. Rather than dispute the meaning of that term, it is simpler, and more useful, to think of him as an Irishman who was educated, and for most of his life worked, in England, though his returns to Ireland were, if brief, frequent and gaudy. His way of life, in fact, acted out the ambivalence which Irish people of his kind of class and upbringing commonly feel about the two countries to which they bear an allegiance.

In England, he was doubly apart from the class whose life he shared. Intellectually, he penetrated their self-deceptions, and he saw them in himself – the fashionable left-wing sympathies, the easy living; as an Irishman, he had a detachment from their culture and their assumptions; he had the mind and the fancy of alien scenes and properties:

In the back of my mind are snips of white, the sails
Of the lough's fishing boats . . .

He remembers, 'Coming across the sea to unknown England', to school, where

sometimes a whisper in books
Would challenge the code, or a censored memory sometimes.

The censored memories – they were often to evade control – were Irish memories. They do not, however, represent a wholly confident experience, a set of invulnerable dogmas on which he could mount his inspection of England: Kathleen ni Houlihan versus John Bull. He said of 'the land of scholars and saints':

Scholars and saints my eye, the land of ambush,
Purblind manifestoes, never-ending complaints.

Unlike Yeats, MacNeice had a stance in a formal political theory – Marxism. MacNeice was not a communist, nor even a communist sympathiser. He detested the monolithic Stalinist orthodoxy of the thirties, the stratagems, the expedients, the dishonesties which a Communist Party, he said, 'allows and even encourages'. Yet he did respond to classic marxist theory. Particularly, it seemed to him to admit the human actor as the essential agent in historical change.

When systems failed, they failed not because of blind determinism, but because the human beings in charge of them had ceased to appreciate their dynamism – the emergence in them of new ideas, new groups, new coalitions.

Two marxist axioms, widely cited in the thirties, summarize forcefully what was in fact the very complex argument which drew MacNeice to Marxism: 'Freedom is the appreciation of necessity'; 'History is nothing but the activity of men in pursuit of their ends'. Writing about marxism in *The Strings are False*, MacNeice had this to say: 'while it attacked human individualism, it simultaneously made the cosmos once more anthropocentric; it – asserted purpose in the world. Because the world was *ours*.' Elsewhere in the same book, he offers a translation of 'Freedom is the appreciation of Necessity' into Aristotelian terms: '*energia* can only be achieved by the canalisation and continued control of *kinesis*.'

It is impossible, reading through MacNeice's poems, to deny in them a kind of translation from his personal experience of these ideas. When, for example, he commends Aristotle:

> The whole town shakes with the peal of living people
>   Who break and build the town.
> Aristotle was right to think of man-in-action
>   As the essential and really existent man
> And man means man in action . . .

Or, even more marxist, talking of the Greeks:

> The days grow worse, the dice are loaded
>   Against the living man who pays in tears for breath;
> Never to be born was the best, call no man happy
>   This side death.
> Conscious – long before Engels – of necessity
>   And therein free
> They plotted out their life with truism and humour
>   Between the jealous heaven and the callous sea.

As a poet of the city, he observed

>   beauty narcotic and deciduous
> In this vast organism grown out of us;
> On all the traffic islands stand white globes like moons,

The city's haze is clouded amber that purrs and croons,
And tilting by the noble curve bus after tall bus comes
With an osculation of yellow light, with a glory like
    chrysanthemums.

There again is a perfectly marxian conceit – 'this vast organism grown out of us'.

It is constantly present in *Autumn Journal*, the sense of a failure in the will which created these monuments, the decline of a purpose and a perception, on which a civilization depended:

And still the church-bells brag above the empty churches
    And the Union Jack
Thumps the wind above the law-courts and the barracks
    And in the allotments the black
Scarecrow holds a fort of grimy heads of cabbage
    Besieged by grimy birds
Like a hack politician fighting the winged aggressor
    With yesterday's magic coat of ragged words,
Things were different when men felt their programme
    In the bones and pulse, not only in the brain ...

The quotation exemplifies very well MacNeice's control of images, of the movement of images, and of the movement of images into ideas.

MacNeice's personal history too seems, like Yeats's, to corroborate the communal frustrations. Sections iv and xi of *Autumn Journal* turn movingly upon memories of a tempestuous love affair. In its failure he sees the same incapacity, in private as in public relationships, to apply the truth that, in his own words, 'action makes both wish and principle come true.' The blame is his that love became a narrow possessiveness, which could not salvage what was good:

For suddenly I hate her and would murder
    Her memory if I could
And then of a sudden I see her sleeping gently
    Inaccessible in a sleeping wood
But thorns and thorns around her
    And the cries of night
And I have no knife or axe to hack my passage
    Back to the lost delight.

What we observe here, in fact, ends by seeming very like Yeats's method of communing between, and assembling, political occasion, private feeling, and sensuously localised scene – or of refracting the former through the latter two. Ideas and feelings assume the forms of what, then and there, was his world of fact – the allotment scarecrow melting into the hack politician who wears 'yesterday's magic coat of ragged words', the city as 'this vast organism grown out of us'; or the shuttling of scene, idea, and feeling at the end of the section in *Autumn Journal* where he waits for his lover, knowing that it is all over:

> It is October,
> The year-god dying on the destined pyre
> With all the colours of a scrambled sunset
> And all the funeral elegance of fire
> In the grey world to lie cocooned but shaping
> His gradual return;
> No one can stop the cycle;
> The grate is full of ash but fire will always burn.
> Therefore, listening to the taxis
> (In which you never come) so regularly pass,
> I wait content, banking on the spring and watching
> The dead leaves canter over the dowdy grass.

But for all its apparent solidity, the tenure of the material scene is precarious. MacNeice compels us to face its collapse into landscapes of neurotic fear, the shadows behind the substance. 'Time and place' MacNeice said, 'our bridgeheads into Reality/But also its concealment!'

The world of the senses was liable always to sideslip into sinister territories of the mind. And that is very much a part of his Irish inheritance, public and private. His reservations about his country of birth were not only the political ones already suggested. But even the political disaffection enters into a region of secret childhood terrors, among goblins and evil fairies, over the boundary between familiar day and disturbing night: 'And I remember, when I was little, the fear/Bandied among the servants/That Casement would land at the pier.' Any one part of his world is an ante-chamber to the rest.

167

MacNeice was disposed to people his childhood world, which he recalls as a lonely one, with demons, whether from the violence of reality or the badlands of the mind. *The Strings Are False* is full of memories of macabre dreams and waking nightmares. So is his poem, 'Autobiography', which begins with auguries of innocence, fated to betrayal:

> When I was five the black dreams came;
> Nothing after was quite the same.
>
> Come back early or never come.

Generally, though not exclusiveley, it is from Ireland that these sombre images come to MacNeice. He has contrasted the English wood, domesticated, 'reprieved from the neolithic night/By gamekeepers or by Herrick's girls at play' with 'the wilds of Mayo'; and concluded – 'These woods are not the Forest'. It might stand as a metaphor of the two countries as they appear in MacNeice's secondary world.

Ultimately, it is in the presence of the forest, the outpost of region or of character, that MacNeice, in Yeats's words, 'names and numbers the passions and motives of men', and finds 'images of his own secret thoughts'. Recognising these images diversely in his experience, he was able to convene them within a single perception. He absorbed political abstractions into places and feelings – and the words for places and feelings – which encounter other emissaries from his engagement with the mutable world of sensible life.

IV

All that supplies a kind of heredity for the Northern writer in these days when once again politics seizes violently upon the imagination. There may be some risk of diminution in making this particular overture to these writers. If one puts one's mind to it, one can always, to adapt Shakespeare, find sermons in stones, Brookes, and even Chichester-Clarkes, in the running books. Nevertheless, the political crisis with its endless cruelties, does confirm its reality in the illusions of art. Restrictive though it may be, I want to illustrate some of the possibilities exploited by the poets in confronting directly their political environment, and 'the common sound-effect of gelignite'.

In Seamus Heaney's 'A Northern Hoard', a sequence of five poems in *Wintering Out*, the detail of riot, tribal hatreds, the 'smeared doorstep' and the 'lumpy dead', directly though intermittently, surfaces. As in 'Roots':

> Leaf membranes lid the window.
> In the streetlamp's glow
> Your body's moonstruck
> To drifted barrow sunk glacial rock.
> And all shifts dreamily as you keen
> Far off, turning from the din
> Of gunshot, siren and clucking gas
> Out there beyond each curtained terrace
> Where the fault is opening. The touch of love,
> Your warmth heaving to the first move,
> Grown helpless in our old Gomorrah.
> We petrify or uproot now.

For Heaney, the mindless violence, eroding even personal love, means exile, ears stopped to the mandrake shriek of roots torn up: 'I deserted,' he says, but his defection is inconclusive, broken by fitful returns, neither return nor absence satisfying. The private torment shelves into and out from public views, each powerfully augmenting the other, of a fragmented society, hard and ravenous:

> flint and iron,
> Cast-off, scraps, nail, canine.

The vistas of *Wintering Out* open on the Northern violence. If the volume has a central question, it is that of Shakespeare's MacMorris, 'What ish my nation?' Repeatedly, here, Heaney invokes the rights and the rituals of language, in places whose names, English and not-English, pronounce a domicile: 'Anahorish, soft gradient-

169

/of consonant, vowel-meadow'; 'the tawny guttural water/spells itself: Moyala'; 'Demesnes staked out in consonants'. Language is divisive too: in Broagh, the final '*gh* the strangers found/difficult to pronounce'; a Protestant neighbour, with a biblical image, speaks a 'tongue of chosen people'; McCracken's hanged body is 'a swinging tongue'. So language draws in a host of other memorials to the troubled inheritance of 'vowels and history', where heir and outcast dispute their roles: 'man-killing parishes'.

The phrase is from 'The Tollund Man', where Heaney finds outside Ireland an archetype of ceremonial dispossession. The sacrificial corpse, preserved in a Jutland bog, is a 'saint's kept body', germinal, an ancestor of

> The scattered ambushed
> Flesh of labourers,
> Stockinged corpses,
> Laid out in the farmyards.

The Tollund Man assumes in death a 'sad freedom'. Visiting his homeland, the poet would confirm a kinship:

> I will feel lost,
> Unhappy and at home.

Heaney is sounding out deeper repercussions in what, to begin with, is merely provincial and present. He looks inward and outward. 'Roots' moves between the exterior spectres of death outside the bedroom, and within it an act of love arrested and compromised. It moves also in time. Both sets of actions are inheritors of an unexorcised past in 'drifted barrows, sunk glacial rock'. Both seem to resurrect old calamities and enter into a cycle of loss and sacrifice, new corroborations of old myths. The figures suggest Heaney's notion of Ireland itself, a compression of paradoxes: deep loughs which kill and preserve; an island looking outward to sea and inexhaustibly in upon itself; a journey within that leads to habitations lost and rediscovered:

> Every layer they strip
> Seems camped on before.
> The bogholes might be Atlantic seepage.
> The wet centre is bottomless.

Heaney, Longley, and Mahon have been described as 'the tight-assed trio', the implication being that they are bound up by words, forms and formalities; that life, vigour, and earthiness are buried under aesthetics. A critic observed in Longley's last collection, *An Exploded View*, a 'lack of commitment to the subject itself'. As to commitment, one might fairly say that all it will lead to is poems which politicians will quote when they need them. And as to aesthetics, it is true that Longley has a remarkable technical command, as in his hold over stanza/sentence relationships. He gives a certain primacy to the act of composition, the poetic shaping which is, so to speak, its own experience. But his consideration of what art may contrive from life implicates life itself, the Northern violence included.

'We are trying,' says the epigraph to *An Exploded View*, 'to make ourselves heard.' One subject that gets a hearing is Ireland and its renascent discontents. In 'Skara Brae' an excavation gives 'an exploded view/Through middens, through lives' to expose strata of the past beneath the present, a mosaic of revelations. So Longley's contemplation of his native country and province enters violence as one of the co-ordinates, one stratum, of the world he maps. It is often a disquieting world, its parts fragmenting. Words like 'splintered', 'fractured', 'detonates', 'splintering', 'lesions', 'dispersals', 'elisions', 'scatter' most obviously state the motif. They run through not only the poems about the violence, though that is their home base.

There is a touch of Grand Guignol in the grotesques of 'The Adulterer', 'Confessions of an Irish Ether-Drinker', 'Nightmare'. In 'The Fairground', various monsters spirit 'the solitary spectator' into their company. 'Caravan' projects reality into uneasy, menacing possibilities. A gypsy caravan suggests a family companionship, which in the poet's mind becomes his own. Watched ('tiny, barely in focus') by – his wife? – he imagines riding off through a blizzard to buy food:

> Or to be gone for good
> Having drawn across my eyes
> Like a curtain all that light
> And the snow, my history
> Stiffening with the tea towels
> Hung outside the door to dry.

171

Episodes like these are disquieting, but not depressing, partly because they have contrary aspects. There are poems of union, of a solacing perfection caught in some balance of objects: when a lake's

> surface seems tilted to receive
> The sun perfectly, the mare and her foal,
> The heron, all such special visitors.

More important, however, whatever afflictions he observes, the poet keeps his head, not aloof but composed. The poems addressed 'To Three Irish Poets' reflect within 'The stereophonic nightmare/Of the Shankill and the Falls', on personal friendships, on memories of places and people which assemble to

> Claim this country mine, though today
> *Timor mortis conturbat me*.

The urbane octosyllabics, by turns strictly and irregularly rhymed, respond to the varying pitch of feeling:

> Blood on the kerbstones, and my mind
> Dividing like a pavement,
> Cracked by the weeds, by the green grass
> That covers our necropolis,
> The pit, the terror . . . What comes next
> Is a lacuna in the text.

In *An Exploded View* Longley moves about a world more apparently 'serious' than that of his first collection. 'Wounds', for example, movingly associates memories of the poet's father in the first world war with the manifold atrocities of Belfast. Delicate, brutal, its memorializes a legion of the dead:

> Now, with military honours of a kind,
> With his badges, his medals like rainbows,
> His spinning compass, I bury beside him
> Three teenage soldiers, bellies full of
> Bullets and Irish beer, their flies undone.
> A packet of Woodbines I throw in,
> A lucifer, the Sacred Heart of Jesus
> Paralysed as heavy guns put out

172

A Rhetoric for Politics in the North

> The night-light in a nursery for ever;
> Also a bus-conductor's uniform –
> He collapsed beside his carpet-slippers
> Without a murmur, shot through the head
> By a shivering boy who wandered in
> Before they could turn the television down
> Or tidy away the supper dishes.
> To the children, to a bewildered wife,
> I think, 'Sorry Missus' was what he said,

So with 'Kindertotenlieder':

> There can be no songs for dead children
> Near the crazy circle of explosions,
> The splintering tangent of the ricochet,
> No songs for the children who have become
> My unrestricted tenants, fingerprints
> Everywhere, teethmarks on this and that.

The political violence is a form of terror with its counterparts in private risks and insecurities. The poems are constantly making such connections. The poet's commitment is to the words and structures which will shape these diversities into his imagined world:

> The accommodation of different weathers,
> Whirlwind tours around the scattered islands,
> Telephone calls from the guilty suburbs,
> From the back of the mind, a simple question
> Of being in two places at the one time.

'Being in two' – or more – 'places at the one time' is the very heart of the problem. Being in reality, and being in the world of art, and establishing a contour between the two. And within that secondary world to authenticate its happenings as events which occur only there. They will not persuade us because something exactly the same happened yesterday. These problems are at their most acute with political matter, for then ideology, dogma, is most favourably placed to subvert the allegiance to language. I have tried to outline some of the ways in which writers have manoeuvred amongst these correspondences. It seems to me that there are continuities between them all. Yeats and MacNeice do not, in any comprehensive way, make a tradition. Two writers hardly could. They did supply an example.

All these writers make their concrete particulars generalize upon themselves. They become both more particular – that is, they recede into the mind that observes them to find synonymous dramas in performance; and they become more expansive: the lighting of their own scenes is set about with shadows from myth, its actors at once distant and familiar. Once it's put like that, however, it is far too schematic. We are dealing, in poetry, with illusions contrived by words. The poet creates figments of reality. But it is with realities that he starts, and through the poem, to realities that he returns us, though his own purposes are enclosed within the act of writing the poem. His intentions is not to gratify or disappoint our own convictions, whatever after-images his poem may impress upon our imaginations. So in a seemingly very simple recent poem by Longley, 'The Greengrocer':

> He ran a good shop, and he died
> Serving even the death-dealers
> Who found him busy as usual
> Behind the counter, organized
> With hollywreaths for Christmas,
> Fir trees on the pavement outside.
>
> Astrologers or three wise men
> Who may shortly be setting out
> For a small house up the Shankill
> Or the Falls, will pause on their way
> To buy gifts at Jim Gibson's shop,
> Dates and chestnuts and tangerines.

The language of poetry is not demonstrative, declarative, litigious. As Yeats said of Synge, its intent is to add 'to our being, not to our knowledge,' and what it adds is itself. It was Yeats, too, who recommended a proper tone of poetic discourse: 'Only that which does not teach, which does not cry out, which does not condescend, which does not explain, is irresistible.'

174

THE IRISH WRITER: SELF AND SOCIETY, 1950–80

THOMAS KILROY

I

I am not going to attempt anything like a conspectus of Irish writing in the period partly because, as you see, our chairman has invited me to talk not only of the present and the past but of the future as well. Actually he has given me licence to treat of this subject in whatever way I choose, a generosity which has been offered to me because I have written a novel and some plays myself.

In a sense, I don't think I'm going to be talking about literature at all but rather about the web of secondary circumstances that lie behind the writing. It is there, if anywhere, that the essentially private activity of writing comes into contact with the shared experience of human beings living in the one culture. I will be particularly interested in the kinds of roles which writers tend to appropriate for themselves or, if you will, the roles imposed upon them by the society in which they live. The kind of discriminations, then, which I would like to make have little to do, directly, with the intrinsic quality of a particular work, although they may have important, indirect bearings upon it.

There is the widely accepted view nowadays among the historians that contemporary Ireland derives from the late fifties, that from that period one can trace the economic, social and cultural changes by which the country, for good or ill, moved from being an essentially rural-based, tradition-bound society to something resembling a modern, urbanized, technological state. Both in Britain and Ireland, in different ways, obviously, and at a different pace, something important appeared to happen in the arts, too, in that decade. Let me offer two occasions by which we might understand this for ourselves. In 1962 Sean O Faolain wrote a review of 'Fifty Years of Irish Writing' for the Dublin periodical *Studies* and in the Autumn of that year, two young poets, John Montague and Thomas Kinsella, edited *The Dolmen Miscellany of Irish Writing*. One, the work of the most distinguished literary figure in the country, might have been a clearing of space for the other.

The brief editorial of the *Miscellany*, you may remember, read, in part, as follows:

> In recent years a new generation of writers has begun to emerge in Ireland, probably the most interesting since the realists of the 1930s. While not forming any sort of movement, they do reflect a general change of sensibility and this Miscellany is an attempt to provide them with a platform. They are, in general, more literary than their predecessors: many of them are poets, and the prose-writers seem to be working towards a more experimental form of story. The main link between them, however, is their obvious desire to avoid the forms of 'Irishism' (whether leprechaun or garrulous rebel) which has been so profitably exploited in the past. In such a context, a little solemnity may be a revolutionary gesture.[1]

The *Miscellany* contained work by Brian Moore, Thomas Kinsella, Aidan Higgins, Pearse Hutchinson, James Liddy, Richard Weber, John Jordan, Richard Murphy, John Montague, Valentin Iremonger, John McGahern and James Plunkett. What was remarkable, at the time, in that collection was the sense of a dividing line, especially the way in which these writers projected themselves in an utterly different way to the beleaguered figure of the Irish writer in O'Faolain's essay. It emerged as a matter of style, the classical precision of Kinsella's 'A Country Walk', Moore's self-conscious, curious piece on the artist as revenger, Higgins' enormously self-confident, pedantic voice, wrestling with the reader's encyclopoedia, the quieter, no less intelligent one of McGahern in the process of transforming the conventional rural-Irish, small-town fiction. It extended to the *Miscellany's* criticism which seemed to promise at once, and perhaps for the first time, a native school of criticism which could command respect. Intelligence had suddenly come to be respectable among Irish writers. It was no longer something for which a struggle had to be waged, nor something to be mocked at with cultivated buffoonery nor something to be squandered through easy sentiment, with what the editorial calls 'Irishism'.

O'Faolain's essay, buttressed by his own reputation as a writer of fiction and especially his work as editor of *The Bell*, describes with characteristic good humour the fate of the Irish writer, the Irish intellectual in the post-revolutionary period.

> The upshot of it was an alliance between the Church, the new
> businessmen, and the politicians, all three nationalist-isolationist
> for, respectively, moral reasons, commercial reasons, and
> politico-patriotic reasons, in themselves all perfectly sound
> reasons. The effect on letters was not good. The intellectuals
> became a depressed group. Possibly they were also infected by
> the atmosphere around them.[2]

It is difficult to measure the debt which this country owes to Sean
O'Faolain; in the more narrow sense, if these new writers could
assume a certain place, could take certain things for granted, they
owed this security in no small part to O'Faolain. Indeed it is some
indication of an uncaring attitude towards these very issues that,
even as he is still with us, O'Faolain does not seem to get the kind of
attention which he deserves except, perhaps, among very young
writers to whom he has shown a graceful reception. It may be
because that, even yet, we are uncomfortable with the writer who
spans several enterprises, the imaginative writer who is also an
intellectual, deeply concerned with both the life of the mind and the
life as it is lived on the street, in the marketplace, in the institutions
of social and political power and in the confrontation with this world
through ideas.

If Irish writing over the past quarter of a century has demonstrated a new confidence, including an intellectual one, then it is also
true that Irish society has responded to it in expansive fashion. It
would appear that a social milieu has developed in this country
which has sought art as something to be cultivated, to be acquired,
without which society would be seen to be impoverished. The artist
in Ireland to-day enjoys the relaxation, both legally and by social
custom, of attitudes which made the life of the writer in the thirties
and forties well-nigh intolerable. He enjoys the disappearance or
virtual disappearance of the censorship mentality; he has a particular standing with the Revenue Commissioners. He has seen the
development of native publishing, native galleries and a network of
native, largely state, patronage. The public position of a Seamus
Heaney, a John McGahern, a Brian Friel is manifestly different to
that of a Brian Coffey, a Patrick Kavanagh, a Brinsley MacNamara.
The change has to do with the earnestness, the sometimes gauche
and embarrassing earnestness, with which the Irish public in these

decades has strained towards its particular conception of modernity. In the narrowest, most pragmatic way it has to do with the opening of the school and college curricula to the teaching of modern literature. All of this has been accompanied, particularly in more recent years, by varying evidence that we are, once more, undergoing the process of redefining the kind of culture which we possess in this country. We might begin this process by looking more closely at this apparently comfortable position of the contemporary writer in our society, questioning what it really means.

As a writer and teacher I am very conscious of being part of an Anglo-Saxon, Anglo-American, Anglo-Irish, a kind of anglic tradition and I am conscious of certain received ideas from that tradition as to how a writer is identified within his community. It seems to me that this shading, this impression of values has had a more tenacious hold on our thinking than we would, perhaps, allow and that this kind of survival is more typical of post-colonial society than it is of the parent one. Historically, this tradition has given particular weight and value to terms such as Imagination, Taste and Culture, a weighting which tends towards exclusiveness in that it arbitrates between the possessor and the dispossessed. It further promotes an idea of literature as a pristine, unitary expression which tends to guard its preserve, firstly, from other forms of intellectual activity, secondly, from other art forms and, thirdly, from human expressiveness which fails to meet the literary criteria of established taste. The idea of High Art and Low Art is deeply rooted within this tradition, a symptom of social presumptions which this country, like each one anglicised through colonization, has inherited.

If I am doing anything in this paper, I am attempting to question the way in which such ideas colour our attitudes towards writing and the writer. One aspect of this, which lies beyond this paper, indeed well beyond my competence, is the phenomenon of two languages in this country, two literatures and of the uneasy relationship between the two. To the many other factors that have contributed to the decline of the Irish language and the ambiguous attitude of large sections of the Irish public towards its literature, one must add the framework of thinking which we have inherited about the writer, about writing, from our colonial experience.

II

The title of this paper implies that there is some kind of relation or measurable transaction in the act of writing between the writer and the social world around him. Not everyone, obviously, would accept this as true or true in all cases or, even if true, as particularly desirable, something which is of significance to the work itself. When we find the idea asserted widely – that literature rests upon an environmental bed and is, in important ways, conditioned by environment and answerable to it – then we know we are in one kind of society. It will most likely be socialist or one congenial to socialist thought. When we turn to a society like our own, however, we find a counter-assertion, that literature is the product of an individualistic mind and the act of writing is popularly associated with a transcending of the ordinary, everyday social facts of existence. The claim, here, is that the writer enjoys a greater degree of freedom of expression whereas, in fact, what it often means is that the writer and society are free of one another in some kind of mutual agreement of self-preservation.

The whole question of the artist and society is one of the more contentious and over-worked issues in twentieth century art and criticism. It lies behind most efforts to make historical sense of the movement from Modernism to Post-Modernist art. In recent times it has become part of the argument surrounding the influence of European, particularly French and through French, German and East European aesthetics on what is called Anglo-American criticism. I want to illustrate this point because I feel it has a direct bearing upon what it is like to be a writer and teacher of literature in Ireland in 1979, if not 1980.

Frederic Jameson who is, by any account, one of the more sophisticated Marxist critics now writing in the English language, describes in his preface to *Marxism and Form*[3] and in the opening chapter on Adorno, the hostility which Anglo-American philosophy and literary criticism nurture towards that other, European tradition. It is the hostility of a tradition which we, however disguisedly, share in, a tradition founded upon a cultivated liberalism in politics, social thinking and literary criticism which would see the arts, firstly, as an adornment upon society and, secondly, as an educative, ameliorizing influence upon the population at large. That art should offer modes of perception which may radically transform the way in which we see, hear and feel about the world around us is something which liberalism embraces as a principle but converts into Culture, that is to say it protects itself from the full, social implications of artistic subversion.

Lionel Trilling has described[4] the calm, the nerveless composure with which his students of Modern Literature at Columbia University read and responded to, in examination, works of profound subversion, subversive, that is, of every assumption about life by which they themselves lived. The most potent energies of literature had been converted into a pedagogic system in which assent costs little more than the transcription of an idea to paper, all the disturbing intuitions have become sanitised. More than anyone else, Trilling tested the elasticity, the tolerance of Anglo-American liberalism and expressed, honestly, his misgivings about the claims which the system made on its own behalf. I simply want to isolate one or two points about the role of the artist in this kind of society and some of the anomalies that derive from it.

In the liberal culture there is the tendency to allow the artist a position as privileged commentator, not out of any particular compulsion on the part of society to find illumination through art but rather because such an image of the artist is immensely gratifying to the liberal conscience and, by extension, to the liberal idea of education. The privileged position of the writer has little to do with the hierarchy of power in society. It is a kind of shared fiction between writer and society which has nothing to do with the reality of privilege and power in society itself. Since any particular set of ideas or themes in an art-work is automatically accepted by the liberal mind, simply because the work is art, the ideas and themes are effectively neutralized. The liberal society has made a particular cult of the artist as an aberrant figure, a provider of alternative, radical ways of re-looking at the world which, given the marketplace of our type of society, can be easily converted into mere occasions of sensation. The Modern Movement, the subject of Trilling's course, began by offering an art which sought nothing less than an acceleration of the evolutionary process, an advance of the species on to a higher level of consciousness. It is depressing to observe how easily that literature has been converted into documentation, decoration, a testimony to the tolerance, the open-ness of the liberal mind. Art has been placed in an insulated, if highly reputable shrine, with no real grounding, no real armature into the mechanics which power the world in which we live.

As a non-Marxist I want to look at that other European tradition which offers an alternative way of looking at the art-work, an alternative way of speaking of the artist. Jameson's book is, for me at any rate, an extremely difficult attempt to introduce the English-speaking reader to the key European texts. It is also an elegant demonstration of the pre-occupations of this tradition in the attempt to establish a dialectical literary criticism. One of its striking features is its eclecticism which is characteristic of this tradition in which literary criticism is seen to proceed, naturally, from philosophy, history and sociology by which the disciplines are inextricably bound-up in the one model. Its chief interest for me is the way in which it re-reads literature in a fashion that challenges the one I'm familiar with and, more specifically, how it grounds this reading in the very nexus that is the subject of this paper: how to relate the integral self of the writer to the society around him.

As our chairman knew in inviting me to this conference, I have an obsessive interest in such matters. I have written one novel *The Big Chapel*[5] and a play, *Talbot's Box*[6] that are very much the result of this obsession. The obsession might be described as follows: I am fascinated and often appalled by what happens when the intense, concentrated hopes, fears, beliefs of the private person are subjected to the fragmenting, diffusionary effects of public life. I now know that both my works are about that division and that both acknowledge a failure to achieve a wholeness of community in the Irish experience which they describe. My question to myself, for the moment, is why has the cult of estrangement become such a convenient form of heroism in our writing?

Let me try to extrapolate three crucial implications from a work like Jameson's which offer me some consolation in all of this. Firstly, this alternative tradition would restore ideas to a proper place in the working of the imagination, and thereby to the activity of criticism, as figures of beauty in themselves, part of human inventiveness and human vision, as available to an aesthetic structure as the image, the metaphor, the subjective intuition. In this sense the movement is a reaction against late forms of romanticism. Secondly, it would radically question the mystique of autonomy of the individual artist and of the individual art-work, seeing them as occupying their places in history, in society, parts of the process of communal living. In this sense the reaction is against the extreme egoism of the modernist. Thirdly, it would take literature or any other art-form as inextricably bound up with all other forms of human expression including those which the liberal tradition would describe as vulgar, tasteless and of a culturally deprived mind. In this way the sovereignity of any one form of human expression becomes suspect, a version of the totalitarian impulse in the human character. In this way, too, literary criticism becomes panoptic and is seen to possess, in the freest possible manner, not only other kinds of art criticism, philosophy, politics, historiography but also social information of all kinds from the ephemeral to the revolutionary.

I think it would be true to say that issues like these have never been really prominent among the concerns of Irish writers in this century, nor among those who write about Irish writing. Our interests are different, we admire our writers for other qualities, very great qualities in some instances. But whatever else one may say about our literature, its peaks of genius, its sheer bulk of output, its dominance over the other arts in the country, one would scarcely describe it as a literature possessed of interesting, dynamic ideas about its local society. In its most characteristic form, it tends to engage society by way of oblique shafts, or, if you will, through the impression of the personality of the writer and the personalised achievement of the work. This is quite different to an art which assumes that it is part of the culture. What Irish writing has said to us, consistently, what it continues to say to us to-day is that such integration is impossible, that the evolving society in this country has persistently fallen behind the finer perceptions of its artists, that it has been and continues to be unworthy of its own art. If this is true it speaks of deep impoverishment in modern Ireland. The response of many of my contemporaries to all of this would be that it is not the business of the imaginative writer to worry about such things, that the kind of concerns I've been talking about are contaminations of the pure imagination. It does not seem to matter then that, despite its public reputation, despite all the recent patronage of the arts, it is extremely doubtful that Irish writing has made any significant impact on the kind of life, the kind of society which we have in this country to-day.

III

Even as I say this I am conscious of so much clamour behind me disputing such extreme opinions. There is the presence of Yeats and the public consciousness of the man, the way in which the career may be defined in terms of a willed progression of encounters between the private and the public man. I think of O'Casey whose quality, finally, as a writer depends upon how we respond to his social conscience and to the ways in which he gave it voice. There are whole areas of prose-fiction and even drama in the late-twenties, thirties and early forties which meet and re-meet the social facts, the concrete details of daily living in this country. There is the work of a poet like Austin Clarke who, particularly in the later work, a volume like *Ancient Lights*,[7] ought properly to be at the centre of this discussion, both from the committed nature of the man's work and the fact that he stands at the portals of contemporary writing, acknowledged and respected by his younger fellows before he died.

But even the way we feel about Clarke is significant: the key-word is respect, not a particularly urgent response to what he has to say, with great skill, about the grotesque, the inhumane and repressive in Irish society, nor even to his technical solution of the problem of finding a poetic form which would admit the rhythms of social habit, social distortion, social protest. It is my experience that young Irish writers do not look at Clarke with any particular degree of interest, despite the fact that he confronted the more obtuse, more vicious elements which were blocking the way of even the modest circulation which younger writers enjoy to-day.

There are, however, other models and the two figures who do have a hold upon the consciousness of the young, providing a continuity with writing of the pre-fifties, are Francis Stuart and Patrick Kavanagh. What is attractive, I think, in both, over and above the considerable achievement of each as a writer, is the projection of a literary persona, the writer as a figure of freedom, of courageous iconoclasm with an unrelenting belief in the unique vision of art, superior in kind to any other form of human vision and exacted at great personal cost in both cases from an uncaring society. I would never question such integrity. What I would suggest, however, is that the type of society in which we live, at this point in the century, has little difficulty in accommodating, even conniving at such an idea of the writer because it remains unscathed by the subversiveness of the exceptional individual and is even flattered by the ease with which it can contain him. Bearing in mind, then, that my subject is not literary achievement but the projection of an artistic persona I want to comment upon the presences of these two writers in our contemporary culture.

You will remember that in the early portions of Stuart's *Black-*

List: Section H,[8] the protagonist H or Luke has a number of shocking encounters with Yeats. They are part of the whole journey of
that amazing book, a movement fuelled at one and the same time by
irresistible purpose and painful disconnectedness. Stylistically, this
split is maintained in the mixture of documentation and inner
journal which is further urged upon the reader in the earlier portions (the style later is more fluid) by abrupt paragraphing and
startling interjections. The journey itself is across a recognizable
map, through a time-span that bristles with modern European
historical data, passing persons that, in so many instances, have
already a public reputation, perhaps especially for the Irish reader.
But it is also a journey refracted through the eye of a highly
idiosyncratic viewer so that while events and persons trail evidence
of existence of one kind or another, including that of autobiography, from outside the book, they are subject within it to this austere
and fevered scrutiny: an effect, as it were, of sameness and difference at once. In the end we realize that this is the very shape, the
potent cause of the novel, to demonstrate an heroic confrontation
between the artist and the world. The work does not seek to annihi-
late history or dissolve its sweeping edges which is the aspiration of
most autobiographical fiction where the central consciousness tends
to subsume historical information and change it into a utility, a domestic image, an extension of the singular imagination. Stuart's style is
much more angular, nothing less than the opposing of one kind of
record to another.

What emerges as positive, then, within the controlling mind of the
book is directly contrary not only to conventional social morality
but also to the common, received version of a particular phase of
Irish and European history. The negatives of common social vocabulary: dishonour, disgrace, failure become positives, values to be
embraced. The artist, then, is offered as a social misfit, stumbling in
and out of life's incidents without a scrap of that shell which makes
social intercourse endurable for most people. What emerges is the
claim that such risk, such exposure as of a wound, is precisely the
very quality which distinguishes the artist from all others.

Now all of this will be familiar to us from Stuart's own work and
from that particular stream of Modernism of which it is part which
reflects back to Blake and a romantic idea of the artist as heroic
victim but would include writers like these who haunt H in the
novel, Dostoevsky and Kafka. What is shocking in the encounters
with Yeats is not the fact that a great poet could be pompous,

absurdly theatrical and the kind of host who wandered in and out of guest bedrooms at odd hours. At this late stage in the century we are well accustomed to the common frailties of genius. What is shocking, what is always shocking in my reading, at any rate, in much of the modernist sensibility is that, despite the shared elevation of the artist, the violent expression of individualism is ruthlessly selective in its view of other artists. It might be said, however, that one of the processes which is being described in the book is the way in which the writer-protagonist has to free himself from the burden of greatness in others. It is not only Yeats but also Joyce who is put aside in several of those parentheses which stud *Black List: Section H*.

I do not refer to Stuart's novel as, as I believe it to be, a work of such command that beside it most Irish fiction of this period appears anaemic. Nor do I offer it as particularly representative, although it is one of two substantial works (Aidan Higgins' *Balcony of Europe* being the other) which charts the progress of an artistic Irish mind in its passage through a complex, modern European situation. What is at stake, however, in this discussion, is its vigorous anti-social version of artistic freedom. The modernist declaration of freedom, of which it is typical, rose out of the clutter of an over-ripe nineteenth century middle-class society. I have tried to argue that, for all its immense achievement, its subversiveness has been effectively assimilated by the remnants of that same society and has become, in effect, one of the ornaments of that society's culture. It stands in opposition to a second declaration of freedom arising out of that same exhausted century which sought a corresponding transformation of human consciousness not by way of extreme individualism but through a revolution of the masses, a recognition of otherness not as something hostile and beyond redemption but as the ground of one's personal salvation. Freedom is the key slogan: it is one of our available words to indicate what is of permanent value in every work of art. What I am questioning is its use in ways that are strikingly at odds with its use in common, social speech, in political discourse, where it implies an admittance into fellowship, not an exclusion from it.

What Kavanagh projects is a different version of the same kind of role as in Stuart, the same mystique of the writer, the same mockery of conventional bourgeois attitudes, the same idea of an artistic vision, mystical and transcendent. The differences, however, are considerable, firstly, in that Kavanagh was a great comic writer and, secondly, in that he is the last in a rich, native rural tradition in which the poetic gift confers a status in the community, the status of waspish eccentricity. There is plenty of evidence in Kavanagh's own work that within the rural community, for all the shafts and frustrations, this role had its communal place and was not some kind of imposed aberration. Kavanagh chose to leave, however and the complexity of his mature personality has something to do with the carrying of that role into a different sector of Irish society: literary Dublin and the surrounding society with its painful repressiveness. He stalks through the fifties like some *cáinteóir* out of the Gaelic past with that sartorial stamp, the swinging coat, the dipped, brooding hat, the notorious cough and splutter, arms akimbo, knotted like an embrace that has lost or crushed its loved object.

He was a man of high intelligence, a lover of stillnesses and epiphanies, a very private man who lived behind this consciously constructed personality. The ridicule, contrariness and contradiction, insult and infamy, formed a kind of mask of power and even of style which protected the grace and delicacy of the poems and the numerous, glittering insights of the letters, journalism, trivia, which we get in the *Collected Pruse* and the posthumous volumes. As the last of our authentic voices out of a rural Ireland that was already changing beyond all recognition he exemplifies in his personality and the circumstances of his life the cost to selfhood of the changes which have characterised these decades. It will be the business of the biographer to analyse the kind of distortions of selfhood which Kavanagh affected in his role as poet and to question the kind of society which impelled him, often with great cruelty and delight in the histrionics, towards the worst caricaturing, a perverse form of self-satisfaction on the part of society itself.

What I have been attempting in this hurried fashion is a look at two forms of potent estrangement in modern Irish writing. It is a crude way, I suppose, to try to exaggerate the illusion that the society in which we live is in any profound way touched by extreme individualism in the writer. Quite the contrary, such individualism, however outrageous, is curiously consoling to the society of liberal aspirations. It is only when the writer assumes a common place in the world about him that that kind of encounter takes place and literature enters into the dynamics of the social process.

186

NOTES

1   *The Dolmen Miscellany of Irish Writing*, ed. John Montague and Thomas Kinsella (Dublin, 1962) Prefatory page.
2   Sean O'Faolain, 'Fifty Years of Irish Writing', *Studies*, Spring, 1962, p. 97.
3   Frederic Jameson, *Marxism and Form*, (Princeton University Press, 1971).
4   Lionel Trilling, 'On the Teaching of Modern Literature', *Beyond Culture*, Peregrine Books (London, 1967).
5   Thomas Kilroy, *The Big Chapel*, (London, 1971).
6   Thomas Kilroy, *Talbot's Box*, Gallery Books (Dublin, 1979).
7   Austin Clarke, *Later Poems* (Dublin, 1961).
8   Francis Stuart, *Black List: Section H* (Southern Illinois Press, 1971).
9   Aidan Higgins, *Balcony of Europe*, (London, 1972).

RHYME IN MODERN ANGLO-IRISH POETRY

PETER DENMAN

The closing lines of Seamus Heaney's first collection, *Death of a Naturalist*, offer a resounding statement of the poet's awareness of his own art.

> Now, to pry into roots, to finger slime,
> To stare big-eyed Narcissus, into some spring
> Is beneath all adult dignity. I rhyme
> To see myself, to set the darkness echoing.

This foregrounding of the rhyme element, in which the particular technique is equated with the essential poetic process, is but one instance of a preoccupation with rhyme which has been evident in Irish poetry from the early Irish lyricists to the assiduous practitioners of assonance in our own century. In this paper I intend to look at ways in which rhyme asserts itself in the work of some Anglo-Irish poets, and by using particular poems as case-studies to isolate some of the effects resulting from its use. I take rhyme to mean any formal phonic resemblances between words; this includes not only the typical full rhyme of a final stressed vowel sound and subsequent phonemes at the end of a verse, but also assonance, alliteration, para-rhymes, and consonance, occurring anywhere in the line.[1] By way of theoretical preliminary to what I have to say, I begin with a reminder of what may seem flagrantly obvious: rhyme is not a property of any one word taken singly. It exists only as a relationship between two or more words. And although the relationship is set up by a certain partial similarity of sound, the words function primarily as areas of signification. In the words of Roman Jakobson 'rhyme necessarily involves the semantic relationship between the rhyming units'.[2] Thus, although a rhyme word may be separated by several lines of verse from its pre-rhyme, and may belong in a wholly

189

different syntactic unit, we inevitably regard a rhyme-word as existing in a context evoked by its partner.

It is this aspect of rhyme which makes it worth isolating – not
rhyme in its musical or mnemonic aspects which, in these days of the
printed poem, are often bypassed, nor rhyme as a closural device,
contributing to the completeness of the structure of a poem, which
belongs more to consideration of conventions of poetic form.[3]

The semantic contribution of rhyme was explored by W. K. Wimsatt, but he was primarily concerned with the way rhyme-words are
played off against the logical statements of a poem. In the tight
couplets of Pope the regularly spaced rhyming units function as a
'fixative counterpoint' to the rhetorically varied argument. It is a
stimulating approach to the topic, but it is based on a limited range
of verse-forms and leads mainly to the limiting conclusion that the
degree of meaning difference between the rhyming-units is directly
indicative of the cleverness of the rhyme.[4] But the Anglo-Irish
poetry with which we are concerned is much more diffuse than
Pope's couplets; it uses internal rhyme irregularly across the line, or
end-rhyme over alternate lines in larger stanzaic forms. Looking
at Anglo-Irish poetry of the past four or five decades it is possible to
trace a shift from internal and cross-rhyming, associated particularly
with Austin Clarke, to the end-rhyme of contemporary poets such
as Heaney and Richard Murphy; this might be represented graphi-
cally as a move from horizontal to vertical rhyme.

In considering the use of horizontal rhyme it is necessary to bear
in mind the distinction between regular internal or cross-rhyme
used as a structural device to generate form, and haphazard internal
rhyme used without reference to its position or sequence in the line
of verse. The former occurs less frequently than one might think. A
poem which Clarke himself once selected to illustrate this feature is
'The Straying Student'[5] in which, he claims, 'the pattern of each line
is a b b a c'[6], a claim which it is worth subjecting to some scrutiny.

The a b b a 'envelope' pattern, with a core of two rhyming units
flanked by two others, is strongly established in the first line:

On a holy day when sails were blowing southward.

The pattern is maintained through four of the six lines of the first
stanza, but after that it is more or less abandoned as a structuring
device. There is discernible assonance or alliteration between two

elements in most lines of the next three stanzas but of the eighteen lines only four (six if one reads indulgently) conform to the a b b a internal rhyme scheme. In the last stanza the pattern drops out of sight, with only a half-hearted substitution of alliteration and one cross-rhyme.

> And yet I tremble lest she may deceive me
> And leave me in this land where every woman's son
> Must carry his own coffin and believe
> In dread, all that the clergy teach the young.

Apart from the horizontal rhymes each stanza is conventionally end-rhymed a b a b, and this continued throughout the entire length and clearly wins out over the attempt to sustain the initial internal envelope pattern. Thus 'The Straying Student' demonstrates in itself the movement from horizontal rhyming across the page to vertical rhyming down it.

Clarke has a number of other poems written about the same time which also use internal or cross-rhyme, but I have selected 'The Straying Student' as a case-study not just because it is so well-known but also because it was the poem he himself quoted when, in a lecture given late in his life, he discussed his earlier attempts to use assonance structurally. He quotes most of the poem but not, I note, the final stanza, and remarks, perhaps wistfully how, 'AE kept reminding us of William Larminie's theory that Gaelic assonance could be used in English to modulate rhyme. But F. R. Higgins and I were the only ones to follow his advice.'[7] Someone else who tried something similar is Louis MacNeice in his short poem 'O'Connell Bridge' but by and large any examples one comes across tend to be exceptions. When Clarke and his contemporaries of the mid-century did attend to Larminie's and A.E.'s exhortations and used assonance as a structural device, they generally used it not as an internal or cross-rhyme operating *within* the line-unit but as a replacement for the usual full end-rhyme. This very effectively increased the range of rhyming units available and offered new phonic possibilities, but had absolutely no effect on formal considerations. Rhyme is a convention, as Levin remarks,[8] and the use of assonance merely extended the scope of the convention without altering its basis. One of the most successful users of assonantal end-rhyme was Patrick MacDonagh.

> This morning I wakened among loud cries of seagulls
> Thronging in misty light above my neighbour's ploughland
> And the house in its solid acres was carried wheeling
> Encircled in desolate waters and impenetrable cloudy
> Wet winds that harried and lost the sea birds' voices
> And the voice of my darling, despairing and drowning
> Lost beyond finding in the bodiless poising.[9]

I would suggest that an underlying reason for the eventual predominance of the vertical rhyme structure is the possibility which rhyme offers for semantic coupling. The particular virtue of such a coupling is that it can exist independently of the grammar of the logical statement contained in the poem, or even, as Wimsatt observed in Pope's verse, in counterpoint to it. Thus rhyme may be suprasyntactical or contrasyntactical. Internal rhyming across the line necessarily involves linking words which are already linked through their contiguity in the syntagmatic structure. As a result any connection between semantic references which is brought about by the rhyme is superfluous or, at best, no more than a reinforcement of what is contained in the logical statement. For instance, in the opening two lines of 'The Straying Student' the rhyme scheme relates 'holy' and 'blowing' 'day and sails', 'bishop' and 'Inishmore', 'sang' and 'mass'. But the only link discernible between 'holy' and 'day' and their respective rhymes is that the pre-rhymes attach a time and an aura of sanctity to the sails which are blown. A rather uninteresting observation, because this is the intent of the logical statement made in line I. 'Bishop' and 'Inishmore' give us an agent and a location: the linking situates one in the other. 'Mass' is not only the rhyme of the sound 'sang' but also the direct object of the verb 'sang'. Rhyme here is neither standing independently nor running counter to the logical statements, but is being submerged by them.

Later in the same poem, when vertical rhyme emerges as dominant, we find two sets of three end-rhymes rhymed alternately:

> They say I was sent back from Salamanca
> And failed in logic, but I wrote her praise
> Nine times upon a college wall in France.
> She laid her hand at darkfall on my page
> That I might read the heavens in a glance
> And I knew every star the Moors have named.

'Salamanca' and 'France' belong in different logical statements, separated by the strongly disjunctive 'but' in the middle of the intervening line. However the two rhyming units show an obvious semantic affinity, both being placenames. Together they encompass the range of the student's lived experience, as against the insular limitation of Inishmore and the imaginatively apprehended Rome and Greece mentioned earlier in the poem. But as well as affinity there is contrast, for Salamanca is a place the student was reputedly sent away from, while in France there was the positive affirmation of the writing on the wall. The final rhyming-unit of this set, 'glance', extends the speaker's range to the cosmos – 'might read the heavens in a glance' – in a careless gesture of knowledge that typifies the confidence of learning. In the alternating set of rhymes one can trace, from 'praise' to 'named', a progress from heady enthusiasm to cool definition, a progress brought about by study, signified by the 'page' which is the intermediate term. Thus the rhymes suggest or indicate a progress of enlargement while remaining independent of the syntactical statements of the verse; the relational emphases of the rhymes amplify the logical statement.

I mentioned earlier that there are two types of horizontal rhyming – the regular, as in 'The Straying Student', and the haphazard. The regular does at least have the virtue of contributing to the form even if it contributes little or nothing thematically. Irregular rhymed verse has the added drawback of being formally null as well. The type of thing found in works such as Robert Farren's long poem *The First Exile*[10] and in W. R. Rogers's *'Europa and the Bull'* soon begins to grate – I quote from the latter:

> Naked they came, a niggling core of girls
> Maggoting gaily in the curling wool
> Of morning mist, and careless as the lark
> That gargled overhead. They were the root
> Of all that writhing air, the frothing rock
> Of that grey sea in whose vacuity
> Footless they stood . . .[11]

In the opening lines there is hardly a stressed syllable which does not have a rhyming partner. Pervasive rhyming of this nature is quite without function. A rather fussy embroidery on the text, at best it imparts a languid musicality, at worst it becomes tedious.

There is one relatively recent instance of a poem which uses irregular horizontal rhyme in a manner which integrates the device into the text's totality of effect: Richard Weber's best-known piece, 'Lady and Gentleman'.[12] This traces the thoughts and attitudes of a couple at a dining-table, a confrontation fraught with love and misunderstanding. The first stanza sets the tone:

> Of himself to think this: she does not
> Know my meaning, nor ever will,
> Though the leaves like late butterflies
> Twist and turn, falter and fall
> In the outside racing, interlacing winds.

Alliteration, assonance and, eventually, full rhyme are all used in this first stanza. In the fourth line we find the word 'falter' acting as pivot: the first, stressed syllable of 'falter' is a homonym presaging its rhyming partner 'fall', while the unstressed second syllable refers back to the second element of the alliterated pair 'twist and turn'. The last line relies on the full internal rhyme of 'racing' and 'interlacing'. At first glance this rhyming pair might be thought devoid of thematic significance. The rhyme links two words already linked by contiguity and equivalence – both are epithets qualifying the same word – and, in part, the rhyme is brought about by homoeoteleuton. There is no opportunity here for rhyme to operate suprasyntactically, to suggest a relationship between elements otherwise disjunctive. But as the meaning of the word 'interlacing' suggests, the general semantic intention is one of convoluted self-regard, and the piling up of rhyme itself 'interlaces' the line. The whole poem is in fact about hesitancy and introversion, and because of this the normally debilitating properties of irregular horizontal rhyme work to appropriate effect.

We have already seen how horizontal internal rhyme tends to have a limiting effect, interfering with the linear progression of the logical statement. At times this may be useful, but more often than not it stunts a poem. It is noticeable that this introverted device was used mainly by poets who wrote in the middle years of this century, when Ireland was politically isolated as never before, and who turned to themes that were historically remote: Rodgers embroidering classical myth, Farren working up the story of St. Colmcille, Clarke assuming the *persona* of an eighteenth-century clerical student. At the same time more internationally-minded poets – Coffey, Devlin, Donnelly – eschewed rhyme as a device. Perhaps this resulted not simply from imitation of modernist free verse; perhaps there was a necessary relationship between attitudes they expressed and the form they adopted. All that is couched in 'perhapses'; what is quite certain is that when Clarke later turned to trenchant commentary on contemporary public issues he simultaneously turned to a new type of rhyme which operated vertically.

I will conclude with an example in which rhyme is to be seen operating integrally, an example again taken from Clarke, a poet whose use of rhyme is unfailingly exploratory. I will take the quatrain published alongside 'The Straying Student', and almost as well-known: 'Penal Law'.

> Burn Ovid with the rest. Lovers will find
> A hedge-school for themselves and learn by heart
> All that the clergy banish from the mind,
> When hands are joined and head bows in the dark.[13]

One first notices the striking internal rhyme of the opening line, the consonance of 'Ovid with' and 'lovers will'. It is effective because of several factors: although in the same line the rhyming units belong to different logical statements, there is an obvious and appropriate link between Ovid's essays in eroticism and the lovers, and yet the assertion being made is that the latter can do without the former.

The next rhyme to establish itself is the end-rhyme of lines 1 and 3. 'find' 'mind'. Semantically the rhyme pair points, or foregrounds, a strong contrast between the discovery of finding and the negative movement of 'banish from the mind'. But apart from the semantic relationship the rhyme has a striking syntactic function, governing our reading of the last line. How does one determine the reference of line 4:

> 'When hands are joined and head bows in the dark'?

Does this refer to the hands of a penitent or clergyman with head bowed in the gloom of a confessional or church, or to the hands of a lover in the friendly obscurity of the night? The reading of the line selected is governed by which of the rhyme words it is attached to – does it depend on what 'lovers will find' or what will be 'banished from the mind'? The natural tendency to attach the final clause to that immediately preceding – to the contiguous clause – is explicitly resisted by the punctuation: the comma at the end of line 3 has no other purpose. Instead, the rhyme 'mind' evokes its pre-rhyme 'find' so that their respective phrases jostle for the temporal clauses of l.4. In prose statement the resultant indeterminancy would indicate slipshod construction; in verse, thanks to the additional structural device of rhyme, the ambivalence is revealed because the linking by rhyme overcomes the essential linearity of syntax.

The other end-rhyme pair, 'heart' and 'dark', makes an approximate rhyme. This set has less to do in the structure of the quatrain, but nevertheless can be seen as contributing to the overall effects. The ambivalent last line is, as we have seen, linked syntactically to both the first and third lines; it is linked to the second line by its rhyme, giving a strong sense of closure to the poem. Going further, we notice that the last line is made up of the syntactically similar statements, 'hands are joined' and 'head bows in the dark'. The latter statement has a pre-rhyme in 'heart', while the former ends with 'joined', an approximate rhyme to the dominant 'find-mind'. And between the two half-lines there are a number of formal links: 'hands' and 'heart' alliterate, they have obvious semantic affinities in being parts of the body, and they are both subjects of their respective clauses. And just as 'heart' is a pre-rhyme to the end-word 'dark', it is also a pre-rhyme to 'hands' and 'head' through alliteration, sharing in the semantic association as well.

There are a number of other rhyme patterns which can be identified within this short poem, but there comes the problem of knowing when to stop the search for ingenious and tortuous patterns. If rhyme is regarded as a foregrounding device, something to suggest relationships, then the rhyme has to assert itself. Rhyme which has to be discovered is non-functional. A poem must not be read in order to discern faint rhyme patterns, but rather the rhyme should be able to guide our reading of the text.

To sum up therefore, I would maintain that our examination of the preoccupation with rhyme in much Anglo-Irish poetry indicates that it is not to be regarded as a musical or mnemonic aid, but that it justifies itself as an aid to and amplifier of meaning. The characteristics of internally or horizontally rhymed poetry show that, as well as suggesting relationships between the semantic associations of rhyming units, it also operates with reference to, although independently of, the syntax, and I would maintain that the often-expressed dissatisfaction with Anglo-Irish internally rhymed poetry can be explained with reference to this.

In Clarke's 'Penal Law' we can see how the rhymes bind the poem to give it strong closural force while simultaneously balancing the ambivalence of the last line to give it resonant signification. There at any rate, if I may paraphrase the quotation from Heaney with which I began, the rhyme serves to set that particular darkness echoing.

NOTES

1   v. G. N. Leech, *A Linguistic Guide to English Poetry*. (London, 1969), Chapter 6.
2   R. Jakobson 'Linguistics and Poetics' in *Essays in Style and Language* ed. Thomas A. Sebeok, (New York, 1960). This essay is fundamental to any modern discussion of rhyme. Marjorie Perloff's *Rhyme and Meaning in the Poetry of Yeats* (The Hague, 1970) demonstrates a practical application of Jakobson's theory, while Christina Brooke-Rose, in *A Structural Analysis of Pound's Usura Canto: Jakobson's Method Extended and Applied to Free Verse* (The Hague, 1976) broadens its scope. See also Samuel R. Levin, *Linguistic Structures in Poetry* (The Hague, 1962) and Nicolas Ruwet's essay 'L'analyse structurale de la poésie' in his book *Language, musique, poésie* (Paris, 1972).
3   v. B. H. Smith *Poetic Closure* (Chicago, 1968).
4   'One Relation of Rhyme to Reason' in *The Verbal Icon* (London, 1970).
5   p. 188 *Collected Poems* (Dublin 1974).
6   'Anglo-Irish Poetry' in *Literature in Celtic Countries* ed. J. E. Caerwyn Williams (Cardiff, 1971).
7   Ibid. p. 168.
8   Samuel R. Levin 'The Conventions of Poetry' in *Literary Style: A Symposium* ed. Seymour Chatman (London, 1971).
9   p. 25 *One Landscape Still and Other Poems* (London, 1948).
10   (London, 1944).
11   p. 57 *Collected Poems* (London, 1971).
12   p. 15 *Lady and Gentleman* (Dublin, 1963).
13   p. 189 *Collected Poems* (Dublin 1974).

THREE IRISH WOMEN STORY WRITERS OF THE 1970s

JAMES H. O'BRIEN

In the past few years several Irish women have turned to the short story, partly in response to new sources of publication, such as the weekly story in the *Irish Press* and the establishment of the Poolbeg Press, Dublin, a firm that publishes in paper new collections of short stories. These women writers do not seem to be attached to any group; they avoid black humour, the grotesque, the apocalyptic, and the sexually sensational. In some ways these writers are social realists, for they write about a recognizable external world, and they respect the conventions of plot and characterization. They do not sentimentalize or romanticize the Irish countryman or the Dublin slum dweller. They concentrate upon domestic friction and conflicts within the individual.

Because of an emphasis on social realism, the stories of three of these women writers reveal significant perspectives on social change and social values in Ireland. The short story has an immediacy, a closeness to daily concerns often unavailable in the novel. The first of these writers is Val Mulkerns, also a novelist. She writes of three generations of Dublin women in *Antiquities*, published in 1978. The second writer, Maura Treacy, writes mainly of rural Ireland in *Sixpence in her Shoe* (1977). The last author is Kate Cruise O'Brien, whose first collection, *A Gift Horse*, was published in 1978. All three women are well aware of currents of change resulting from the civil rights movement, from the women's movements, from the EEC and Vatican II, and from the increasing prosperity and declining emigration. Only rarely do they touch upon the present agony of Ireland, the violence that erupted in 1969 in the North.

I

Val Mulkerns's *Antiquities* has a suggestive subtitle, 'A Sequence of

199

Stories'. Like Sherwood Anderson's, *Winesburg, Ohio, Antiquities* contains stories which are inter-related and bound together by a central figure. This character, Emily, a woman in her fifties, appears in various stories as a girl, a wife, and a mother. Emily looks backward to the idealism of her mother's era of the Easter Rising and forward to the personal freedom and prosperity of her daughter's era. Like others born in the 1920s, Emily discovers in retrospect how her personality was formed by the economically and culturally restricted Dublin of the 1930s and 1940s. Emily's mother married a young patriot imprisoned for his part in the Easter Rising, but Emily's daughter Sara learns Irish in the west; she becomes at age fourteen an exchange student in France, attends university to become an architect, and has her first job in Paris. By contrast, Emily's growing up was lackluster and drab, but she searches for meaning in antiquities, the vanished world of her childhood and youth.

Like Mary Lavin, Val Mulkerns has a gift for portraying the intimacy of family life in Dublin. Emily and her mother share a passion for Dublin homes and neighborhoods. In the first story, 'A Bitch and a Dog Hanging', Emily blends this love for houses and her search for meaning in the past as she, a grown woman, looks for a thatched cottage in Dublin, a cottage once owned by her nanny. The cottage has disappeared – the area is filled with housing estates and paved roads. As a girl, Emily found what she later discovered to be the rhythm of country life right in Dublin. Each summer as a child Emily spent two weeks at the nanny's cottage, a herdsman's house set in fields and trees. Here she gathered eggs, saw the birth of a red calf, played in the fields, and delighted in a swing set high in an oak tree. Emily became attached to the nanny's family, especially to her epileptic son. The nanny told stories of elemental joy and fear, one of which Emily partially remembers. This story deals with a man who tried to cut his sons out of his will. The man opened the door of an outbuilding to find a bitch and a dog hanging from a pair of ropes, a sign of ill luck for the miserly old man. Emily forgot the rest of the story, but she could not put out of her mind the image of the bitch and the dog.

Like other Irish women writers, Val Mulkerns does some of her best writing when she treats women as victims of cruelty. In 'The Sisters', Emily's mother has domineering relatives who provide moral guidance for their wayward brothers and sisters. Emily's mother endures patronizing insults and humiliations because she has made the mistake of marrying an Irish patriot who has only a menial job in the gas works. For this failure, Emily's mother, Fanny, must accept the tyranny of her sister Harriet, known as Aunt Harry. Aunt Harry married late in life, is childless and is jealous of Emily's mother and her family. To Aunt Harry, poverty is evidence of moral failure. She has a series of issues on which she baits her younger sister. For example, Aunt Harry chides Emily's mother for not wearing her wedding ring, a ring Emily's mother frequently takes to the pawn shop. The climax of 'The Sisters' comes when Aunt Harry makes a shattering proposition to Emily's mother; Aunt Harry wants to take Emily, then about eight, into her house and provide clothes and tuition for school. Emily's mother is outraged; she refuses, saying that their mother would not let one of her eight children out of the household. Then Emily's mother bursts into tears, helpless and crestfallen.

The inter-related stories of Val Mulkerns's *Antiquities* reveal several lost worlds of Emily as she searches for meanings in her life. But the family stories exemplifying values and attitudes of the 1920s to the 1970s are subordinated to Emily's review of the past and her capacity to transform previous loss and pain into illuminating images. Stories like 'The Sisters' and 'A Cut Above the Rest' are presented through the narrator's re-examination of the past. Other stories narrated as if the action were present seem to lack the compression and concentration of those with a framework of memory. Yet Mulkerns's first volume is remarkable for its large design, its intricate relationships, and its warm yet unsentimental approach to the joy and sadness in Dublin houses and neighborhoods. Emily could not help learning a great deal about Dublin houses, for she characterizes her mother in these terms: '. . . and it was the ambition of my mother to rent a bigger house in a more acceptable district which would land us in debt but do us justice.'

II

Maura Treacy's first book of stories, *Sixpence in her Shoe*, was published in the author's thirty-first year. Born in Co. Kilkenny, Maura Treacy writes of the frustrations and reverses of people in rural Ireland. Her characters do not rebel or flee from the countryside; they are compelled by circumstances and their own lack of understanding to settle for less. They lack the inner resources for assessing and gaining at least partial control over situations thrust upon them. For instance, an elderly woman living alone on a farm waits in vain for a visit from her nephew. The old lady has a simple and rigid schedule. She sends messages by a creamery truck driver; she attends Sunday Mass; she visits her sister-in-law each week in the district hospital. Although the old woman longs for company, she contributes to her own isolation because she presents to visitors only a shyness and a timid agreeableness. In another story, a husband whose ideal wife is a woman conspicuous for tidiness finds no way to reform his slovenly wife, except to strike her. Treacy plays adroitly upon the nexus of social convention and individual desires, stressing the inability of her characters to respond constructively to a crisis.

Treacy's ability as storyteller is evident in the title story, 'Sixpence in her Shoe', a treatment of the jagged friendship of two old women in the country. Their friendship serves as a metaphor of the uneasy concessions and tolerance at the base of many friendships. At the start of 'Sixpence in her Shoe', an old woman, Mrs. Frewin, resents her secondary position in her household since she has become subordinate to her daughter-in-law. Mrs. Frewin has a single gesture to demonstrate her frustration: she grinds a hot poker into the new tiles of the kitchen floor. Mrs. Frewin has one friend in the neighborhood, Mrs. McLoughlin. The friendship began many years before when Mrs. Frewin and Mrs. McLoughlin were young brides; on the surface the two women seemed destined to provide consolation for each other. But Mrs. Frewin did not want to divulge her intimate secrets to Mrs. McLoughlin, who wanted a confidante. For a time the friendship was dormant, for Mrs. McLoughlin told her stories to others in the neighborhood – only to have her stories returned in disturbing forms to her mother-in-law. Then Mrs. McLoughlin returned to Mrs. Frewin, satisfied to have an audience who would not spread her secrets. Another difference between the two old women inhibits their friendship. Mrs. McLoughlin romanticizes memories of the early days of their married life, a time when they knew where the children were. But Mrs. Frewin will not sentimentalize this period because she does not want to betray the prosperity of the present time. The delicacy of their present relations is indicated when Mrs. McLoughlin pays a visit, presenting a jar of marmalade, with apologies for its imperfections.

An achievement in itself, Maura Treacy's first volume provides solid evidence that her future stories on rural Ireland may have increased passion and depth. Treacy skilfully controls a descriptive sketch of a family working in a sugar-beet field in 'A Time for Growing'. In 'The Pet of the Family', she elaborates, with closely observed details, a plot in which a wife creates years of family strife by attempting to turn her husband into a farmer when he would like to be a carpenter and builder. In her stories, Treacy raises several aspects of a perennial issue: Why do many Irish women have such limited inner resources for contending with the obstacles of marriage? One of her women characters awakens to the point that she 'finds her own lack of prescience remarkable'. In addition, Treacy endeavours in various ways to portray the inner consciousness of her character. In 'The Weight of the World', an adolescent farm girl broods as she sits in a windowsill. As she reviews the recent past, largely in the form of accusations against the members of her family, she speaks to herself as 'you', thus crudely but effectively struggling to comprehend her role in family quarrels.

III

Kate Cruise O'Brien published her first collection *A Gift Horse* in 1978. She may well become a leading figure in Irish letters if Sean O'Faolain's prediction comes true. O'Faolain said her stories reveal something much more than a special talent; they reveal 'a seed of genius'. Kate Cruise O'Brien is a discerning analyist of human reactions and a weaver of complex stories. Her characters have no sudden epiphanies or moments of recognition; instead they make delayed, painful discoveries of their confusion, selfishness, or obtuseness. They belong to a well-educated, suburban world; their realities emerge from personal interests rather than from social or political matters. Like many of Chekhov's characters, O'Brien's are afflicted with a psychic blindness, an inner numbness preventing them from comprehending their powers and limitations. One of her characters refers to 'the glass wall that has come between me and the outside world'.

O'Brien's stories are often taut and lean. In a few pages she presents a critical juncture in an individual's life. Her fiction may not warm or intrigue the reader by its abundant details; it does not immerse the reader in a new world in which he would like to dwell. Yet her stories accomplish an essential work of fiction by thrusting the reader immediately into a dilemma he may have only half recognized as his own.

Kate Cruise O'Brien treats a current preoccupation such as the enthusiasm for egalitarianism or anti-elitism with a penetrating grasp of its implications. In previous decades a headmaster, a father, an employer, or a priest controlled a decision almost ex-officio. But with the declining influence of institutions and their figures of authority, individuals previously in subordinate position may indirectly or directly control a situation. In some cases an individual may assume dominance because of position or age and then be compelled to surrender control. For example, in O'Brien's story, 'Losing', an antique dealer, a man in early middle age, assumes that he will manage his young mistress. As an antique dealer, he has her wait at dinners and meetings while he arranges purchases and sales. But after five years of such waiting, the mistress, out of boredom, takes courses at a university. She becomes fascinated with the orderly girls in a small Protestant school and accepts a position as a teacher. This decision infuriates the antique dealer; he cannot bear the thought of his mistress as a person with interests of her own. In another story, 'Pieces of Silver', a schoolboy gains attention and love from his recently widowed mother who seems to be waiting for someone to compel her to care for her son. In 'A Matter of Principle', another schoolboy punctures the clichés of his father who constantly speaks of rebellion against oppressive authority but in practice bows meekly to his superiors.

In Kate Cruise O'Brien's most ambitious story, 'Some Rain Must Fall', she lays bare the narcissism that corrodes love and marriage. In this story an intelligent young couple seem to be building a harmonious marriage. The wife is the daughter of a wealthy indulgent father; the husband, a lecturer at Sheffield, is the son of a mother immersed in lower middle-class morality. The narrator of the story, however, explains flaws in their initial attractiveness to each other:

Gerald had been entranced with her money and her sports car and her careless rich ways, which made her appear both more generous and more secure than she really was. She'd met him when she was about to graduate and by then she'd found out about Daddy's big girls and it felt as if her only security was gone. So Gerald didn't know what he was getting. Well, neither did she. She hadn't known that money made all the difference between being cossetted and being used. The trouble was that she hadn't been brought up to insist on her rights as a person. Her father had always implied that there was some kind of advantage in being a woman, in being his little girl. So she hadn't known how to teach Gerald about equality because she didn't really know what equality was.

In this story, wife and husband cause each other a great deal of suffering because they perceive each other according to their own desires; they see only an autonomous individual and fail to assess the obviously conditioned qualities of their parents. Wife and husband were each blind to the character of their future in-laws despite many encounters with them. The bonds joining daughter to father and son to mother were invisible to the couple until conflicts arose at the birth of their child.

Kate Cruise O'Brien's first stories surprise the reader with their insights into the blindness of her urban and suburban characters whose self is dominated by false image and values – from home, school, church, and the mass media. O'Brien has an exceptional ability in structuring her stories, often pitting the blindness of an older person against the fresh, uncomplicated view of a child or an adolescence. Such stories as 'Ashes', 'A Matter of Principle', and 'Pieces of Silver' are among her most provocative stories. Within the confines of the short story, she unfolds what often takes months or years to evolve, that is, the casting off of layers of prejudice or ignorance. Although O'Brien can so deftly expose the false images and idolatries of the modern self, in some instances she seems so intent on the structure that she fails to develop adequately character and scene, thus limiting the impact of her perceptive designs.

CHANGE AND THE IRISH IMAGINATION

PATRICK RAFROIDI

The non-stop debate as to whether literature should be committed to reflecting current society and problems or aspirations (the Marxist creed) or should remain entirely gratuitous and only echo the personal concerns of the individual artist (say, Francis Stuart's position as expressed in his paper for the Lille Symposium[1] or in a recent issue of *The Crane Bag*[2]) seems to me to be both quite irrelevant as regards Ireland, and the cause of one of those false dilemmas that badly stifle criticism of Irish literature – like the all too famous identity problem raised by the change in language suffered by a whole nation, or the overwhelming majority of it – even though the Irish may find in relishing such difficulties a masochistic faithfulness to the spirit of the Celtic race 'always ready to react against the despotism of fact' as Matthew Arnold had it, quoting the French scholar Henri Martin[3]. For facts are stubborn things and literature in Ireland had next to no choice.

Gratuity, on the one hand, is the aesthetic luxury of more or less 'stable' countries, an epithet that hardly applied to the Ireland of the past and can't either to the Ireland of to-day, as long, at any rate, as the situation in the North has not been clarified: witness the bad conscience of contemporary Irish men of letters who cannot face it, try to ignore it or dismiss it for a while – the latter attitude leading John Montague to preface his collection *The Great Cloak* with the apologetic lines

> while my province burns
> I sing of love[4]

just like Thomas Moore, a century and a half before (John, I am sure, won't enjoy the comparison) had begged his readers' pardon in the following terms:

> Oh! blame not the bard; if in pleasure's soft dream,
> He should try to forget what he never can heal[5].

Committment, on the other hand, cannot be in Ireland or elsewhere a free political or ideological option but is borne out of historical necessity, a point that hardly needs to be expatiated upon.

Should Irish literature, then, with so few writers capable of sufficient detachment or insensitive enough to avoid the pitfalls of such a necessity, one way or another, whether to plead, or accuse, or condemn, or laugh, or just describe, be contemptuously relegated to 'post-colonial' status? Are there, in any case, any such writers even among those who are generally considered as innocent of the sin of parochialism? Neither Yeats, nor the author of 'Ivy-Day in the Committee Room', nor Flann O'Brien, nor Francis Stuart himself (vide *Black List, Section H.*, or, more recently, *Memorial* and *A Hole in the Head*) nor even Beckett, who may hate it but expresses himself vividly on the subject in *First Love*[6] – and this is already too much:

> What constitutes the charm of our country, apart of course from its scant population, and this without the help of the meanest contraceptive, is that all is derelict, with the sole exception of history's ancient faeces. These are ardently sought after, stuffed and carried in procession. Wherever nauseated time has dropped a nice fat turd you will find our patriots, sniffing it up, on all fours, their faces on fire. Elysium of the roofless.

A study of 'change' and its impact on Irish imaginative creation may give us a clue as to the possible answers.

The subject is a capital one, and yet, let us agree, for a start, that change – whether political, social or ethical – bears on the non-essential. It is a long time since we have entered the age of the existential.

Let us also agree that over-emphasis on what goes on outside one's own personality tends to unfocus the work of art and turn it into one-sided polemics apt to cause the writer to lose 'the somnambulate state of consciousness out of which art comes' – to quote Francis Stuart again[7]. But this is not absolutely evident in the individual products of this country and it is even less so in Irish literary production considered as a whole. The single track is definitely absent and the usual dialectics are in the foreground, the mental division in as far as change is concerned, those who cannot and will not choose, those who accumulate the pros, those the cons – the movement depending on periods, perhaps, but not on the essence of such periods: certain eras, known for their stability, produce conservatism – but also a desire for change; others, famed for being unstable, produce a craving for novelty but also a longing for the status quo or even a return to the past.

The latter wish, we shall see, is not as rare, even in our own time, as one may be induced to think at first, and it is a constant trait of Irish letters throughout the previous centuries.

The episode of Oisin's visit to Tir-na-nOg already contains – beside a number of other elements – a protest against a changing civilization in which the crosier has replaced the sword. Even the non-Gaelic scholar is aware of the presence of the same theme in much later poetry written in the original language: Maurice Fitzgerald lamenting the changed manners of the new century (the seventeenth), David Ó Bruadair, in 'A wound that has made me a vessel of sadness' mourning – again – the passing of heroic life after the Cromwellian war and, of course, Egan O'Rahilly:

> That royal Cashel is bare of house and guest,
> That Brian's turreted home is the otter's nest,
> That the kings of the land have neither land nor crown
> Has made me a beggar, before you, Valentine Brown[8]

while a contemporary of his heralded both the modern ecologists and the campaign in favour of Georgian Dublin when he wrote:

> Cad a dhéanfaimid feasta gan adhmad?
> Tá deire na gcoillte ar lár;
> Ní'l trácht ar Chill Chais ná a teaghlach
> 'S ní cluinfear a cling go bráth.

> What shall we do without timber?
> The last of the woods is down;
> Kilcash and the house of its glory
> And the bell of the house are gone[9].

Eighteenth and nineteenth century Anglo-Irish literature can provide as many examples of Irish writers' fundamental dislike of change, which turns them neither into better nor into worse artists than their more progressive colleagues. Or, for that matter, unconcerned authors.

Swift comes evidently to mind with, particularly, the third book of *Gulliver's Travels*, and, at any rate to a French academic, Anglo-

Irish reaction to the 1789 Revolution. Is there any passage more sentimentally attached to the past than Burke's famous outburst on Marie Antoinette in his *Reflections on the Revolution in France*?

It is now sixteen or seventeen years since I saw the Queen of France, then the dauphiness, at Versailles, and surely never lighted on this orb, which she hardly seemed to touch, a more delightful vision. I saw her just above the horizon, decorating and cheering the elevated sphere she just began to move in – glittering like the morning star, full of life and splendour and joy . . . Little did I dream that I should have lived to see such disasters fallen upon her in a nation of men of honour and cavaliers. I thought ten thousand swords must have leaped from their scabbards to avenge even a look that threatened her with insult. But the age of chivalry is gone. That of sophisters, economists, and calculators has succeeded, and the glory of Europe is extinguished forever[10].

Other examples, though none so passionate, could be found in the realm of the essay, from the pages of the *Dublin University Magazine* or the leaves of Father Prout's *Reliques*[11], in drama, in poetry and in the novel – with Maria Edgeworth for instance. Her *Madame de Fleury* – one of the *Tales of Fashionable Life* – published in 1809, is a bitter indictment of democratic rage, and – to match such political conservatism – there is her stand against a number of other novelties, including the literature of sensibility, the changes in educational methods advocated by Rousseau and his admirers (cf. *Belinda* (1801)) and the first attempts at woman's lib put forth by Mme de Staël and a few others (cf. *Leonora* (1806))[12].

Irish reaction to change, whether it goes as far as wanting to resurrect the distant past or not, could be illustrated throughout the 19th and the beginning of the 20th century in Ascendancy and Gaelic circles alike: through Somerville and Ross and Lord Dunsany to Elizabeth Bowen on one side, down to Pearse and Corkery on the other. And it is still there.

I was amused on first reading Brian Friel's *Philadelphia, Here I Come* to find the dual hero Gareth O'Donnell using as a leitmotif the passage from Burke which I quoted above. I was even more amused to hear from the horse's mouth that the least progressive of all writers of utopias in the 20th century, Anthony Burgess, considered himself an Irishman, like his God Joyce. It added spice to my reading of *1985* which I happened to take up immediately after *The*

Non-Stop Connolly Show[13]: up with the unions, down with the unions – in reverse order – and brings us back to Francis Stuart, defending as it does 'the right of man to loneliness, eccentricity, rebellion, genius; the superiority of man over men'[14].

May I be allowed two more illustrations, one from a so-called 'novel' of present life in Ireland, the other also a utopia?

The blurb of David Hanly's *In Guilt and in Glory* points to change in every direction, and two or three things, at least, have struck me as fairly new or fairly typical of new trends: the overt satire, the introduction of recognizable public characters, their name their only disguise, like Freddy Barton (ex) Minister for Posts and Telegraphs, the free use of joyous sexual descriptions. But the author's obvious spokesman, Crossan – sexuality apart – remains a complete Irish traditionalist. *In matters of religion.* While visiting St Patrick's College, Maynooth, with an American television crew, he leaves the hall where President Thomas Paschal O'Meara displays his 'very diplomatic and even-tempered public face', issuing unhectoring statements markedly different from 'the too-frequent utterances of Cro-Magnon bishops such as Lucey and Newman'[15] and he makes his way to Father Vincent Keegan's study. Although he has himself lost the faith, he is appalled when he learns that his old schoolfriend, a specialist of Mariology, has followed the same path and is about to leave and get married. *In psychological matters.* In spite of the advice of a gorgeous American female, he refuses the American psychoanalytical orthodoxy:

> 'You . . . you modern person'

he exclaims:

> 'I like my inhibitions . . . I don't want any neurotic clomping around my mind with a torch, pretending to understand me, telling me to shed my inhibitions. Inhibitions are the root and glory of civilization, and I love inhibitions. If I didn't have inhibitions, Virginia, if I weren't weighed down with all kinds of guilts and complexes, I'd be a very unhappy man indeed[16].

In matters of literary taste. Again, unlike Irish-Americans but like most true-born Irishmen, he hates Joyce and Beckett.

> 'Mr Joyce is a burden on me',

Crossan says, and his friend replies:

> 'Mr Joyce is a burden on us all',

before describing Beckett thus:

> 'Mr Beckett is an evangelical zombie, preaching for years to an empty church. Then the word gets out, the church fills to over-flowing, and when they hear his sermon he is telling them that they shouldn't listen to preachers'.
> . . .
> 'Do you think of Mr Beckett as Irish?'
> 'He's a Protestant of English blood, educated at Trinity, a cricket player who lives in Paris and writes in French. Of course he's Irish'[17].

In matters of scientific and industrial development. If change is to come to Ireland in that respect, for better or for worse, it won't evidently come through the artist. David Hanly symbolises the situation well when he has his artistically-minded tourists gaze disconsolately on the destruction in Bantry Bay while a fisherman – of all people – exults at it as his boat and his exertions to spread the detergent on the oil that covers the surface of the sea are worth gold:

> 'I never thought I'd land a windfall like this . . . There's may be a fortnight's work out there, or more. A few more spillages and I could retire for life. Send my children to the university. Well, we can only hope for the best'[18].

In Brian Moore's *Catholics* 'the fishing is grand again'[19] on the coast of Kerry. The year is 1984 or after and the water has been cleaned out, but not the regret in the mind of an author who has also shed his fidelity to the Church, that the successive Vatican Councils should have turned sacraments into symbols, abandoned the time-honoured, liturgical tradition and rendered it impossible to sing 'Faith of our fathers'[20] anymore.

I haven't yet read T.P. O'Mahony's *Sex and Sanctity*[21] (which I bought for the present congress!) and cannot say therefore whether that new episode of church-fiction follows the same or opposite tracks. Brian Moore, anyway, is an interesting man to stay with for a while as he can be quoted in each of my three divisions on the study

212

of change. *Catholics* places him among the conservatives, *The Doctor's Wife* among those who rejoice at the fact that the combined influence of the mass-media, the Council and the Northern conflict should have proved liberating forces, particularly in as far as sex is concerned; an earlier book, *The Emperor of Ice Cream* makes him one of the final exponents of Ireland's incapacity for change.

In that novel set in Belfast at the beginning of the Second World War, the young hero, Gavin Burke, is left to meditate, on one occasion, in a hospital parlour:

Nothing had changed in this room since 1930. Nothing would change . . . The care of this room would continue, as would the diurnal dirge of Masses all over the land, the endless litanies of evening devotions, the annual pilgrimages to holy shrines, the frozen ritual of Irish catholicism perpetuating itself in saecula saeculorum. Yeats was wrong in '16 to think that he and his countrymen,

> Now and in time to be,
> Wherever green is worn,
> Are changed, changed utterly:
> A terrible beauty is born.

This room denied that boast. Even Hitler's victory would not alter this room. Armageddon would bypass Ireland: all would remain still in this land of his forefathers. Ireland free was Ireland dead. The terrible beauty was born aborted[22].

One immediately recognizes the mood that prevailed in the South as well, throughout the Bourgeois State, the mood of Sean O'Casey's 'A Terrible Beauty is Borneo'[23], the mood of Frank O'Connor's 'The American Wife' (1961). The woman of the title has got her nation's propensity for improvement:

she had apparently discovered a great many things wrong with Ireland, and Tom, with a sort of mournful pleasure, kept adding to them.
'Oh, I know, I know,' he said regretfully.
'Then if you know, why don't you do something about it?'
'Ah, well, I suppose it's habit'[24]

213

And when his friend urges him to join his wife in the States where she has retired in disgust:

'I'm too old, Jerry,' Tom said so deliberately that Jerry knew it had been in his mind as well.
'Oh, I know, I know,' Jerry repeated. 'Even ten years ago I might have done it myself. It's like gaol. The time comes when you're happier in than out. And that's not the worst of it' he added bitterly. 'The worst is when you pretend you like it'[25].

The mood did not start, however, as everyone knows, with the disillusions of the post Civil War era: it is already to be found in another Moore, George, and, of course in Joyce's famous study in paralysis: *Dubliners*.

Far from losing their integrity as artists, Irish writers who have expressed their qualms at changes they could not welcome or at a kind of hemiplegia of the will which they refused to accept, have played their rôle, again in Francis Stuart's words, as a 'disturbing influence'[26], even though they were not good or bad in proportion of the disturbances they caused: literary greatness lies elsewhere: either it has nothing to do with efficiency and this, in spite of Marcuse, should be understood in a positive as well as in a negative sense, or it has – in which case, why should we refuse to consider the rest of the crowd, also a mixed one?

One reason that is often advanced is that there is no art without tension. And it is quite true that some of the most recent literature to come out of Ireland, revelling with a vengeance in the new permissiveness of the late seventies, seems completely to lack any backbone.

Hymns to affluence are understandable enough from a people that starved yesterday and the day before, dreaming, as late back as the middle-English period – in as far as Anglo-Irish is concerned – (*vide*: 'Cokaygne'[27]) of a Land of Plenty, even earlier than that in Gaelic, this being also one of the aspects of Tir-na-nOg. Paeons to sexual liberation are equally comprehensible in a country that is supposed to have been priest-ridden for so long, the victim of Protestant Puritanism and Catholic Jansenism alike and the only nation in the world, till 1967, where the local censorship was far stricter than the Roman index itself. But to what kind of artistic greatness is either type of song of praise likely to lead? Let us confess candidly that Ireland doesn't seem to have given birth to any

214

D. H. Lawrence, Jean Genet or Henry Miller as yet (to confine myself to the second source of inspiration). But who knows? Eleven years ago, a work like Benedict Kiely's *Dogs Enjoy the Morning* was well on the way and I could also mention at this point a very delicate short story called precisely, 'The Change', by a writer who, on the whole, is neither 'delicate' nor particularly modern in his subjects, John B. Keane. The story is to be found in a 1976 collection called, after John Donne, *Death Be Not Proud*[28]. It is born of a very fleeting image: a sports car stops for a second in a remote Irish village, a girl steps out to change her clothes and reveals part of her beautiful body; but it has duration, for the change of clothes changes the attitudes of all the staring villagers.

The objection to literature devoted to the political changes already achieved or to be brought about by victory – on the field of battle, through a movement, a protest march, an election or whatever – is, of course, of a different nature and a much more difficult one to refute. The subject under attack had, it is true, nearly ceased to be relevant, at any rate for the student of contemporary Irish letters. But the troubles in the North, with their long track, not only of treatises and pamphlets, but of poems, novels and plays, have put the problem into the foreground again, and it is bound to creep up, anyway, in any study of the works produced in Ireland before the 1920s.

The objection cannot be, of course, to the fact that the political or social situation is taken into account within the author's or the narrator's or the characters' total experience, but that such a situation should be substituted for the experience in a utilitarian desire to preach and convince. But it is not easy to draw the line, whether for the creative artist or the critic, and the latter – where Irish literature is concerned – has probably been too prone to condemn without judgment.

His intolerance can easily be explained. Not only has the literature he is dealing with sent forth to the printer hundreds of ballads in the style of those to be found in *The Spirit of the Nation*, but the innate didactic tendency engendered by the country's situation has kept spoiling some of the best artists as well and particularly the novelists, not excluding William Carleton of whom Yeats very sensibly remarked a propos of *Valentine Mc Clutchy* (but the statement holds good for most of his works):

215

Carleton was a man of genius, but the habit of dividing men into sheep and goats for the purposes of partisan politics made havoc of what might have been a great novel[29].

Not excluding either – to come back to our time – some very fine writers who did not recollect enough in tranquillity before venting their views on Ulster (whichever side they were on): Terence de Vere White in *The Distance and the Dark*, Eugene McCabe in *Victims*, Benedict Kiely in *Proxopera*, the list could be continued but should not blind us to the merits of Francis Stuart already mentioned on the subject or Jennifer Johnston's *Shadows On Our Skins* or playwright Brian Friel's *The Freedom of the City* . . .

Granted the value of much incidental writing is outside the realm of art proper: a reflection of things that be or to come, conducive to more changes: send out certain men the English will shoot, bring peace or war or revolution or what not in our time, it is not that 'incidental' quality that excludes it from Literature with a capital L, which can choose any time, any setting, any environment it likes. Besides, the purposes of literature, and, for that matter, the fore-seen or unforeseen effects of the written word can be multiple. *Cathleen ni Houlihan* may have been composed for art's or love's sake – it became propaganda. Conversely propaganda can become a work of art. If it is good propaganda it is bound to organize things, arrange reality into a pattern which is available to human under-standing, and interpret life. And to this intellectual value, to the soothing or enervating quality of its treatment of given situations, it can add an imaginative dimension through hope and projection.

In whose name should Irish writers be condemned for being more interested in their own society – whether changing or paralysed?

In the name of Dostoevsky who wrote about Russia, Balzac about France – and particularly Paris, the most provincial of cities –, Hawthorne about New England, Hardy about Wessex?

In the name of such Irish writers whom their imaginative great-ness and their mastery of idiom, irrespective of the setting of their works, have made famous abroad?

Yeats, who used to say that

The grass-blade carries the universe upon its point?

216

Joyce, who, for once, agreed with him and told Arthur Power:

> For myself, I always write about Dublin, because if I can get to the heart of Dublin I can get to the heart of all the cities in the world. In the particular is contained the universal

adding that all great international artists

> were national first and it was the intensity of their own nationalism which made them international in the end?[30]

The act of writing remains a personal process – but not an isolated one. No writer is an island: he must react to his society, often in opposition – but not necessarily so, in spite of the Gospel according to Marcuse – sometimes in symbiosis, always in interrogation.

And, for the sake of originality, variety, sincerity, readability, it is a good thing that it should still be the case in Ireland. Take a Frenchman's word for it.

NOTES

1   Francis Stuart: 'Politics and the Modern Irish Writer', in P. Rafroidi and P. Joannon, eds: *Ireland at the Crossroads*, Lille, P.U.L., 1978–9, pp. 41 seq.
2   'Novelists on the Novel. Ronan Sheehan talks to John Banville and Francis Stuart', *The Crane Bag*, vol. 3, no. 1, 1979, pp. 76 seq.
3   Matthew Arnold: 'On the Study of Celtic Literature' in *Lectures and Essays in Criticism* ed. R. H. Super, Ann Arbor, The University of Michigan Press, 1962, p. 344. *The Complete Works of Matthew Arnold*, vol. III.
4   John Montague: *The Great Cloak*, Dublin, The Dolmen Press, 1978, p. 7.
5   Thomas Moore: *Irish Melodies*, 1st series, 3rd number, London, J. Power, 1810.
6   London, Calder, 1973.
7   'Politics and the Modern Irish Writer', op. cit., p. 44.
8   Frank O'Connor's translation in *The Fountain of Magic*, London, 1939, p. 62.
9   Quoted by Frank O'Connor in: *The Backward Look*, London, Macmillan, 1967, p. 113.
10 First edn: 1790. T. H. D. Mahoney & O. Piest, eds: Indianapolis & New York, Bobbs-Merrill Co., 1955, p. 86.
11 See my own *Irish Literature in English: The Romantic Period*. Gerrards Cross, Colin Smythe, 1980, ch I & II. 'Father Prout's' (Francis Sylvester Mahony's) *Reliques* were first published in London (1836) by James Fraser.
12 Id., and H. D. Paratte: 'Maria Edgeworth's *Madame de Fleury*, an Anglo-Irish View of the French Revolution' in P. Rafroidi *et al.*: *France-Ireland: Literary*

Relations, Lille, P.U.L.; Paris, Editions Universitaires, 1974, pp. 69 seq.
13 Margaretta D'arcy & John Arden: *The Non-Stop Connolly Show*, London, Pluto Press, 1977, etc.
14 Anthony Burgess: *1985*, London, Hutchinson, 1978, p. 166.
15 David Hanly: *In Guilt and in Glory*, London, Hutchinson, 1979, p. 93.
16 Id., p. 219. Italics are in the text.
17 Id., pp. 91–2.
18 Id., p. 245.
19 Brian Moore: *Catholics*, London, Jonathan Cape, 1972, p. 9.
20 Id., p. 73.
21 Swords, Co. Dublin, Poolbeg Press, 1979.
22 Mayflower edition (1967), pp. 176–7. The novel was first published in New York, in 1965, by the Viking Press.
23 *Inishfallen, Fare Thee Well, Autobiographies*, II, London, Macmillan, 1963, pp. 125 seq.
24 Frank O'Connor: *Collection Three*, London, Macmillan, 1969, p. 19.
25 Id., p. 27.
26 'Politics and the Modern Irish Writer', op. cit.
27 In George Ellis: *Specimens of the Early English Poets*, London, 1811, I, 83.
28 Dublin & Cork, The Mercier Press, pp. 51 seq.
29 To the Editor of *United Ireland*, Dec. 23, 1893. *Uncollected Prose* by W. B. Yeats, collected and edited by John P. Frayne, London, Macmillan, 1970, I, 306.
30 Arthur Power: *From an Old Waterford House*. Quoted by Richard Ellman: *James Joyce*, New York, Oxford University Press, 1959.

NOTES ON THE CONTRIBUTORS

SUHEIL BADI BUSHRUI is Professor of English and Anglo-Irish Literature at the American University of Beirut, Lebanon, and received his Ph.D. from Southampton University where he was a British Council Scholar and Research Fellow 1959–62. He has taught at Oxford University, in Nigeria at Ibadan University and at the Universities of Calgary and York in Canada, as well as lecturing in many other countries. In 1963 he was awarded the Una Ellis-Fermor Prize for his work on W. B. Yeats, on whom he has written four books, including the first full-length critical study in Arabic. He has also written on English, Arabic and African literatures. He is an authority on Kahlil Gibran, the Lebanese poet, has published two volumes of his own Arabic poetry and is a regular broadcaster in the Arab world. He is president of the Association of University Teachers of English in the Arab World, and is the Collector for the English Association's 1982 volume of Essays and Studies, as well a joint editor of *James Joyce, An International Perspective*, to be published this year to mark the centenary of Joyce's birth.

PETER DENMAN lectures in the English Department at St. Patrick's College, Maynooth. He studied at University College, Cork, Université de Caen and Keele University. He was a winner of an Eric Gregory Poetry Award in 1978, and his collection of poems *Sour Grapes*, was published in 1980 by Honest Ulsterman Publications.

DECLAN KIBERD is Lecturer in Anglo-Irish Literature and Drama at University College, Dublin. He is the author of *Synge and the Irish Language* (1979) and a commentary on *The Merchant of Venice* (1980). He is a graduate of Trinity College, Dublin, where he was later Lecturer in Irish. He holds a doctorate from Oxford University and has also held a post as Lecturer in English at the University of Kent at Canterbury.

Literature and the Changing Ireland

THOMAS KILROY is a novelist and playwright as well as being Professor of Modern English at University College, Galway. He is a Member of the Irish Acadamy of Letters and a Fellow of the Royal Society of Literature. He has been awarded the Guardian Fiction Prize, the Heinemann Award for Literature, the Irish Academy of Letters Prize for Literature and the American-Irish Foundation Award for Literature. His publications include *The Death and Resurrection of Mr. Roche*, *The O'Neill*, *The Big Chapel*, *Tea and Sex and Shakespeare*, and *Talbot's Box*. He is Editor of the Sean O'Casey 20th Century Views Series.

KLAUS LUBBERS was educated at the Johannes Gutenberg-Universität, Mainz, where he is now Professor, the University of Birmingham and the University of Michigan. His particular interests are in American literature and he has written full-length studies on Poe, Hemingway, and Emily Dickinson, as well as many shorter works and essays.

D. E. S. MAXWELL was educated at Foyle College, Derry and Trinity College, Dublin, where he took his B.A. and Ph.D. He has been a Lecturer at the University of Ghana, Assistant Director of Examinations, Civil Service Commission, London, Professor of English at the University of Ibadan and is now Professor of English at York University where he was Master of Winters College 1969–79. He was a Visiting Professor at Trinity College, Dublin 1979–80. His publications include *The Poetry of T. S. Eliot*, *American Fiction*, *Cozzens*, (as co-editor) *W. B. Yeats Centenary Essays*, *Poets of the Thirties* and *Brian Friel*. His work in progress is a critical history of Irish drama.

VIVIAN MERCER is a Professor of English at the University of California, Santa Barbara. His publications include *The Irish Comic Tradition*, *The New Novel from Queneau to Pinget*, and *Beckett/ Beckett*. He is now working on a two volume critical history of Anglo-Irish Literature, 1878 to the present.

JAMES H. O'BRIEN is Professor of English at Western Washington University. He has written articles on Yeats, the Bucknell University Press books on Liam O'Flaherty, and (with Richard M. Kain) on G. W. Russell – AE, and is currently working on Irish short story writers. He is an exchange professor at the University of Haifa, 1981–82.

CATHAL G. Ó HÁINLE studied at St. Patrick's College, Maynooth, at University College, Dublin and at the University of Munich. He was Professor of Modern Irish at Maynooth before becoming Associate Professor in the School of Irish at Trinity College, Dublin in 1977. He is the author of *Promhadh Pinn* (1978) and *Gearrscéalta an Phiarsaigh* (1979), and of many articles on modern literature in Irish.

PATRICK RAFROIDI is presently Director of the Institut Français du Royaume-Uni in London. He was President of L'Université de Lille III 1974–79, and a visiting Fellow at the Humanities Research Centre, Australian National University, Canberra, 1980–81. He was Chairman of IASAIL 1976–79. He is author of the two volume *Irish Literature in English, the Romantic Period*, as well as editor of a number of books on Ireland, and *Études Irlandaises*.

STAN SMITH is a lecturer in English at Dundee University, and was previously a lecturer at Aberdeen University. He was born in Warrington, Lancs., and educated at Jesus College, Cambridge, where he took his Ph.D. with a thesis on the work of Edward Thomas. He has written widely on modern Irish, English and American literature, and is author of *A Sadly Contracted Hero: the Comic Self in Postwar American Fiction* (1981) and *Twentieth-Century Poetry* (1981). His *Inviolable Voice: History and Twentieth Century Poetry* will be published in 1982, and he is currently working on a study of Irish poetry since Yeats. He writes regularly for and is Poetry Review Editor of *The Literary Review*.

PETER CONNOLLY is Professor of English at St. Patrick's College, Maynooth and was host-organiser of the 1979 IASAIL Conference held there.

Index

This index only covers the essays themselves, not their notes.

223

Index

City, 216; *Philadelphia, Here I Come*, 210
Froude, J.A., 92
Furlong, Thomas, 48–9, 51

Gaelic League, 6, 7, 8, 9, 10, 11, 15, 19, 37
Gaelic Society (founded 1807), 37
Gaelic Union, 7
Gaeltacht, the, 7, 8, 9, 10, 15, 16
Gayer, Rev. Charles, 72
Genet, Jean, 215
Gentleman's Magazine, 33
George III, King, 29
Gladstone, W.E., 87
Godkin, James, 81, 82, 84, 85
Goldsmith, Oliver, 17, 75
Gonne, Maud, *see* MacBride, Maud Gonne
Goodman, Rev. J., 91
Gorki, Maxim, 23
Grangegorman Parish Church, 85
Grattan, Henry, 124
Greece, King of, 160
Green, Alice Stopford, 76–7
Green, J.R. 76
Greene, David, 9
Gregg, Bp. John, 82
Gregory, Isabella Augusta, Lady, 16, 22, 87, 94, 110, 111, 118, 125, 129
Gregory, (William) Robert, 115–6, 121
Griffin, Gerald, 26, 35
Griffith, Arthur, 5
Groves, A.N., 79
Gwynn, Stephen, 109

Hales, Rev. William, *Essay on the Origin and Purity of the Primitive Church*, 88; *New Analysis of Chronology*, 88
Hanly, David, *In Guilt and Glory*, 211–2
Hannay, Rev. G.O. ('George Birmingham'), 8, 9
Hardiman, James, 39, 40, 48, 50; *Irish Minstrelsy*, 39, 48, 49, 50
Hawthorne, Nathaniel, 216
Heaney, Seamus, 177, 190; *Death of a Naturalist*, 189; 'A Northern Hoard', 169; 'Roots', 169, 170; 'The Tollund Man', 170; *Wintering*

Out, 169
Henn, T.R., 118, 119
Heslinga, M.W., 15
Hibernian Bible Society, 71, 97
Hibernian Church Missionary Society, 71
Hiberno-Celtic Society (founded 1818), 38
Higgins, Aidan, 176; *Balcony of Europe*, 185
Higgins, F.R., 191
Hinkson, Katharine Tynan, 109
Hogarth, William, 35
Hume, David, 124
Hunt, Leigh, 29, 30
Hutchinson, Pearse, 176
Huxley, T.H., 93
Hyde, Rev. Arthur, 59, 60, 64
Hyde, Arthur, 64, 65, 66
Hyde, Douglas ('An Craoibhin Aoibhin'), 6, 7, 8, 9, 10, 11, 12, 13, 14, 38, 48, 59, 60, 63, 64, 65, 76, 94; *Casadh an tSúgáin*, 13, *Love Songs of Connaught*, 55
Hyde, Oldfield, 64

Inniu, 9
Iremonger, Valentin, 176
Irish Church Act (1869), 59
Irish Church Missions to the Roman Catholics, Society for, 72, 74
Irish Free State, 118, 120
Irish Home Rule Party, 64
Irish Language, Society for the Preservation of, 37
Irish Literary Revival, 16, 59
Irish Literary Society, 38, 107
Irish Literary Theatre, 74
Irish National Literary Society, 107
Irish Parliamentary Party, 8
Irish Society, 71
Irish Times, The, 4
Irish Worker, The, 11
Irlande Libre movement, 23

Jacks, L.P., 93
Jakobson, Roman, 189
Jameson, Frederic, 179; *Marxism and Form*, 179, 181
Jesus, the Christ, 69, 70

225

Index

227

Index